Business and the Greater Good

STUDIES IN TRANSATLANTIC BUSINESS ETHICS

Series Editors: Laszlo Zsolnai, *Corvinus University, Hungary* and George Brenkert, *Georgetown University, USA*

Over the past several decades the importance of ethical issues in business has become widely acknowledged. Business scandals, globalization, the Internet, outsourcing of production, environmental concerns, and a growing appreciation for business responsibilities for human rights have led to a greater appreciation of the importance of business ethics. In addition, increased concern for trust, humanity and purpose in an age of crisis leads us to ask fundamental questions about the role of business ethics and the legitimation of business. In this setting, there is an obvious need for more refined studies of business ethics as informed by an international perspective. Though American and European business ethics have developed differently, many problems are similar on both sides of the Atlantic. Based upon this insight we established the TransAtlantic Business Ethics Conferences (TABEC) in 2000 for promoting exchange and collaboration between American and European scholars and practitioners.

The first TABEC was held in Budapest in 2000 at the Budapest University of Economic Sciences. The second one was organized in Washington, DC in 2002 at Georgetown University. Subsequent conferences have been held at such prominent locations as the ESADE Business School (Barcelona), the Wharton School (Philadelphia), the SDA Bocconi School of Management (Milan), York University in Canada, and NHH Norwegian School of Economics (Bergen). The intention in each case was to bring together a group of distinguished business ethicists from Europe and North America to address current and central problems of business ethics.

The purpose of the *Studies in TransAtlantic Business Ethics* series is to publish some of the best thinking on business ethics that is currently available on either side of the Atlantic. Though the main engine behind the series is TABEC, the series is not limited to papers presented at one of the TABEC conferences. Other contributions from prominent business ethicists are welcome too. It is our hope that our series can catalyze fresh and innovative thinking and practices in America, Europe and beyond.

Titles in the series include:

Business Ethics and Corporate Sustainability
Edited by Antonio Tencati and Francesco Perrini

Business and the Greater Good
Rethinking Business Ethics in an Age of Crisis
Edited by Knut J. Ims and Lars Jacob Tynes Pedersen

Business and the Greater Good

Rethinking Business Ethics in an Age of Crisis

Edited by

Knut J. Ims

Professor, NHH Norwegian School of Economics, Norway

Lars Jacob Tynes Pedersen

Associate Professor, NHH Norwegian School of Economics, Norway

STUDIES IN TRANSATLANTIC BUSINESS ETHICS

Edward Elgar
PUBLISHING

Cheltenham, UK • Northampton, MA, USA

Published by
Edward Elgar Publishing Limited
The Lypiatts
15 Lansdown Road
Cheltenham
Glos GL50 2JA
UK

Edward Elgar Publishing, Inc.
William Pratt House
9 Dewey Court
Northampton
Massachusetts 01060
USA

A catalogue record for this book
is available from the British Library

Library of Congress Control Number: 2014954949

This book is available electronically in the **Elgar**online
Business subject collection
DOI 10.4337/9781784711771

ISBN 978 1 78471 176 4 (cased)
ISBN 978 1 78471 177 1 (eBook)

Typeset by Columns Design XML Ltd, Reading
Printed and bound in Great Britain by T.J. International Ltd, Padstow

Contents

Contributors

George G. Brenkert, PhD, is Professor Emeritus of Business Ethics at the McDonough School of Business at Georgetown University. He is former President of the Society for Business Ethics, past Editor-in-Chief of *Business Ethics Quarterly*, and co-founder of the Capital Area Business Ethics Network, an association of ethics officers from profit, non-profit and government organizations in the Washington, DC area. Among his publications are *Marketing Ethics* (Blackwell), The *Oxford Handbook of Business Ethics* (Oxford), and *Corporate Integrity and Accountability* (SAGE). He has published numerous articles pertaining to business ethics and corporate social responsibility. He is a co-founder of the TransAtlantic Business Ethics Conference.

Johannes Brinkmann holds a PhD in sociology and is a Professor of Business Ethics at the Norwegian Business School (BI). Beyond textbooks and essays written in Norwegian most of his articles are published in outlets such as the *Journal of Business Ethics*, the *Journal of Business Ethics Education*, *Business Ethics: A European Review* and the *Electronic Journal of Business Ethics and Organization Studies*. His main research interests are within descriptive consumer and marketing ethics, insurance customer and insurance business ethics, and within interdisciplinary risk research.

Wesley Cragg is a York University Professor Emeritus and Senior Scholar in Philosophy at the Schulich School of Business. He has written and edited a number of books including: five editions of *Contemporary Moral Issues*; *Ethics Codes, Corporations and the Challenge of Globalization*, 2005; *Corporate Social Responsibility*, 2009; and *Business and Human Rights*, 2013. He has published widely on a variety of business ethics themes including corporate governance, corporate codes of ethics, corporate social responsibility, sustainability, environmental ethics and business and human rights. A recent research theme is the ethics of resource extraction mining, with a particular focus on Aboriginal rights, and economic development in the Canadian North.

Georges Enderle is the John T. Ryan Jr. Professor of International Business Ethics at the Mendoza College of Business, University of Notre

Dame, and former President of the International Society of Business, Economics, and Ethics (ISBEE; 2001–2004). He is a Guest Member of the Business Ethics Innovation Group at the Shanghai Academy of Social Sciences. Educated in Philosophy (Munich), Theology (Lyon), Economics (Fribourg), and Business Ethics (St. Gallen), he has extensive research and teaching experiences in Europe (1983–1992), the United States (since 1992), and China (since 1994). He serves on the Board of Advisors of several academic journals and Centers for Business Ethics in various countries and has authored and edited 18 books and over 140 articles. He conducts research on the ethics of globalization, wealth creation, business and human rights, corporate responsibilities of large and small companies, with a view on developments in China. His website is www.nd.edu/~genderle.

Knut J. Ims is Professor in Business Ethics at the Department of Strategy and Management at NHH Norwegian School of Economics. He is a member of the Business Ethics Faculty Group of the Community of European Management Schools (CEMS). Some recent publications include: "From Welfare to Well-Being and Happiness" in *Handbook of Business Ethics: Ethics in the New Economy* (Ed. L. Zsolnai), Oxford, Peter Lang, 2013, "Initiating an Open Research System based on Creativity" (with O. Jakobsen) in *Responsible Economics* (Ed. H. Opdebeeck), Oxford, Peter Lang, 2013, and "Deep Ecology" in *The Palgrave Handbook of Spirituality and Business* (Eds. L. Bouckaert and L. Zsolnai), Palgrave Macmillan, 2011.

Kevin T. Jackson, J.D., PhD, holds the Daniel Janssen Chair in Corporate Social Responsibility at Solvay Brussels School of Economics and Management, Université Libre de Bruxelles (ULB). He is Professor of Law and Ethics at Fordham University in New York City. Author of several books and many scholarly articles, he has been on the faculties of Princeton University, Georgetown University, Peking University in Beijing, China, and École des Ponts in Paris. Jackson's book, *Charting Global Responsibilities: Legal Philosophy and Human Rights* (University Press of America) was presented to His Holiness the Dalai Lama by the US State Department as a gift.

Ove Jakobsen is Professor in Ecological Economics at Bodø Graduate School of Business (HHB), University of Nordland. He is co-founder and leader of the Centre for Ecological Economics and Ethics at HHB. He is a member of the National Committee for Research Ethics in the Social Sciences and the Humanities (NESH). In addition to holding a PhD in economics from the Norwegian School of Economics, he holds three master degrees; in philosophy, marketing, and administration and leadership. In 2000, Jacobsen received the SAS and the Norwegian Economics Association prize for the best integration of environmental and societal responsibility in lectures at Norwegian Business Schools. His major research interests are ecological economics/circulation economics, business ethics/CSR, holistic science and development based on sustainability. He has published a number of scientific articles and books both nationally and internationally.

Josep M. Lozano is Professor and URL Associate Professor at ESADE Ramon Llull University. He has published five papers and seven books. Among his books, *Danone en Ultzama* won the MSD Award for Business Ethics Research in 2005 and his book *Ètica i empresa* received the Joan Sardà Dexeus Award in 1998. He has also collaborated on a further 33 books. He is the Director of the Observatory on Ethical, Ecological and Social Investment Funds in Spain; co-founder of Ética, Economía y Dirección (the Spanish branch of the European Business Ethics Network); a member of the international board of Ethical Perspectives and of the Society and Business Review; he is also a member of the board of trustees and on the advisory board of various foundations and associations. He was recognized as a highly commended runner-up in the Faculty Pioneer Award (2003), granted by EABiS and the Aspen Institute (USA).

Eleanor O'Higgins (BA, MSc, MBA, PhD) is on the faculty of the School of Business at University College Dublin. She specializes in teaching, research and publications in social issues in management, including corporate social responsibility, business ethics, corporate governance, and strategic and public management. She is the author of numerous papers in academic and professional journals, newspaper articles, book chapters and case studies. She is a member of the Business Ethics and of the Public Management & Governance interfaculty groups of the Community of European Management Schools (CEMS) and serves on the editorial boards of a number of international management journals. She has received a number of international awards for peer reviewed articles in the social issues in management area. Her case studies and research work on the airline industry and on Ryanair have also received prestigious international awards.

Lars Jacob Tynes Pedersen is Associate Professor at the Department of Accounting, Auditing and Law at NHH Norwegian School of Economics, and Chairman of its Center of Ethics and Economy. He teaches and does research on a variety of topics in business ethics, corporate responsibility and behavioral finance. He has published in journals like the *Journal of Business Ethics* and *Business Ethics: A European Review*, and his most recent book is *Accounting Ethics* (Wiley, 2014).

Peter Pruzan is Professor Emeritus at the Department of Management, Philosophy & Politics, Copenhagen Business School (CBS). He has been the president of an innovative international business and professor at the Technical University of Denmark, the University of Copenhagen and CBS. Recent books include *Research Methodology for the Reflective Practitioner of Science* (in process), *Rational, Ethical and Spiritual Perspectives on Leadership: Selected Writings by Peter Pruzan* (2009), and, together with his wife Kirsten, *Leading with Wisdom: Spiritual-based Leadership in Business* (2007/2010). Among his organizational initiatives are co-founding/designing: AccountAbility in London (1995); CBS's Center for Corporate Social Responsibility (2002) and the European Academy of Business in Society (2002). He and his wife share their time between a small historical Danish town and a university campus/ashram in southern India.

Donald H. Schepers is Associate Dean for Academic Affairs and Professor of Management at Baruch College, City University of New York. His teaching specialty is Social and Governmental Environment of Business, Corporate Governance, and Business Ethics. His present research interests include corporate governance and codes of conduct, corporate political campaign contributions, socially responsible investing and the impact of nongovernmental organizations on business policy. Recent research has focused more specifically on multi-stakeholder codes of conduct. His articles have appeared in *Organizational Behavior and Human Decision Processes*, *Human Resource Management*, *Journal of Business Ethics*, *Business and Society* and *Business and Society Review*, and authored book chapters and case studies as well.

S. Prakash Sethi is University Distinguished Professor at the Zicklin School of Business, Baruch College, at the City University of New York. He has written several books and articles on corporate social accountability and international codes of conduct, and has advised numerous corporations, nongovernmental organizations, and national and international governmental bodies on the conduct of competitive markets and the role of large corporations in economic activities. He is also President of the International Center for Corporate Accountability (ICCA), an independent educational organization affiliated with the Zicklin School of Business.

Antonio Tencati is Associate Professor of Management at the Department of Economics and Management, Università degli Studi di Brescia. Between 2005 and 2012 he was Assistant Professor of Management and Corporate Social Responsibility at the Department of Management and Technology, Università Bocconi, with which he continues to collaborate. He is a member of the Steering Committee and a Research Coordinator at CReSV, the Center for Research on Sustainability and Value at Università Bocconi, and a member of the Business Ethics Faculty Group of the CEMS (Community of European Management Schools – The Global Alliance in Management Education). His research areas include business and society, management of sustainability and corporate social responsibility, environmental management, innovation and operations management. His work has been published in leading international journals and academic books.

Laszlo Zsolnai is Professor and Director of the Business Ethics Center at the Corvinus University of Budapest. He is Chairman of the Business Ethics Faculty Group of the CEMS – The Global Alliance in Management Education. He serves as President of the European SPES Institute in Leuven, Belgium. He has been guest professor or visiting scholar at University of Cambridge, University of Oxford, UC Berkeley, Georgetown University, University of Richmond, University of St. Gallen, Bocconi University Milan, and Netherlands Institute for Advanced Study. His website is http://laszlo-zsolnai.net.

Acknowledgements

This book is published thanks to the manifold contributions of numerous people and institutions who have helped us realize the project.

First, we are very grateful to Laszlo Zsolnai and George Brenkert for inviting us to host the Seventh TransAtlantic Business Ethics Conference in Bergen, as well as to edit this volume. As founders of the TABEC initiative and editors of the Studies in TransAtlantic Business Ethics book series, their passion, personal involvement, and constructive suggestions have not only made this book possible, but a pleasurable project.

We are also grateful to several persons and institutions who contributed to the realization of the conference and to the publication of this book. We would like to thank all the participants at the conference for bringing their knowledge and creativity to work in illuminating the topic of the conference. It is our hope that the dialogues at the conference will stimulate further work on these important issues.

We are thankful for support from NHH Norwegian School of Economics, where the conference was hosted. We thank the Center of Ethics and Economy at NHH and our respective departments, the Department of Strategy and Management and the Department of Accounting, Law and Auditing, for financial, practical and collegial support.

Several NHH students volunteered for the conference and for the work with the book and we are grateful for their contributions. In particular, we thank Ingvild Orheim and Kamilla Korsnes. Ingvild played an important role during the conference in taking care of our guests and their spouses, and Kamilla has done invaluable work with preparing the manuscripts of this book for publication.

There were several participants at the conference whose work for different reasons are not included in this book. We are grateful for the contributions of these participants to the conference, and thereby to the intellectual content of this book, to which they indirectly have contributed through dialogues at the conference: Thomas Beschorner, Andrew Crane, Tom Donaldson, Josep Lozano, Wayne Norman, and Antonio Tencati.

Finally, we would like to acknowledge our editors at Edward Elgar Publishing for publishing this book as part of the Studies in TransAtlantic Business Ethics series, as well as for their constructive help, engagement and commitment to the book project.

Knut J. Ims
Lars Jacob Tynes Pedersen

1. Rethinking business ethics in an age of crisis

Knut J. Ims and Lars Jacob Tynes Pedersen

1.1 INTRODUCTION

The new millennium has been plagued by several crises, of which the financial and climate crises have gained most public attention. The financial crisis cast a vast number of people into unemployment while their lifetime savings evaporated and many lost their homes. The inequality between the poor and the rich significantly increased. During the last decades in the US, the top 1 percent managed to obtain a fifth of the national income; wealth became even more unequally distributed than before (Stiglitz 2012). Among the manifold consequences of this growing inequality are lower health and lower life expectancies in many countries. In this respect, the real price of the financial crisis is not first and foremost an economic problem, but rather a serious human one (e.g., Kentikelenis et al. 2011).

However, the financial crisis is perhaps only a symptom of even more profound problems in our time. We are facing an environmental crisis due to the consequences of an economy dependent on oil and coal, which pollutes the soil, water and air, and that ultimately threatens the climate by heating the atmosphere to an unprecedented level. Thereby, biodiversity and the life prospects of future generations on earth are threatened. Corporate recklessness has played a part in this picture. A prominent example of corporate environmental transgressions is Deepwater Horizon – the BP oil spill in the Mexican gulf in 2011. Also, we increasingly see controversial business cases related to novel practices like oil sands extraction and so-called fracking. Such cases further endanger the environment, lead to considerable clean-up operations for residents, and in many instances threaten communities by forcing people to move or by creating social instability.

There has been widespread hope that the political system could repair the economic system. However, the political system also seems to be failing. At the time of writing, vast numbers of youth in Southern Europe are unemployed, which has led to mass protest movements that have shaken European democratic institutions. The "Occupy Movement" has drawn attention to the deficiencies and dysfunctionalities of the capitalistic system. The economic system is criticized for not being efficient, since it has vast underutilized resources. Furthermore, it is criticized for not being fair, as the system does not meet even the basic needs of those at the bottom. In this age of crisis, protesters are asking for the right to decent work for decent pay, as well as for a more just economy and society. When the political system amplifies the voice of wealth, gives the wealthy better opportunities to design and administrate laws and regulations, and is unable to prevent large-scale corporate transgressions or protect those at the bottom, we see the interconnectedness of the failures in the economic and the political system. As Stiglitz (2012) maintains, "[r]ather than correcting the market's failures, the political system was reinforcing them". Similarly, economic forces are to an increasing extent colonizing parts of the culture and the life-worlds of citizens. In the US, the Supreme Court has approved corporate campaign financing, thus allowing corporations to exercise "free speech" in supporting candidates and causes much like individuals – only with vast financial powers at their disposal.

In affluent countries, there is talk of "affluenza" – the obsessive quest for material gains in an endless effort to "keep up with the Joneses" (de Graaf et al. 2005). On this hedonic treadmill (Eysenck 1990), many argue that we are confronted with a *moral and spiritual crisis*, wherein a materialistic value orientation becomes ever more dominant. One of the consequences of this orientation, Kasser (2011, p. 204) argues, may be lower personal well-being and more "manipulative, competitive, and ecologically degrading behaviors". Goodpaster (1991, p. 94) termed the strong emphasis on a limited purpose *teleopathy* – a kind of moral disorder that erodes integrity and leads to the disintegration of character. Finally, one of the implications of such crises is unstable social environments, which inevitably erode trust (Shiller 2008). An economy that leads to an erosion of trust may also lead to a loss of respect.

Crises are not only a contemporary phenomenon – rather, financial, environmental and sociocultural crises have occurred repeatedly throughout the centuries (e.g., Galbraith 1994; Lamb 1995). However, the present convergence of crises, "in money, energy, education, health, water, soil, climate, politics and the environment" is a "birth crisis, expelling us from the old world into a new" (Eisenstein 2011, p. xx).

That is, the comprehensiveness and interconnectedness of our current crises, and of their causes and potential solutions, are arguably unprecedented. The premise of this book is that we need new thinking in order to correct the deep failures of economics, business and politics that we are currently witnessing in our societies. The book presents novel ideas and concepts from the frontiers of business ethics, which illuminate a number of the problems we are facing and sketch solutions that are strongly needed. As such, the book attempts to provide a rethinking of business ethics in an age of crisis, as reflected in the book's subtitle. We believe the contributions in the anthology give genuine insights about the causes of the current crises as well as new directions and fruitful solutions that may contribute to our societies' ability to move in the direction of aligning business with the greater good.

1.2   BUSINESS AND THE GREATER GOOD

The anthology comprises chapters that in different ways deal with the problems discussed above. Taken together, they provide insight into the causes, nature, and potential solutions to major ethical problems in contemporary business. The contributions by the authors share some fundamental features that reflect a rethinking of central elements of business ethics in theory and practice. In the following, we outline three central dimensions that run through the chapters of this book, and that together constitute the message of change that is suggested by the contributors. The three parts suggest new directions both in mindset and in practice: (1) from inequality to equality, (2) from the technical–materialistic to the ecological–spiritual, and (3) from compliance and enforcement to autonomy and responsibility. In outlining these three dimensions, we also provide an overview of the contributions of each of the chapters.

1.2.1   Part I: From Inequality to Equality

The first stream of thought in the book deals with the problem of (in)equality. Increasing inequality is a widely discussed phenomenon in the contemporary economy, and it is arguably one of the most important drivers of social activism today. In at least three important ways, inequality is a central problem when it comes to business and its externalities. Since the chapters in this part of the book were developed, inequality has been subject to considerable academic and public debate, not at least following the publication of Thomas Piketty's (2013) *Capital in the Twenty-First Century.* The chapters presented here are in different ways relevant to this debate.

First, inequality in opportunities may create systematic difference in the degree to which different groups are able to participate in business activity and the workforce. In the current economic climate, a considerable number of workers are unable to get employment and, at the bottom of the pyramid, entrepreneurs struggle to get financing and other necessary infrastructure in order to create small businesses.

Second, inequality in exposure to risks and externalities of business may lead underprivileged and poor communities to carry a disproportionate weight of the social and environmental costs of business. Generally, the world's poor do not have power to protect themselves from significant externalities of businesses that increasingly migrate to low cost markets, and they are similarly more likely to be exploited by corporate transgressors than are people in countries with stronger background institutions (Yunus 2007). Similarly, the effects of financial crises are often most strongly detrimental to the poor (Baldacci et al. 2002).

Third, the net effect of the two former issues is increasing inequality in outcomes. There is both philosophical and empirical discussion about what is most important – *inequality of opportunity* on the one hand versus *inequality of outcomes* on the other hand (e.g., Sen 1992; Lefranc et al. 2008). Clearly, however, the current increase in unequal outcomes is a source of considerable social uproar and activism, and, as such, it constitutes an ethical as well as a political challenge across societies.

The chapters in the first part of the book address these issues of (in)equality. They discuss the sources and consequences of inequality, and in particular how the mental models and market institutions of the capitalist system have contributed to increasing inequality. The chapters discuss dominant perspectives like shareholder primacy and principal–agent theory as well as the institutions that embody these principles. They also problematize the nature and distribution of wealth. Finally, the chapters in this part of the book address the question of how mental models and market and governance institutions could – and perhaps should – be changed in order to move from inequality to equality.

Inequality itself is the theme of the book's chapter by *George G. Brenkert* (Georgetown University), who addresses the role played by business in creating inequality. The point of departure is that during the last decades more than 80 percent of total increase in Americans' income went to the top 1 percent. The "great divergence" that is the result damages the trust people have in others in society, and may result in a serious threat to a well-functioning economy. Brenkert considers the increased inequality of income and wealth in the US, with special regard to the responsibilities of business. Two different approaches – that inequality is a "natural" and a desirable result of markets and business transactions – are discussed and rejected. The libertarian bottom-up view and Hayek's top-down account are described.

Brenkert's conclusion is that these mental frameworks are not acceptable, and until such mental models are rejected, the problem will continue. Brenkert sketches several reasons to ground the beliefs that business does have direct as well as indirect responsibilities for increased inequality. For example, business did not adequately inform or take the financial condition of customers of mortgages into consideration. Thereby, business increased the inequalities between different ethnic groups in the US. Based on the view that with great power comes great (moral) responsibility, Brenkert suggests that businesses should be more active in implementing various laws and regulations that will have an effect of increasing equality in society. Businesses could lobby for a higher minimum wage law, executives could do what they can within their own spheres, and they could seek to solve problems that can only be solved collectively. Referring to the general ethical guidelines discussed by De George, special attention could be given to developing fair background institutions that support greater equality, which ultimately might lead to higher trust.

Shareholder primacy and its role in creating inequality is the theme of the chapter by *Wesley Cragg* (York University). He discusses why management theories on which the profit maximization model is based are "fatally flawed". Cragg presents a history of the firm and emphasizes that there is a pressing need for reassessing the currently dominant management theories and practices. Business as investor-owned corporations has not always followed the dogma of profit maximization. Cragg argues that "incorporations" in their early modern phase were a kind of a formal social contract between the company and public interests. The potential for private enrichment should be balanced by the assumption of generating public benefits. Underlying this view was an expectation of reciprocal benefits for the public and the company that was given "the exclusive right to trade and commerce."

Cragg describes the rise of shareholder primacy theories, by referring to agency theory's implication that the purpose of the firm is to maximize shareholder value. One of the consequences was that stock-based compensation became seen as a way of aligning the interests of executives with those of the shareholders. Cragg discusses the normative implications of the profit maximization model, the moral hazard conundrum, and analyzes the issues in a societal perspective. Finally, Cragg discusses the theoretical and practical implications of the shareholder primacy approach for ethics and makes suggestions for how to rebuild the foundations of ethics and trust. Cragg's main critique is that profit maximization represents a dogma that undermines the ethical foundations of corporate behavior, and that may ultimately threaten our economic and social system. This will erode trust and result in a loss of respect. According to Cragg, we need a new understanding of the purpose of business, which is to provide goods and services ethically and profitably.

The nature of wealth and its implications for market institutions and economic actors is the theme of the chapter by *Georges Enderle* (University of Notre Dame). Enderle clarifies the notion of "the greater good", by placing business organizations into the broader systemic context. Business is part of the economic system but not the whole of it, since the purpose of the economic system is the creation of wealth in a comprehensive sense. Enderle emphasizes the fact that the economic system mediates between business and society, and that the market is often mistaken for the entire economy. He characterizes and evaluates economic systems as consisting of three basic components: ownership and decision-making, information and coordination, and motivation. Concerning the motivational structure, Enderle emphasizes that self-interest is insufficient in producing public goods. Other-regarding motivations are indispensable, together with entrepreneurial spirit. Defining wealth as a combination of private and public wealth, Enderle draws implications for the motivational structure, the role of markets and collective actors. One implication is the very fact that market institution is efficient in producing private goods, but fails in generating public goods.

One essential part of wealth creation is the innovative activity that constantly searches for improvement. By referring to Grameen Bank in Bangladesh and Medtronic in the US, Enderle shows that wealth creation includes both material and spiritual aspects. In sum, wealth consists of physical, financial, human and social capital. In this way, there is a mutual dependence of private and public wealth. Finally, Enderle stresses that corporations have a moral obligation to recognize business enterprises as responsible to respect human rights and to help "remedy human rights violations".

The theme of the chapter by *Eleanor O'Higgins* (University College Dublin) is whether there may be alternative economic models that to a lesser extent promote inequality and short-term horizons. O'Higgins investigates "gatekeepers" and intermediaries who brought on the global economic crisis, and thereby takes the system of capitalism and its theoretical underpinnings from economics as her point of departure. She discusses how principal–agent logic facilitated the production of perverse incentives and conflicts of interest throughout markets and value chains, and contends that this was an important factor leading to the global financial crisis. Specifically, O'Higgins argues that trust eroded in the financial markets as a consequence of the market-based relationships in the financial sector's investment value chains. Thus, the participation of both investors and savers may be threatened.

On the basis of this understanding of the problem, O'Higgins maintains that a new model of business and capitalism is needed. O'Higgins argues that its purpose should be to create value for all, in a context of social solidarity. This implies placing strong emphasis on developing investment value chains in a manner that promotes the trust between actors in the value chain. According to O'Higgins, the professional ethics of actors in the value chain plays an important role in achieving this end. O'Higgins suggests that such a reconfiguration of the investment value chain is necessary in order to ensure a long-term view that enhances value creation. Thereby, argues O'Higgins, a new movement in fund management – that of "slow finance" would be enabled to flourish.

The four chapters in Part I together constitute an argument that the current mental models, market and governance institutions, and corporate behavior promote inequality rather than equality, and that this is detrimental from economic, social and environmental points of view. The authors of these chapters argue for laws and regulations that promote fairness, a broader purpose for corporations, market and governance institutions that provide incentives for generating public wealth, and market mechanisms that stimulate longer-term thinking promoting equality in business and society.

1.2.2 Part II: From the Technical–Materialistic to the Ecological–Spiritual

The second stream of thought in the book deals with the values and beliefs that are embedded in the current approaches to business in general and business ethics in particular. Any understanding of a problem is based on a set of beliefs and a corresponding set of values, since a problem reflects our understanding of the gap between the current and the desired state (Eierman and Philip 2003). In this respect, the values we strive to realize or to protect are central to how we act as individuals and organizations, and to how we design organizations, markets and governance mechanisms.

The chapters in Part II of this book address the role of values and beliefs in business ethics along several dimensions. First, values are central to the way in which individuals and thereby organizations conceive of and approach problems (Mitroff 1998; Ims and Zsolnai

2006). Thus, values in large part determine the choices and behavior of individuals and firms, whether this relates to consumer behavior, investor behavior or managerial choice (cf. Van Lange 1999). Therefore, the value orientations of individuals and organizations are significant both from an economic and ethical point of view, since they influence the economic, social and environmental outcomes of economic behavior.

Second, the boundaries we set for what is considered relevant types of value in decision contexts matter for decision-making purposes. Broadening the set of values considered in the decision-making process is arguably likely to increase the set of stakeholders considered and the breadth of norms taken into account (e.g., Zsolnai 2011). The value set considered, then, has an impact on the outcomes of decisions along several value dimensions, which implies that value plurality increases the adequateness of decision-making.

The chapters in the second part of the book address issues related to different value dimensions and beliefs in business. They discuss the values that are embedded in current management models and theories, and the implications they have for economic decision-making and behavior. In doing so, they contrast materialistic and non-materialistic – and in particular spiritual – value orientations. The chapters further address how beliefs about reality relate to our conceptions of what is ethical. In this respect, issues of consciousness, man's place in the world, the notion of time and our different worldviews are all addressed. Finally, the chapters address the metaphysics of business and the metaphysics of the environment, and how our understandings thereof may stand in the way of our ability to design organizations that promote socially and ecologically viable business. In this way, the chapters in the second part of the book are interconnected in their emphasis that for business to be sustainable, there is a need for a shift from technical–materialistic perspectives to ecological–spiritual perspectives.

The theme of the chapter by *Laszlo Zsolnai* (Corvinus University of Budapest) is the value orientation of decision makers. Zsolnai argues that the dominant management model of today's business is based on a materialistic conception of man in which greed and an "enrich yourself" mentality play a key role. The economic and financial crisis has given insight into the problems of mainstream business that is based on this model. With this point of departure, Zsolnai criticizes the notion of profit as the sole measure of economic success. One of the problems with profit as a success criterion is that the value of natural assets and important human and social values cannot adequately be expressed in monetary terms. Another problem is created when money is used as the main motivational source for economic activities. By using the "crowding" theory, Zsolnai emphasizes that strong profit motivation may be counter-productive, because it decreases the intrinsic motivation of economic actors, which may lead to manipulation of others and oneself via mechanisms of moral disengagement.

In opposition to the dominant value orientation, Zsolnai suggests a spiritual value orientation characterized by interconnectedness and transcendence. A spiritual person – a *homo spiritualis* – is "genuinely aware of the interconnectedness of all living beings", experiencing love and compassion toward others. Zsolnai points out that this kind of behavior can be seen in spiritual-based leadership, which is a holistic approach that provides a framework for an organization's values, ethics and responsibility. The non-materialistic management model assumes that a human being has materialistic and non-materialistic motivation. Zsolnai further discusses examples of non-materialistic management – the Grameen Bank in Bangladesh and Triodos Bank in the Netherlands – which demonstrate that spiritually driven, non-materialistic management models are based on intrinsic motivation and measure success in a multidimensional way. In this manner, argues Zsolnai, organizations are able to serve the common good.

The sources of ethical competency in an Eastern perspective is the theme of the chapter by *Peter Pruzan* (Copenhagen Business School). His chapter concerns what it means to be ethical, how it can be realized, and its relevance for organizational leaders. Pruzan's intention is to present a chapter that is "both academically acceptable and yet is based upon personal mystical experiences as well as on a metaphysical starting point". Accordingly, he seeks to integrate spirituality as an overall framework for understanding central leadership concepts.

A crucial question for Pruzan is the following: "What is the source of our competence to behave virtuously and wisely so as to transcend the limitations of our ego-minds?" Pruzan supplements the modern Western approaches to ethics with wisdom and spontaneous knowing. The Buddhist and Hindu teachings provide a non-dual perspective on reality where we are simply one with an underlying total reality. It follows that ethical behavior does not just concern the relationship between humans, but also between humans and all of reality, including future generations. The goal of life is to identify one's self with the Self, to *be* the unity in all the diversity. Pruzan sketches the relevance of the concept of ethical competency to the field of business ethics. He asserts that the world of business can provide a fertile context for spiritual development, and the ability to integrate and balance rational actions with one's inner source of ethics. Spirituality can inspire business leaders to re-consider how they and their organization formulate the core-meaning of their existence.

In his chapter, *Kevin T. Jackson* (Fordham University) takes an existential approach to exploring philosophical and practical aspects of *time*. Jackson draws together issues of time as they relate to *aesthetics* (temporal relationships between economic value and moral values), *human rights* (time's impact on our capacity for well-being), and *economic life* (comprehending business as a temporal art). Jackson argues that living with time-balance is a vital existential need – a prerequisite for flourishing in a state of physical and mental health. He further draws on the relationship between music and business, in order to grasp how business (like music itself) is a complex, pulsating temporal art that engages our whole being in multiple layers of time cycles. Both music and business happens *in time* and have specific rhythms. Moreover, they may both have aesthetic, economic, and spiritual value. As such, they are central to our well-being. However, time is also associated with specific problems, and Jackson introduces the notion of *chronopathy*, which is a state of temporal dysfunction that afflicts not only individuals but also organizations. It can be manifested in individuals as busy-ness, and can be seen as a species of "invisible" human rights deprivation.

Jackson further argues that because they are linked to markets, and because markets are in flux over time, the objects to which we assign economic value undergo changes in valuation in a continuous temporal flow. According to Jackson, it is important to recognize that there is some overlap between economic and aesthetic value. Accordingly, he proposes that one of the important characteristics of the moral value of human rights is that it remains constant over time. It is not subject to "market swings." Therefore, argues Jackson, human rights have a special *axio-logical atemporality*, even though they may well undergo change over time.

The theme of the chapter by *Ove Jakobsen* (Bodø Graduate School of Business) is ecological economics. Jakobsen argues that the negative side effects of the modern industrial society are largely unintended consequences of the dominating mechanistic worldview. The ecological losses put a strain on both economic and social systems. Jakobsen points to the fact that degraded ecosystems increase the risk that these systems will be pushed over the edge. The problems are to a large extent due to shallow approaches aimed at the symptoms of the problems. Jakobsen argues that solving such serious challenges by one-sided treatment of the most visible symptoms could lead to a number of paradoxical outcomes. For example, an attempt to solve the financial crisis by stimulating economic growth will increase the current environmental problems. Growth in production and consumption in rich countries often leads to reduced resource efficiency, the life cycle of products becomes shorter, the distance between production and consumption increases, and the amounts of waste grow dramatically. According to Jakobsen, the tendency to overexploit resources is currently reinforced by powerful technologies, as well as by cultural norms, particularly those associated with today's globally dominant economic growth paradigm. Jakobsen argues that we are consequently in need of a paradigm shift.

According to Jakobsen, most developed countries are currently in a period of uneconomic growth, in which further growth in economic activity actually reduces well-being. He argues that addressing the climate crisis suggests additional measures that are difficult to implement without changing from a growth to a de-growth economy. Jakobsen proposes new solutions based on a change from a competitive to a cooperative economy, based on an ongoing dialogue between all concerned stakeholders. He distinguishes between different interpretations of economic growth along the variables "green economy" and "ecological economics" versus "short term" and "long term" action plans. Jakobsen concludes that the failure to address metaphysical questions has led to many of the central errors of conventional economics.

The four chapters in Part II together constitute an argument that the beliefs and values embedded in current management theories as well as in the behavior of managers, employees and customers are largely based on a materialistic worldview and a corresponding technical mindset. The authors argue that there are detrimental side effects of this orientation, and that a much broader value orientation and mindset is needed. The authors argue that an emphasis of the spiritual sources of ethics in business as well as on the aesthetical values that may inform business activity has the potential to broaden the horizon and deepen the thinking of decision makers. Furthermore, the authors argue that a longer-term orientation that emphasizes the ecological dimension of business is necessary in order to arrive at more sustainable business practices.

1.2.3   Part III: From Compliance and Enforcement to Autonomy and Responsibility

The third and final stream of thought in the book deals with the question of whether mandated or voluntary approaches to business ethics are more effective. At a deeper level, this relates to the question of how ethical behavior is motivated, facilitated, and sustained. Increasingly, governments, professional bodies, and other actors argue that mandatory practices related to business ethics and corporate responsibility are necessary in order to enforce responsible practices and ensure compliance with desired standards. For instance, there is an expectation that social and environmental reporting (or integrated reporting) will become mandatory in the coming years (Ioannou and Serafeim 2011). The development of institutions like UN Global Compact, Global Reporting Initiative, and the ISO26000 standard has also moved reporting practice in the direction of standardization and thereby created more emphasis on compliance.

On the other hand, many scholars and practitioners argue that voluntary approaches to business ethics and corporate responsibility are more appropriate for motivating and fostering ethical practices. First, it is possible that mandating responsible practices will lead firms to do only what is mandated and abstain from doing more (cf. Pogge 1992). Second, there is a risk that enforcing responsible practices may crowd out any genuine moral commitment on the part of the actor, and thus reduce the act to pure compliance or opportunism (Ims et al. 2013). This may transform the vibrant nature of ethical reflection and dialogue into a more narrow "quasi-legalistic" system of rules and requirements. Finally, a heavy reliance on mandatory standards requires a comprehensive system to follow-up and develop such rules and regulations in order to sustain ethical practices over time.

The chapters in the third part of the book address issues related to how ethical and responsible behavior can be fostered and sustained. They address the question of what constitutes responsible behavior and how personal values determine choices of personal responsibility. The chapters further discuss the individual's autonomy and power to act in line with one's convictions. Furthermore, they analyze how voluntary versus mandatory regimes stimulate firms to act in accordance with societal expectations. The authors also address the importance of legitimacy in driving behavior. Finally, the chapters stress the importance of free and open dialogues for stimulating ethical reflection and action. In this way, the chapters in Part III together emphasize the importance of autonomous and responsible choice, which stimulates moral commitment and accountability, rather than compliance and enforcement regimes that may undermine such commitment.

The phenomenon of personal responsibility in organizational life is the theme of the chapter by *Knut J. Ims* and *Lars Jacob Tynes Pedersen* (NHH Norwegian School of Economics). Ims and Pedersen aim to explore how individuals in organizations arrive at heroic acts of taking personal responsibility despite inflicting considerable costs on themselves (and potentially on others). The chapter investigates a particular type of personally responsible behavior – acts that are characterized by autonomous, value-driven choice in business settings. In doing so, Ims and Pedersen shed light on the relationship of personal responsibility and the greater good, as well as on how the individual's moral sensitivity is translated into action.

Ims and Pedersen investigate the case of Inge Wallage, who used an *exit strategy* in order to take personal responsibility. Wallage left her former position as vice president of communications in the Norwegian oil company Statoil, and chose to work as communications director of Greenpeace. The authors discuss the nature and scope of personal responsibility, and shed light on how acting personally responsibly is related to promoting and protecting the common good.

The theme of the chapter by *S. Prakash Sethi* and *Donald H. Schepers* (Baruch College, CUNY) is the codes of conduct in multinational firms. Sethi and Schepers investigate numerous non-state regulatory regimes (e.g., UN Global Compact and the Equator Principles) that have been developed to promote responsible business practices. Their point of departure is the manifold critique directed at these initiatives. A fundamental distinction is made between input and output legitimacy of codes of ethics, where the former refers to the degree to which the code has been developed in a manner that ensures (for example) stakeholder representation and voice, while the latter refers to the real world impact of the code.

The framework proposed by Sethi and Schepers involves an evaluation that combines an emphasis on measures in the code itself weighed against the cohesiveness of the member group that governs the code. These two criteria are indicators of the effectiveness of the code. Based on this framework, Sethi and Schepers identify eight pre-conditions for identifying strengths, weaknesses, and pitfalls related to different types of codes. In a systematic way, Sethi and Schepers analyze and evaluate four different codes of conduct – all of which are industry-wide codes. By means of their analysis, the authors highlight key differences between codes, and how their strengths and weaknesses relate both to issues of internal and external legitimacy.

The theme of the chapter by *Johannes Brinkmann* (Norwegian Business School) is how individuals learn to develop business ethics competence. Brinkmann explores the methodology of Socratic dialogue in the tradition of the German philosophers Leonard Nelson and Gustav Heckmann. The Nelson–Heckmann tradition is a small-group conversation process inspired by Plato's classical dialogues of Socrates. According to Brinkmann, the Socratic dialogue may promote the individual's understanding of how to "walk the talk", by offering the dialogue participants a learning-by-doing experience of what an ideal moral conversation looks like.

Brinkmann outlines four indispensable features of the Socratic dialogue methodology: (1) starting with the concrete and remaining in contact with concrete experience, (2) full understanding between participants, (3) adherence to a subsidiary question until it is answered, and (4) striving for consensus. That is, the methodology takes as point of departure the concrete experiences of the individual. Brinkmann uses three examples of actual Socratic dialogues in order to illuminate how such processes may be carried out, and which features promote their success. Brinkmann concludes that we may successfully employ Socratic dialogues in order to reach well-justified consensus about a variety of ethical issues, and thereby we may get closer to reducing the theory–practice divide.

The three chapters in Part III together constitute an argument that an important challenge for business ethics is to stimulate ethical reflection, judgment, motivation and commitment over time, and that this challenge requires autonomous choice and personal accountability. The authors thus argue that individuals sometimes need to be able to make heroic moral choices in organizational life. They further argue that firms should be given considerable degrees of freedom to design and implement appropriate ethical institutions that stimulate commitment and competence in the face of difficult issues related to business ethics and corporate responsibility. Finally, the authors argue that open, but structured ethical dialogues can stimulate reflection and commitment to foster genuine and sustained ethical behavior.

As a forward-looking epilogue to the three main themes outlined above, the book culminates in all the contributing authors' perspectives on what ought to be the future of business ethics. The final chapter gives an account of the structured dialogue that concluded the TABEC conference in Bergen, in which the conference participants had a roundtable discussion about the future of business ethics. The dialogue thus dealt with the question of how business ethics ought to develop in order to be suited for the challenges of the future of business. The anthology's concluding chapter summarizes the viewpoints of the conference participants, and thereby points towards the horizon in discussing how business ethics needs to be developed in order to regain trust and purpose in the post-crisis era, as well as to foster the ability of business to contribute to and to protect the greater good of humanity.

REFERENCES

Baldacci, E., L. De Mello and G. Inchauste (2002), *Financial Crises, Poverty, and Income Distribution* (No. 2002–2004), Washington, DC, USA: International Monetary Fund.

de Graaf, J., D. Wann and T.H. Naylor (2005), *Affluenza: The All-consuming Epidemic*, San Francisco, CA, USA: Berrett-Koehler Publishers.

Eierman, M.A. and G.C. Philip (2003), 'The task of problem formulation', *International Journal of Information Technology & Decision Making*, **2** (03), 353–372.

Eisenstein, C. (2011), *Sacred Economics: Money, Gift and Society in the Age of Transition*, Berkeley, CA, USA: Evolver Editions.

Eysenck, M. (1990), *Happiness: Facts and Myths*, Hove, UK: Lawrence Erlbaum.

Galbraith, J.K. (1994), *A Short History of Financial Euphoria*, New York, NY, USA: Penguin.

Goodpaster, K.E. (1991), 'Business ethics and stakeholder analysis', *Business Ethics Quarterly*, **1** (1), 53–73.

Ims, K.J. and L. Zsolnai (2006), 'Shallow success and deep failure', in L. Zsolnai and K.J. Ims (eds), *Business within Limits: Deep Ecology and Buddhist Economics*, Bern: Peter Lang.

Ims, K.J., L.J.T. Pedersen and L. Zsolnai (2013), 'How economic incentives may destroy social, ecological and existential values: The case of executive compensation', *Journal of Business Ethics*, **123** (2), 353–360.

Ioannou, I. and G. Serafeim (2011), 'The consequences of mandatory corporate sustainability reporting', *Harvard Business School Research Working Paper* (11-100).

Kasser, T. (2011), 'Materialistic value-orientation', in L. Bouckaert and L. Zsolnai (eds), *The Palgrave Handbook of Spirituality and Business*, New York, NY, USA: Palgrave Macmillan.

Kentikelenis, A., M. Karanikolos, I. Papanicolas, S. Basu, M. McKee and D. Stuckler (2011), 'Health effects of financial crisis: Omens of a Greek tragedy', *The Lancet*, **378** (9801), 1457–1458.

Lamb, H.H. (1995), *Climate, History and the Modern World*, New York, NY, USA: Routledge.

Lefranc, A., N. Pistolesi and A. Trannoy (2008), 'Inequality of opportunities vs. inequality of outcomes: Are Western societies all alike?', *Review of Income and Wealth*, **54** (4), 513–546.

Mitroff, I.I. (1998), *Smart Thinking for Crazy Times: The Art of Solving the Right Problems*, San Francisco, CA, USA: Berrett Koehler.

Piketty, T. (2013), *Capital in the Twenty-First Century*, Cambridge, MA, USA: Belknap Press.

Pogge, T.W. (1992), 'Loopholes in moralities', *The Journal of Philosophy*, **89** (2), 79–98.

Sen, A. (1992), *Inequality Reexamined*, Oxford, UK: Oxford University Press.

Shiller, R.J. (2008), *The Subprime Solution: How Today's Global Financial Crisis Happened, and What to do About It*, Princeton, NJ, USA: Princeton University Press.

Stiglitz, J.E. (2012), *The Price of Inequality: How Today's Divided Society Endangers our Future*, New York, NY, USA: W.W. Norton & Company.

Van Lange, P.A. (1999), 'The pursuit of joint outcomes and equality in outcomes: An integrative model of social value orientation', *Journal of Personality and Social Psychology*, **77** (2), 337–349.

Yunus, M. (2007), *Creating a World without Poverty: Social Business and the Future of Capitalism*, Philadelphia, PA, USA: Perseus.

Zsolnai, L. (2011), *Responsible Decision Making*, New York, NY, USA: Transaction Publishers.

PART I

From inequality to equality

2. The business of inequality

George G. Brenkert

2.1 INTRODUCTION

Increased inequality of income and wealth between those at the top and those at the bottom of the economy has been one of the noteworthy features of US society in the last several decades. "From 1980 to 2005, more than 80 percent of total increase in Americans' income went to the top 1 percent. Economic growth was more sluggish in the aughts, but the decade saw productivity increase by about 20 percent. Yet virtually none of the increase translated into wage growth at middle and lower incomes" (Noah 2010, p. 2). Stiglitz claims that "by 2007, the year *before* the [latest financial] crisis, the top 0.1 percent of America's households had an income that was 220 times larger than the *average* of the bottom 90 percent." Beyond this, "wealth was even more unequally distributed than income, with the wealthiest 1 percent owning more than a third of the nation's wealth" (Stiglitz 2012, p. xii). Lansley claims that "little more than a thousand individuals commanded a sum equivalent to a third of the output of the American economy" (Lansley 2011, p. 9).

This economic inequality has also been the object of many best seller books, academic articles, public essays, and popular movements such as Occupy Wall Street. In his State of the Union address (Eichler 2012) President Obama said that a level economic play field is "the defining issue of our time."[1] According to Bower, Leonard and Paine, corporate executives also see the increase in income inequality as a major issue (Bower, Leonard and Paine 2011, pp. 56–62).

The increase in inequality has become so significant in recent decades that some have taken to calling it the "great divergence" (Noah 2010). And though this inequality is widely acknowledged, there is much less agreement upon its sources, ethical implications, and appropriate responses.

The most common response of those who find this disparity ethically unacceptable has been to invoke government action. A wide variety of governmental responses have been proposed to curb current levels of inequality. For example, some have urged higher or more progressive taxes on consumption (Frank 2007, p. 9). Others have sought governmental action to require businesses to permit stockholders to have a say on compensation packages of top executives.[2] And some have defended the adoption of a constitutional amendment to reduce (or prohibit) the use of corporate money in lobbying.[3]

Few of these kinds of measures have been adopted, or are currently likely to be adopted. Those that have been adopted have not obviously altered the economic disparity at issue.

An important reason for this situation is, I believe, a widespread acceptance of a mental model or framework, strongly influenced by libertarian views, regarding business, the market, and inequality. These views see inequality as a natural and even desirable result of business transactions. Ludwig von Mises wrote that "inequality of wealth and incomes is the cause of the masses' well-being, not the cause of anybody's distress ... . Where there is a lower degree of inequality, there is necessarily a lower standard of living of the masses."[4]

The implication for those who hold this view, or mental model, is that business does not have any responsibility to redress income and economic inequality, at least insofar as it proceeds from capitalist transactions. Further, not even the government should intervene to alter the distribution of income and/or wealth in society.

This topic is an important one for several reasons. First, as noted above, many political and business leaders have indicated that they are concerned about the level of inequality in society today. The importance of this topic for them is simply a reflection of its wider significance. Second, current levels of inequality have been said to be unfair or unjust. If correct, these moral reasons would establish the importance of this topic. Third, current levels of inequality are said to have negative impacts on the functioning of the economy (see Lansley 2011). It has also been argued that great degrees of inequality damage the trust people have in others in their society (see Wilkinson and Pickett 2010). Since trust is said to play an important instrumental role in societies, great inequality imperils an important part of a well-functioning economy.

Finally, this issue poses an important question about discussions of business ethics (as a field) and the ethics of business. If such a major issue as inequality that comes about through the actions of business lies outside the purview of (the field of) business ethics and the businesses that are part of the economy, then this points to a major limitation of business ethics as well as of business itself in addressing such issues. It would seem that, on this libertarian view, greater equality could only be viewed as an external constraint on business that must be imposed by some other agency, for example the government, and not something that should or does play a role within business itself.

In this chapter, I consider the increased inequality of income and wealth in the US with special regard to the responsibilities of business for such inequality.[5] To do this, I consider two rather different approaches to the view that inequality, rather than equality, is a "natural" and desirable result of markets and business transactions. I argue that their defense of inequality is not acceptable. Unless and until such views and the mental models are rejected (or at least modified), the problem of the great divergence will continue. In the latter part of the chapter I sketch several reasons to believe that businesses do have an ethical responsibility, in part, for the increased inequality that currently attracts so much attention.

2.2 LIBERTARIANISM, NARVESON, AND BUSINESS

In considering the issue of equality, the claim at stake is not that everyone should be absolutely equal with regard to the income they earn or the wealth they are able to accumulate. That is a non-issue. There are all-too-many familiar reasons why this is not a plausible alternative. Rather the issue has to do with how those inequalities come about and the implications and consequences of great disproportions in incomes and wealth.

One major obstacle that stands in the way of efforts to redress these great divergences is an underlying view of business that has been greatly shaped by libertarianism. On this view, businesses acting in a free market have responsibilities not to engage in fraud or to violate current law, but may otherwise act in any self-interested manner they choose (the virtue of selfishness) to maximize their profits. The result may be significant inequalities that are viewed as just (they are part of the workings of the market).[6]

This viewpoint is expressed and defended in different ways. Here I wish to consider two rather different accounts. The first (Narveson) builds upon an account of the basic business transaction and derives its views from the bottom up. The second (Hayek) begins with a spontaneous market order and asks whether we can make any sense of demands for social justice (and equality) of a society with such a structure. In short, it views the matter from the top down.

Both views capture elements of a mindset that many people hold and that reject objections to inequality. These views not only permit but encourage great disparities of income and wealth in (US) society.

In the following I want to briefly sketch these libertarian views and draw out their common stance regarding equality and inequality. In this discussion, I do not deny that libertarians also believe that certain forms of equality are important, however, for them it is the equality of individual rights (Nozick 1974) or the equal respect for individual agreements (Narveson) that is crucial.

I will take a brief essay by Narveson as one example of the libertarian view. Narveson begins with the view that the nature of business is "transactions [that] occur between free and independent persons presumed to be rationally seeking to promote their own advantage" (Narveson 1971, p. 63).

There is an impersonal character to these exchanges, since one can do business with people one loves, hates, or doesn't even know. "The free exchange of goods or services which is the essence of business is possible because each party has something which the other party values *more* than what he already has" (Narveson 1971, p. 64). Since we cannot engage the vast majority of people as either the object of our love or as enemies, the best basis upon which to have these relationships is that of "mutual profit and advantage" (Narveson 1971, p. 65). Accordingly, Narveson even suggests that "there is a great deal to be said for business transactions as the paradigm cases of human relationships" (Narveson 1971, p. 64).

Given these views of individuals and transactions, inequalities are not only a natural result, but also are viewed with equanimity. Narveson says of the relations of people on this model, "we are not presumed to *owe* each other anything more than to leave each other in peace, to go about, as we say, his business; and if we do relate to each other, then we do so on terms of mutual advantage" (Narveson 1971, p. 65). This is not to say that business people engage in unlimited self-seeking; they can cooperate with others. However, when they do so they are simply acting to achieve "the best deal possible for himself" in the long run (Narveson 1971, p. 65).

On this view, free and uncoerced agreements are of the essence of just transactions. Accordingly, if two people, or a business and some executive or worker, agree to a particular compensation package then that package is just. Narveson claims

> if we each make and reliably keep the best deal we can, there is no certainty, and indeed small probability, that the result, even in the long run, will be to yield approximately the same level of income, wealth, welfare, or happiness for everyone. Indeed, there is no limit to the discrepancies which could in principle arise as the result of successive just dealings, on this view of the matter. (Narveson 1971, p. 65)

The upshot is that, on this view, "justice has no necessary connection with Equality" (Narveson 1971, p. 65). Consequently, the world that involves significant inequalities is a just world, so long as it results from free transactions between mature people. Contrariwise, "a world in which such transactions are substantially 'interfered with' in the interests of equality is ... an unjust world. For ... to intervene forcibly in an activity carried on between mature people who have freely agreed to do what they do and who are not working for the detriment of anyone else is unjust" (Narveson 1971, p. 66).

In this world there is nothing for business to do regarding inequalities.

This view, or some variant of it, underlies a significant part of current views regarding inequality and the lack of responsibilities that business has for a situation in which inequalities have greatly increased. There are, however a number of serious problems with this view.

To begin with, it doesn't follow that because you can do business with people you don't know or love, that therefore business is impersonal in the sense that no other moral conditions or requirements are involved. Just because one despises or doesn't know the person one deals with in business it does not follow that other norms and values are not relevant in these relations.

Narveson's view here appears to derive from the fact that his account of business relations abstracts the agreements people make from any social context and set of understandings, assumptions, and norms within which they take place. The transaction that Narveson identifies as the essence of business "between free and independent persons presumed to be rationally seeking to promote their own advantage" (Narveson 1971, p. 63) necessarily occurs in some particular historical period and in some society (or between two or more societies). The individuals engaged in these transactions are members of some (or other) society; they have relations of different kinds with different members of their (and other) societies. As such, who they are has been formed through certain values and norms. The actions, choices, etc., they undertake occur within this moral milieu. Of course that milieu and its values and norms may be subject to criticism; but that is not to say they do not exist or that they can be left behind when people make various (self-interested) choices and decisions. Suppose that both Juan and Pedro agree (separately) to work for Smith in his business under certain working conditions doing the same job, perhaps they are to dig a ten foot trench. Without further explanation, surely Smith has (ethical) responsibilities regarding the safety of their working conditions and level of pay.

Further troublesome implications of this view emerge when Narveson suggests that "there is a great deal to be said for business transactions as the paradigm cases of human relationships" (Narveson 1971, p. 64). On the contrary, if the business transaction (as Narveson characterizes it) is one that characterizes family, friendship, or professional relationships, then we have lost a great deal of their content and significance. These relationships are not simply about self-interest and the exchange of mutually interested goods or favors. One can hardly understand the relation of Antigone to her dead brother, or many whistleblowers to their firms, if one simply considers the rational exchange of self-interested goods. Any such attempt is a form of reductionism that destroys the phenomenon in order to save the theory.

In short our engaging in transactions in which products and services are exchanged that are in our self-interest can only be understood in a context in which a host of other values and norms are also relevant and need to be brought to the fore in order to understand and appraise those transactions. Narveson and libertarians cannot simply assert the opposite without some demonstration that these norms and values are not relevant. They cannot – as they try to do – simply wipe them away and begin with the abstracted relation Narveson identifies.

Second, most business transactions today are not simply between individuals but between businesses that are licensed, incorporated, or otherwise socially and legally formed. There is a danger that we transfer our views on the ethics of individual transactions to those of the transactions of organizations that are businesses.

An organization that is incorporated or has legal protection has different relations in society and to society. This is obvious from US history in which the corporation has gone from an organization that must have a social purpose to one in which it can have almost any (legal) purpose. In addition, it has been given (legal) personhood and, most recently, in the US even a voice in elections through the unlimited use of any funds it wishes to place into the political process (so long as it takes certain forms).

Now many of these organizations have great powers to make agreements of self-interest with other such organizations as well as individual job applicants. Such agreements might vary considerably between individuals, groups, or organizations. It stretches the imagination that we must conclude that, without any further ado beyond what Narveson has noted, that those agreements and their results must be said to be just or that considerations of equality might not be relevant. There may be unintended consequences of these agreements that result, for example, in lower wages for entire groups of people; unwitting historical or personal biases might play a role in the opportunities that some, but not others, receive, etc. My contention here does not seek to establish what those other considerations might be, but only that we have not been given sufficient reason to believe that they must exclude matters of equality.

Third, Narveson's view depends on prior agreements. It is on the basis of these agreements that we have (or don't have) various responsibilities. For example, Narveson claims that in the business world "we do not *owe* each other even a minimum standard of living, let alone an equal one. I may be starving in the gutter and in rags: this still does not make it your obligation to feed and clothe me, even if you are exceedingly wealthy" (Narveson 1971, p. 67). When we ask the reason for this view, his answer is: "Because there is no antecedent agreement, struck on terms of mutual self-interest, which requires me to do this" (Narveson 1971, p. 67).

However, it is clear that we have any number of responsibilities without having come to agreement with someone else, let alone on the basis of rational self-interest. Parents have responsibilities to their children even though they have not engaged in some prior agreement that has been based on mutual self-interest. Friends have responsibilities to other friends even though, again, there has been no explicit agreement that is based on rational self-interest. And the owner of a dog or cat has responsibilities to that animal, not based on any prior agreements. In short, we can have responsibilities to other people and even to animals even though we do not have (antecedent) agreements with them. Accordingly, Narveson's view does not show that businesses may not have responsibilities regarding equality even though they have not arrived at agreements with those who experience inequality of income or wealth.

In short, Narveson's starting place is a very abstract relation between two individuals. In building theories one may begin with any number of different starting points, but they need to be tested against the phenomenon they are aimed to explain or evaluate. For this it is important to recognize that the actual business relations of individuals and businesses are much more complex than Narveson begins with. The conclusions he draws from this framework conflict with other reasonable views and involve problems that they cannot handle. When defenders of the geocentric view of the universe argued that their view was a simple starting place – the earth in the center of the universe and everything else circling around it – they did have simplicity on their side – until they confronted the fact that the motions of the planets and stars were much more complicated and involved further complexities that made the geocentric view increasingly implausible. So too with Narveson's libertarian account. Once we recognize these complexities, we also may recognize other responsibilities people have to each other that would not exclude responsibilities regarding equality and inequality.

2.3 HAYEK, SOCIAL JUSTICE, AND EQUALITY

Hayek takes a very different approach. Though he admits that the proposition cannot be proved, he argues that the notion of "social justice" – by which he refers to the concept of a distribution of goods across a society that "should treat all equally well who have deserved equally well of it" (Hayek 1976, p. 63; quoting J.S. Mill) – is an empty, meaningless term.[7] It is, at the same time, dangerous because it "leads straight to full-fledged socialism" (Hayek 1976, p. 64).

His primary argument that social justice (or equality at the societal level) is a mirage is that "those [distributive] shares are the outcome of a process the effect of which on particular people was neither intended nor foreseen by anyone when the institutions first appeared – institutions which were then permitted to continue because it was found that they improve for all or most the prospects of having their needs satisfied" (Hayek 1976, pp. 64–65). However, Hayek maintains, "the attribute of justice may be predicated [only] about the intended results of human action but not the circumstances which have not deliberately been brought about by men" (Hayek 1976, p. 70).

This leads Hayek to two interrelated conclusions: First,

> [j]ustice has no application to the manner in which the impersonal process of the market allocates command over goods and services to particular people: this can be neither just nor unjust, because the results are not intended or foreseen, and depend on a multitude of circumstances not known in their totality to anybody. The conduct of the individuals in that process may well be just or unjust; but since their wholly just actions will have consequences for others which were neither intended nor foreseen, these effects do not thereby become just or unjust. (Hayek 1976, p. 70)

Second, he claims that "there are no principles of individual conduct which would produce a pattern of distribution which as such could be called just" (Hayek 1976, p. 70).

Consider the second conclusion. Even if there could be a principle of individual conduct that, in the market, would lead to a "just" pattern of distribution, this does not mean that individuals might not adopt principles of justice that would set up a societal structure which would impose limits or constraints on the market so that it would have a resulting pattern of distribution different than one without such constraints. Such principles have, in fact, been offered by Rawls' two principles of justice, the second of which mandates that economic inequalities are to be to the "greatest benefit of the least advantaged" (Rawls 1971, p. 302).

Further, simply because the results of individual actions have not been foreseen, it does not follow that we may not ethically evaluate those results. Individual banks may (or may not) approve mortgage applications from various customers seeking to buy homes within a city. It is possible to examine the results of these mortgages and the customers who have acquired them. Now suppose that, without intending it, this distribution of mortgages reveals various biases and discrimination against certain groups of individuals. This is a situation for which the government would be said to have a responsibility to intervene to insure that such discrimination does not take place. However, the banks themselves would also have a responsibility to examine their own mortgage lending practices to ensure that they are not discriminating.

Further, Hayek's argument is based on the assumption of a spontaneous order resulting from individual actions having unintended (but beneficial) results. However, the spontaneous order he assumes is, at least in part, a fiction. There is not a pure, spontaneous order. Instead, government and its policies have affected individual and corporate decisions and actions that have resulted in a current "order" with greatly unequal distributions of wages and wealth.

Second, Hayek argues that people object to wage inequalities since the wages some received don't really reflect their merit or what they deserve. To this, Hayek has an interesting twofold response.

To begin with, Hayek maintains that rewarding merit or desert is not what wages do. "The function of the market order of particular prices or wages is not due chiefly to the effects of the prices on all those who receive them, but to the effects of the prices on those for whom they act as signals to change the direction of their efforts" (Hayek 1976, p. 72). He continues, "their function is not so much to reward people for what they *have* done as to tell them what in their own as well as in general interest they *ought* to do" (Hayek 1976, pp. 71–72).[8] This latter point Hayek states in a different way – one's wages aren't messages regarding their own and the general interest, but the interests of their fellows: "Men can be allowed to decide what work to do only if the remuneration they can expect to get corresponds to the value their services have to those of their fellows who receive them; and that these values will often have no relations to their individual merits or needs" (Hayek 1976, p. 72). Nevertheless, he thinks that this will work out to what "in fact most benefits others" (Hayek 1976, p. 72).

The other point he makes begins by acknowledging that the belief in being rewarded based upon one's merit or desert is a long-standing view, which he links with Calvinism (Hayek 1976, p. 74). He grants that "this belief has beneficial effects: few circumstances will do more to make a person energetic and efficient than the belief that it depends chiefly on him whether he will reach the goals he has set to himself" (Hayek 1976, p. 74). Nevertheless, he thinks it is an erroneous belief, one that "bodes ill for the future of the market order" (Hayek 1976, p. 74). This poses a dilemma for Hayek: should we continue "to support this ['erroneous'] belief, or rather emphasize that inevitably some unworthy will succeed and some worthy fail" (Hayek 1976, p. 74). Should we keep this useful myth, or explode it for what Hayek seeks as the reality of the market?!

If one defends the market then it would seem wise to place that defense within a (psychological) context that supports the market. This is, supposedly, what the appeal to self-interest does. One wonders why an appeal to the belief that wages should reward one for what they do would not fit also into this category. We all recognize that this does not always happen, for various reasons. If that is all Hayek wishes to assert, there can be little disagreement. But he defends a stronger view, that desert or merit are not what is really at stake – it is simply what is in the interest of one's fellows, where he seems to suggest that this is meant to be all one's fellows (including oneself). In short, he defends a utilitarian view of wages.

However, there are any number of articles and books that examine "the cost of inequality" in today's society.[9] They maintain that the current distribution of wages and income impose costs on society that need to be reduced. Further, this argument seems to be at odds with the view that whatever results from the spontaneous order of wages cannot be said to be just or unjust. Here Hayek seems to be allowing that this spontaneous order of wages is just, at least insofar as it "most benefits others." It would seem to follow that if a greater level of equality of income and wages would have greater benefits that Hayek should turn his argument around.

Third, consider Hayek's views on equality of opportunity. This is, he contends, at best, a thin idea; beyond that it is "apt to produce a nightmare" (Hayek 1976, p. 85). The government may, on an equal basis, provide the means for schooling of minors, but even this he thinks is subject to grave doubts (Hayek 1976, p. 84).

His main argument is that for a government to create equality of opportunity it would have to control the entire physical and human environment of all persons and seek, thereby, to provide them with equivalent chances (Hayek 1976, p. 84). To this Hayek responds that "this is an attractive phrase at first, but once the idea is extended beyond the facilities which for other reasons have to be provided by government, it becomes a wholly illusory ideal and any attempt concretely to realize it apt to produce a nightmare" (Hayek 1976, p. 85).

However, no one maintains that governments have to produce absolutely equal opportunities in each and every aspect of human life: height, good looks, intelligence, physical capability, as well as income, loving parents, loyal friends, etc. It can be admitted that there are not bright, shining lines with regard to efforts to foster equality of opportunity. Certainly preventing racial and gender discrimination in the work place is an important effort. So too ensuring that children receive education of high quality is another. There are others as well. But the fact that matters of equality of opportunity become less clear and admit shades of gray does not mean that the preceding equality of opportunity responsibilities are dubious. It simply means that reasonable people must make judgments, over which they will disagree, and regarding which reasons, evidence, consequences, etc. must be taken into account. Hayek's argument is simply an instance of a slippery slope form of fallacious reasoning.

Hayek's views are based on a legitimate concern of governments over-reaching and attempting to make decisions for individuals that make their situation worse off. But Hayek oversteps this important insight. His response to equality of opportunity is based upon threats he perceives that even one step in this direction will lead us to a nightmare of government intrusiveness. He wants bright, clear, sharp lines to be drawn between government and private individuals and organizations. Again, given the experience of fascism one can understand his concerns. But to demand black and white separations is to impose a demand that undercuts important ethical insights and demands that have long received widespread recognition and defense.

The upshot is that, according to the preceding (libertarian) views, inequality – and even great inequalities – is built into the market/ capitalist system. The actions of individuals and individual businesses may result in inequalities, but they cannot be considered unjust (Hayek) and do not imply that we owe anything to those who are poor or at the low end of the inequality spectrum (Narveson). On each of the preceding views, though for different reasons, inequality is either an innocent by-product of market (or capitalist) relations or a beneficial by-product. Not only does business not have any responsibilities regarding the level of inequality that derives from its actions, the government also would seem to have minimal (if any) responsibilities in these regards. Of course individuals may give to charity to help those who are poor. Individual businesses will not. Those businesses will leave such actions to the individuals who are their shareholders. Charity is not a social responsibility of business.

In response to Narveson, I have maintained that it does not follow from the fact that two people engage in a transaction to which they both agree that we might not morally question and disapprove of the results of that transaction. We do this in the case of drugs, prostitution, young children, vulnerable participants, and the destruction of public goods. Further, most business transactions are not simply between two independent individuals, but between businesses that are embedded in different social, economic and political contexts.[10]

Contrary to Hayek, I argued that unintended individual actions can have unjust consequences. That is, they can produce states of inequality that can be morally appraised and said to be wrong. Surely this happens in other ways in daily life. We do things that have unintended consequences that we regret since they harm people, or are taken in ways we did not intend or foresee. I did a certain action and that action caused harm, even if the action I intended was not to cause harm. I still regret it. I apologize for what I did. We might recall, in these regards, the Australian radio DJs who made a fake call to the hospital in London pretending to be the Queen and asking about the medical situation of the Duchess of Cambridge. The nurse who was tricked into revealing the Duchess's medical condition felt so embarrassed she committed suicide. The results of the actions of the DJs were unintended, but they were also harmful and wrong. Similarly, there are other actions by business that end up, for example, harming people through lower wages for entire groups of people that they did not intend. Businesses that follow Hayek's prescriptions to oppose equality of opportunity and to divorce pay performance from merit might well fit this category. Still, we may say that those consequences were unjust and need to be addressed. Even though they did not intend these consequences they need to be remedied.

Accordingly, when we consider business activities that create inequality, we may consider them not simply from the perspective of government, but also the perspective of business.

2.4 OLD ISSUES AND NEW DIRECTIONS

In the preceding sections I have argued that those who hold that equality (or inequality) is not (or should not be) a concern of business are mistaken. However, are there other positive arguments that business has responsibilities regarding inequality? In this chapter I cannot lay out these arguments in any detail. Instead, I will proceed with the more restricted aim of sketching the general outline of a more complete account of business's responsibilities regarding equality and inequality.

Whether in this sketch or a complete argument, I do not contend that business's responsibilities replace or are even more important than the government's responsibilities in this sphere. Instead, my position is the more modest one that business does have responsibilities regarding inequality (and equality) that have not been given appropriate attention in current discussions. These responsibilities are both indirect and direct, and they are significant.

Indirect responsibilities that are relevant to equality but are focused on different stakeholders of business might include a business's responsibilities regarding customers of major purchases, such as mortgages. Does the business adequately inform potential customers of the hazards that they might face given their financial situation and the nature of the mortgage? We know that the failure of many mortgages because their purchasers could not sustain them given their financial condition has led to a significant increase in inequality between whites, blacks and Hispanics in the US. For example, "the Pew Research analysis finds that, in percentage terms, the bursting of the housing market bubble in 2006 and the recession that followed from late 2007 to mid-2009 took a far greater toll on the wealth of minorities than whites. From 2005 to 2009, inflation-adjusted median wealth fell by 66% among Hispanic households and 53% among black households, compared with just 16% among white households" (Kochhar et al. 2011, pp. 1–2).

Other responsibilities relate to business resistance to employee unions. The right of employees to form associations and unions to represent them is widely recognized, both legally and ethically. In the US, the National Labor Relations Act gives employees this legal right. The UN International Covenant on Economic, Social and Cultural Rights recognizes the right to form trade unions. We also know that the decline in unionization has contributed to the current stagnant employee wage situation in the US. For example, Mishel writes that

> the last decade has … been characterized by increased wage inequality between workers at the top and those at the middle, and by the continued divergence between overall productivity and the wages or compensation of the typical worker. A major factor driving these trends has been the ongoing erosion of unionization and the declining bargaining power of unions, along with the weakened ability of unions to set norms or labor standards that raise the wages of comparable nonunion workers. (Mishel 2012, p. 1)

Nevertheless, many US businesses actively and forcefully resist unionization not only through providing employees with information about unions that the employers think is undesirable but also through veiled threats regarding the loss of jobs and the impact on employee careers that unionization might bring about, closing plants that become unionized, and making unionization as difficult as possible.

Yet another area of responsibilities has to do with compensation. The extraordinarily high levels of compensation of various executives, hedge fund managers, etc. have been the focus of a great deal of popular discussion and dissent. Charges of cronyism, conflicts of interest, a lack of connection between pay and performance, inequity between different pay levels, etc. have been leveled. Criteria such as these speak to the issue of the nature and size of compensation an individual might receive. The issues here are complex, but what is clear is that businesses do have responsibilities in this area. The only question is how extensive and how demanding they are.

These are three examples of different responsibilities that businesses have regarding consumers, unions, and executive compensation. They are responsibilities that are, indirectly, connected to issues of equality and inequality. It is a striking feature that our concerns for and responsibilities regarding inequality are more often than not captured through other more particular and indirect responsibilities regarding other aspects of business than general or direct responsibilities for equality itself. It is perhaps this aspect of inequality (and equality) that makes it less obvious in many contexts what the responsibilities of business are in these regards. Nevertheless, this is not a unique situation.

Consider a parent's love for a child. This might be captured in (or involve) providing healthy meals for the child, a secure home, educational opportunities, praising his or her accomplishments, helping him or her overcome other weaknesses or deficiencies, etc. Though each one of these kinds of actions might be said to respond to various other responsibilities the parent has, they may also be said to be part of the way the parent expresses his or her love for the child. Of course, we might also look for the affective way in which these actions were undertaken – but it would be a mistake to simply focus on some very positive affective relation the parent has for the child. For supposing the parent had such an affective relation but did nothing for the child, we might wonder how real that love is. "You say you love your child, but you don't do anything for him. Do you really love him?" Similarly, fulfilling (or not fulfilling) other more direct responsibilities regarding consumers, equality of opportunity, levels of wage compensation, unionization, etc. may also be ways in which businesses express their concern (or lack of concern) for equality.

However, business's responsibilities regarding equality extend beyond these indirect and particular responsibilities. They regard equality in a more direct and general sense that regards the economic and political system within which they operate. If this more general system doesn't have various structures, rules, etc. individual businesses may find it more difficult to fulfill their other responsibilities that indirectly relate to equality.

If they pay more for employees than a minimum wage, then they may be at a competitive disadvantage; accordingly the level of the minimum wage is important.[11] If businesses are allowed certain ways of defeating unions, then those employers who take advantage of these methods may gain over those who do not. If boards of directors are permitted or encouraged to pay certain forms of compensation due to present laws and regulations then those who do not may lose out when they seek to hire executives with top talent, etc. In short, the laws and regulations within which businesses compete play an important role in affecting the issue of inequality in a society.

This observation raises the question whether businesses (as well as individuals and other organizations) have moral responsibilities for the social systems within which they live and operate? If the answer is "no", then they are simply the recipients of whatever happens in "their" society; they don't participate and they don't seek to have any say in how things go. They live and die according to structures and systems that are external to them. On this view, it wouldn't matter how "small" or how large they were. Whether a single individual or a large organization, they don't have ethical responsibilities for the social systems in which they live and operate. Perhaps they have self-interests that are in play that lead them to act in various ways to influence the social system. But they don't have any moral or ethical responsibilities to shape the social system.

Suppose then, on such a view, that businesses – either by themselves or with other like-minded organizations – seek to have implemented various laws and regulations that have the effect of increasing inequality in society. Perhaps they lobby for a low minimum wage law, seek to block equality of opportunity initiatives, oppose efforts to give various stake-holders a greater say in executive compensation, or provide funding for political candidates that support views that increase inequality. Suppose also that they are successful and inequality increases in society. In effect, businesses have through these organizations, and sometimes on their own, shaped government rules and regulations that promote this situation. In this way they have helped to mold the shape of distributive justice in current society.

Do we conclude that business does not have any moral responsibilities for this result? I think the answer is "no." On the contrary, we should hold that the larger and more powerful a business (or any organization) is and the more influence it is able to wield, the greater are its moral responsibilities for conditions that its actions help to foster in society through its direct actions and indirect actions (e.g., lobbying to set the rules by which the direct actions take place).

Business through its actions regarding wages for employees, opposing unions, not warning customers about dangerous financial products (e.g., mortgages, CDOs), resisting equality of opportunity, and giving exaggerated compensation to top executives have fostered high levels of inequality in the US. To say that it is the sole responsibility of the government to take steps to correct the resulting inequalities distracts us from a major source of the problem. To focus solely on the government's responsibilities here is something like arguing, prior to laws or regulations against baseball players using performance enhancing drugs, that those players who do so are simply following their own desires to win and that it is the responsibility of the Major League Baseball organization to take steps to correct this situation. Clearly Major League Baseball has a role here, but the players also have a responsibility in this situation as well.[12]

Business bears important responsibilities with regard to equality in society. It is true, of course, that due to competitive market pressures a single business cannot (in various situations) prevent the resulting inequalities without risking its competitive situation – though many times this is used as an excuse not to do something or to follow a business plan or strategy that omits these responsibilities. But this does not mean that the business does not bear responsibilities here. They have a twofold set of responsibilities. On one level they have a responsibility to do what they can within their own spheres to act and develop policies that do not create unjustified forms of inequality. On another, more general level, they have responsibilities to seek other remedies through joint action to address the problem that can only be addressed collectively.

However, some might respond that the government is the one that must take responsible action here because the problem is caused by government actions, not those of business. The rationale behind this position is that absent government intervention in the market, these problems would either not arise or would solve themselves through market action. In short, the market is self-correcting. It is government intervention that creates the inequality problem.

This response is implausible. First, neither Narveson nor Hayek holds such a view. They maintain that the market itself creates these inequalities. Further, the plausibility of this view was surely undercut by the recent financial crisis. Even Alan Greenspan was brought to acknowledge the limits of the self-correcting view of the market when he testified before the House Committee on Oversight and Government Reform: "Those of us who have looked to the self-interest of lending institutions to protect shareholders' equity, myself included, are in a state of shocked disbelief" (Andrews 2008).

A different kind of argument that has a similar result regarding the responsibilities of business has been offered by Richard De George. He defends, in *Competing with Integrity*, seven general ethical guidelines for multinational businesses that apply not only to business in countries other than the home country but also the countries where MNCs are head-quartered. For example, he argues that "G2. Multinationals should produce more good than harm for the host country." He also contends that "G4. Multinationals should respect the human rights of their employees" (De George 1993, pp. 46–51). In addition, he argues that MNCs are to cooperate with local government to develop and enforce just background institutions: "G7. Multinationals should cooperate with the local government in developing and enforcing just background institutions" (De George 1993, p. 54).[13] Such institutions, De George explains, are intended "to guarantee fair competition, the protection of human rights, and the conservation of the country's resources" (De George 1993, p. 54). However, he also says that this norm prohibits firms from opposing labor unions, the institution of minimum wage laws and environmental protection measures" (De George 1993, p. 54). He thinks this derives from Guidelines 2 and 3, as well as principles of utilitarianism and justice.[14]

De George asks whether this doesn't ask MNCs to act in ways opposed to their self-interests. He answers:

> [i]n the absence of adequate background institutions to promote fairness and efficiency, unscrupulous firms exploit peoples and nations, make gains by bribery and extortion, and succeed not on their efficiency or merits but on their ability and willingness to take advantage of the situations in which they operate. Equitable background institutions would preclude any company from gaining a competitive advantage by engaging in unethical practices. Firms interested in acting with integrity have a vested interest in playing on a level field, where they compete on their merits. (De George 1993, p. 55)

This overarching approach includes the kinds of measures advocated above as moral corrections to the increased inequality that has developed in recent decades.

Part of the preceding argument was that the responsibilities of business regarding inequality are dependent, in part, upon their abilities to exercise influence regarding background institutions. Businesses have responsibilities, *simpliciter*, because they are members of society. They are participants in a system from which they benefit. They act within and have impacts upon that society. They are not simply Leibnizian monads not influencing or being influenced by anyone or anything outside themselves. Accordingly, it would seem to follow that the greater their ability to exercise influence the greater their responsibilities. Certainly large businesses seek to have influence in society through various organizations and associations such as the Chamber of Commerce and the National Manufacturers Association. In this way they seek to shape and alter government policy and social opinion regarding conditions important to business (and equality).

Does this means that (theoretically) a person (or a business) could avoid responsibilities by avoiding and/or not seeking ways in which to enhance his or her abilities to have influence, for example working in cooperation with others through different forms of collective action? The answer is both "yes" and "no." Different circumstances (proximity to power or important events) and conditions (greater powers or abilities) will give rise to greater – or lesser – responsibilities. Beyond this, if a business does not have or cannot develop ways to influence the shape of a society's background institutions then its responsibilities in these regards would be lessened. However, by virtue of being a member of the social, economic, and political system each member retains at the least minimal responsibilities. These responsibilities include not engaging in actions that anyone or any business could readily undertake that foster unjustified inequalities through societal laws and regulations.

It might be objected that those opposed to current levels of inequality should be defending a very different view since businesses are unlikely to change their stripes and defend truly socially responsible policies, for example involving greater distributional justice or equality. Instead, they should support libertarian views that business should not be involved in social responsibility efforts at all since they will see this as opportunities to enhance their own (narrow) self-interests. They will use the public forum to seek rents that benefit them at the expense of the public realm.

However, this objection is implausible since it is the self-interested actions of business (e.g., objecting to minimum wage laws, fighting unions) that have contributed to the current problem. Further, the objection could be turned back on itself, since it could also be argued that inasmuch as businesses are unlikely to change their stripes, their efforts to influence politics are also unlikely to change. Hence, the best stance is to get them to alter their narrow, self-interested pursuits by structuring them in ways that better enhance broader social responsibility aims! Through the actions of the social media, demands for transparency in government and business interactions, it may be possible, and more likely, to bend their efforts in some more ethically justifiable way. In fact, given the concerns of business executives regarding inequality,[15] this might be an area in which self-interests and ethical interests merge.

Finally, if we believe various studies that contend that inequality is not in the interests of even the top 1 percent, then this counter-argument would be strengthened (see Wilkinson and Pickett 2010; Reich 2013). For example, there is a variety of arguments that extremes of inequality are harmful for all of society, the well-off as well as the poor. If these arguments are good, they would not necessarily point to particular responsibilities that any individual business has, but would support the preceding argument in that there are more general prudential consider-ations and responsibilities that businesses have with respect to the background institutions within which they operate.

For example, Robert Reich argues that "wealthy Americans would do better with smaller shares of a rapidly growing economy than with the large shares they now possess of an economy that's barely moving" (Reich 2013). His reason is that "70 percent of economic activity in America is consumer spending. If the bottom 90 percent of Americans are becoming poorer, they're less able to spend. Without their spending the economy can't get out of first gear" (Reich 2013).

A different perspective relates to trust. Everyone in society is affected by levels of trust, not only the poor but also those who are well-off. Given low levels of trust, time and money must be spent to defend one's business from untrustworthy employees, customers, and clients; expen-sive security systems must be put in place; gated communities become a refuge from those that can't be trusted; etc. It is striking then that the level of trust in the US has declined from 60 percent in 1960 who agreed that "most people can be trusted," to less than 40 percent in 2004 (Wilkinson and Pickett 2010, p. 54). During this period the level of inequality has, as noted above, increased dramatically. Is there causality here? The issue is complex and difficult. Certainly there may be reciprocal effects in various circumstances. However, Eric Uslaner, a political scientist, has argued that it is inequality that affects trust and not the other way around (see Wilkinson and Pickett 2010, p. 55).[16]

In short there are a number of additional studies and arguments being explored that could be seen as contending that business organizations also have a prudential interest in background institutions that support a society with greater, rather than lesser, inequality. Obviously this does not show that for any particular business at some specific time less inequality would be in its self interest. These considerations relate to continuing background institutions within which business would operate on an ongoing basis. However, viewed in this manner it would seem that businesses have not only ethical but also self-interested reasons to support efforts to create background institutions of greater equality than we presently experience.

2.5 CONCLUSION

I am under no illusion that the preceding arguments will change the views of libertarians or of the many people who wittingly or unwittingly share their views. However, these objections should give them pause.

I have maintained that the arguments two libertarians such as Narveson and Hayek offer on behalf of inequality (and hence in opposition to business responsibilities for moderating inequality) ought to be rejected. Instead, I have contended that businesses have both indirect and direct responsibilities that relate to the issue of inequality. In addition I have noted that there are prudential considerations that may also underlie business responsibilities for moderating current levels of inequality.

It is time that we reject the mental model that the likes of Narveson and Hayek have offered us for another framework in which equality has a role for business. It would be both practically and ethically a superior position to occupy.

NOTES

1. See: http://www.huffingtonpost.com/2012/01/24/state-of-the-union-address-2012_n_12295 10.html (accessed: February 16, 2012). Larry Summers has said that when the US economy finally recovers "issues relating to inequality are likely to replace cyclical issues at the forefront of our economic conversation", *The Washington Post*, July 16, 2012, A15 (accessed: July 16, 2012).
2. Minow (2012).
3. See Jeff Faux (2012, Chapter 12).
4. Cited in Lansley (2011, p. 36). The quotation comes from Ludwig von Mises. Lansley offers the reference for von Mises' statement as coming from *Ideas on Liberty*, New York: Irvington, 1955. I believe that a more correct reference would be: "Inequality of Wealth and Incomes", *Ideas on Liberty*, No. 1. Irvington, NY: Foundation for Economic Education (May 1955), 83–88. Reprinted in *Essays on Liberty, III*. Irvington, NY: Foundation for Economic Education (1958), 123–131.
5. Though I concentrate on the US, the arguments I offer should have application to other similar societies.
6. See the work of Jan Narveson, Friedrich Hayek, David Gauthier, Milton Friedman, and Robert Nozick.
7. "The basic contention ... [that] the term 'social justice' is wholly devoid of meaning or content, is one which by its very nature cannot be proved" (Hayek 1976, p. 96).
    "In a free society in which the position of the different individual and groups is not the result of anybody's design ... the differences in reward simply cannot meaningfully be described as just or unjust" (Hayek 1976, p. 70).
8. In a spontaneous order the question of whether or not someone has done the "right" thing cannot always be a matter of merit, but must be determined independently of whether the persons concerned ought or could have known what was required. [But WHAT is this spontaneous order? This is an abstraction. The order we exist in is not spontaneous!]
9. See Lansley (2011); Stiglitz (2012); Noah (2010); Frank (2007); Wilkinson and Pickett (2010).
10. See Granovetter (1985).

11. This need not be the case. Costco pays its employees more than Wal-Mart and yet Costco has been very successful in the marketplace. Businesses can compete on various bases – low price is one basis, but quality of service can be another.
12. They could avoid using such drugs themselves, insist their team members do not, urge Major League Baseball to ban the use of these drugs, and so on.
13. Among other guidelines De George mentions: (a) MNCs not to do intentional direct harm!? (De George 1993, p. 46); and MNCs to do more good than harm (De George 1993, p. 47). Neither of these is much help with inequality.
14. See De George, 1993, p. 55 (his endnote 24). In general, he believes that these guidelines regarding MNC responsibilities " are not derived from any single high-level principle that might be supposed to be the only proper one. Most of them are overdetermined, in that one can derive or defend them from a variety of high-level principles" (De George 1993, p. 45).
15. See the results of Bower, Leonard, and Paine on inequality.
16. More speculatively, David Moss is examining whether income inequality contributes to financial crises. Do they, for example, "create perverse incentives that put the financial system at risk" (Story 2010, 2/3). "For instance, inequality, by putting too much power in the hands of Wall Street titans, enable them to promote policies that benefit them – like deregulation – that could put the system in jeopardy" (Story 2010, 2/3). This would be yet another instance in which less inequality would benefit everyone, even if the perspective required for this view is the long-run, rather than the short haul.

REFERENCES

Andrews, Edmund L. (2008), 'Greenspan Concedes Error on Regulation', *The New York Times*, retrieved from http://www.nytimes.com/2008/10/24/business/economy/24panel.html?_r=0 (accessed February 8, 2013).

Bower, Joseph L., Herman B. Leonard and Lynn S. Paine (2011), *Capitalism at Risk: Rethinking the Role of Business*, Boston, MA, USA: Harvard Business Review Press.

De George, Richard T. (1993), *Competing with Integrity*, New York, USA: Oxford University Press.

Eichler, Alexander (2012), 'State of Union Address 2012: Obama Calls Income Inequality "The Defining Issue of Our Time"', *The Huffington Post*, retrieved from http://www.huffingtonpost.com/2012/01/24/state-of-the-union-address-2012_n_1229510.html (accessed February 16, 2013).

Faux, Jeff (2012), *The Servant Economy*, Hoboken, NJ, USA: John Wiley & Sons.

Frank, Robert (2007), 'Falling Behind: How Rising Income Inequality Harms the Middle Class', retrieved from http://democrats.financialservices.house.gov/hearing110/htfrank051607.pdf (accessed February 14, 2013).

Granovetter, Mark (1985), 'Economic Action and Social Structure: The Problem of Embeddedness', *American Journal of Sociology*, **91** (3), 481–510.

Hayek, Friedrich A. (1976), *Law, Legislation and Liberty, Vol. 2: The Mirage of Social Justice*, Chicago, USA: The University of Chicago Press.

Kochhar, Rakesh, Richard Fry and Paul Taylor (2011), 'Wealth Gaps Rise to Record Highs Between Whites, Blacks, Hispanics', *Pew Research Center*, retrieved from http://www.pewsocialtrends.org/2011/07/26/wealth-gaps-rise-to-record-highs-between-whites-blacks-hispanics/ (accessed February 20, 2013).

Lansley, Stewart (2011), *The Cost of Inequality*, London, UK: Gibson Square.

Minow, Nell (2012), 'More Shareholders Are Just Saying No on Executive Pay', *Bloomberg.com*, retrieved from http://www.bloomberg.com/news/2012-07-19/more-shareholders-are-just-saying-no-on-executive-pay.html (accessed February 14, 2013).

Mishel, Lawrence (2012), 'Unions, Inequality, and Faltering Middle-Class Wages', retrieved from http://www.epi.org/publication/ib342-unions-inequality-faltering-middle-class/ (accessed January 31, 2013).

Narveson, Jan (1971), 'Justice and the Business Society', in Tom L. Beauchamp and Norman E. Bowie (eds) (1979), *Ethical Theory and Business*, Englewood Cliffs, NJ, USA: Prentice Hall, pp. 63–71.

Noah, Timothy (2010), 'The Great Divergence', *Slate*, retrieved from http://img.slate.com/media/3/100914_NoahT_GreatDivergence.pdf (accessed February 14, 2013).

Nozick, Robert (1974), *Anarchy, State, and Utopia*, New York, USA: Basic Books.

Rawls, John (1971), *A Theory of Justice*, Cambridge, MA, USA: Harvard University Press.

Reich, Robert (2013), 'The Non Zero-Sum Society: How the Rich Are Destroying the US Economy', *Common Dreams.org*, retrieved from https://www.commondreams.org/view/2013/01/29-2 (accessed February 20, 2013).

Stiglitz, Joseph E. (2012), *The Price of Inequality*, New York, USA: W.W. Norton & Company.

Story, Louise (2010), 'Income Inequality and Financial Crises', *The New York Times*, retrieved from http://www.nytimes.com/2010/08/22/weekinreview/22story.html?_r=0 (accessed February 12, 2013).

Wilkinson, Richard and Kate Pickett (2010), *The Spirit Level*, New York, USA: Bloomsbury Press.

3. The profit maximization mantra and the challenge of regaining trust, humanity and purpose in an age of crisis

Wesley Cragg

3.1 INTRODUCTION

In a recently written book, Roger Martin, the Dean of a leading Canadian business school and a highly regarded commentator, argues that, in examining the cause of the 2008 stock market meltdown and the ethical misconduct that accompanied it, we have failed to explore in sufficient depth "the broader theories that underpin our economy". The theories that define the "fundamental goal of corporations and the optimal structure of executive compensation" he goes on to say, "are fatally flawed" (Martin 2011, p. 10). The problem with the theories that dominate management and management education, he argues, is the thesis that the purpose of the firm is to maximize profits for owners and shareholders.

Roger Martin is one of many business theorists and commentators who have come to this conclusion. They include luminaries like Peter Drucker and Harry Mintzberg. What these theorists do not explore is the impact of the logic of profit maximization on the logic of ethics. The purpose of this discussion is to examine the role of ethics in management where the goal of management is the maximization of profits. What will emerge from this analysis is the conclusion that the role assigned to ethics by profit maximizing theories is incompatible with the role required of ethics for the building of justified trust. I will conclude by pointing to the implications of this fact for corporate conduct and corporate leadership and argue that only if the dogma of profit maximization is jettisoned can the ethical principles on which a market economy is grounded be reintegrated into corporate management, governance and leadership.

3.2 A SHORT HISTORY OF THE FIRM

Shareholder primacy theories of the firm have not always played the role they play today in management theory or practice. As Jim Gillies points out in *Boardroom Renaissance* (1992):

> the way in which corporations operate, the way in which they are controlled and the things that they are expected to do has changed dramatically throughout the years. The corporation is not static, but a dynamic institution and like all dynamic institutions it is always changing. (Gillies 1992, pp. 27–28)

This is an important starting point for this discussion since the fundamental conclusion to be drawn from the argument that follows is that a continuing evolution in how society understands why corporations exist and what is expected of them has become a pressing need in the world in which we currently find ourselves.

Given the need for a reassessment of currently dominant management theories and currently dominant approaches to management practice, a brief review of the history of the modern investor-owned corporation is in order.

Business and the production of goods and services has always been a fundamental feature of human history. Business, however, has not always taken the form of what we know today as the modern investor-owned corporation, a business entity that emerged only in the early period of modern European history. What gave rise to the corporation as we know it was the concept of legal incorporation carried out in the first instance through the device of "letters patent".[1] As James Gillies (1992, p. 29) points out:

> Monarchs normally granted authority to form (business) organizations in the form of letters patent. The grant usually permitted the creation of a monopoly for the purpose of achieving some specific public goal such as the building of a road or canal. As time went on the public purposes for which charters were granted constantly expanded and, eventually, chartering private corporations became the common way to deal with public needs.[2]

An example is the charter granted to the Governor and Company of Adventurers Trading into Hudson Bay which assigned the company "the exclusive right to trade and commerce", "possession of the lands, mines, minerals, timber, fisheries, etc." as well as the "full power of making laws, ordinances and regulations at pleasure and of revoking them at pleasure" (Myers 1914, p. 39).

The purpose of the early modern corporation was to engage in business activities specified in their act of incorporation with a view to advancing public interests while generating private economic benefits for their investors. Indeed, it could be argued that incorporation in its early modern phase is most accurately described as a formal social contract in which the privilege of engaging in profitable business activities is granted to a group of investors in return for their assumption of a specific set of public responsibilities. The expectation of reciprocal benefits required that the privileges associated with incorporation along with their potential for private enrichment be balanced by the assumption of responsibilities designed to generate public benefits. Clearly, notions of profit maximization and shareholder primacy were not originally what defined the purpose of corporations as originally conceived by investors or the state or the public generally.

However, this is not the end but only the beginning of the story of the modern corporation. The legal framework within which corporations operate underwent significant modifications in the nineteenth century in response in part to charges of favouritism, corruption and unfair monopolies. As a result, the mercantile idea that corporations should be chartered only where their activities would advance public interests was gradually replaced with a regulatory framework requiring only that those wishing to incorporate register their companies following a set of largely formal and non-demanding bureaucratic procedures.[3] Incorporation thus became a legal right that could be activated with minimal effort. It is these changes, Horwitz claims, which laid the foundations for the emergence of big business or the large, modern, shareholder-owned corporation.[4] These changes also had the effect of disentangling incorporation from the notion that corporations, in return for the privilege of incorporation, should serve public interests as identified in their charter of incorporation.

What emerged in law to take its place was the view that the primary obligation of corporations was to serve the interests of their owners and shareholders. The result was a shift in law from the idea that incorporation was a privilege to the idea that incorporation was a legal right to be conferred by law upon the performance of a set of legal formalities. Emerging with this shift in law was the assumption that the primary obligation of corporations was to those who created them, along with the view that the primary, perhaps even the sole obligation of managers, was to maximize profits for the benefit of shareholders.[5]

Development in United States corporate law at the turn of the twentieth century is often cited in support of this view of the corporation. An excellent example is the Michigan Supreme Court judgement, *Dodge* v. *Ford Motor Co.*[6] in which the court takes the position that:

[a] business corporation is organized and carried on primarily for the profit of the stockholders. The powers of the directors are to be employed for that end.

Margaret Blair (1995) takes this decision to be "as pure an example as exists" of what she describes as the "financial model" of the corporation. It is a model associated with the Chicago School of law and economics which saw the firm as a "nexus of contracts". On this view, the corporation was the property of its shareholders for whom corporate boards of directors and managers served as agents "with no legal obligations to any other stakeholders" (other than of course those with whom it had entered into contracts) (Clarkson 1998, p. 51).

This view of the corporation did not go unchallenged and with the challenge came the earliest examples of the use of the language of corporate social responsibility.[7] Neither could it be said to become the dominant view of managers and boards of directors at least in the United States until much later in the twentieth century. For, as Archie Carroll notes citing Howard Bowen's 1953 book entitled *Social Responsibilities of the Businessman*,[8] 93.5 per cent of the businessmen responding to a *Fortune* magazine survey in 1946 agreed that the responsibilities of business went beyond financial bottom line considerations (Carroll 1999, p. 270).

3.3　THE RISE OF SHAREHOLDER PRIMACY THEORIES

It was not until the late 1960s and early 1970s that what has been described variously as "the property conception", "the financial model", "the economic model" and the "shareholder primacy model" of the corporation assumed a dominant role in defining the purpose of the firm. Much of the credit for the entrenchment of this view of the firm should probably go to the advocacy of Milton Friedman, who, alarmed by the growing influence of the CSR (corporate social responsibility) movement in the United States, published a rebuttal in the *New York Times Magazine* entitled "The Social Responsibility of Business is to Increase its Profits" (Friedman 1970). As a member of the Chicago School, Friedman did not reject the idea that corporations had social responsibilities. Rather, his goal was to attack the expansive views then influential with a much more constrained view that limited the social responsibilities of business to maximizing profits within the confines of the law and "the rules of the game", or alternatively "local ethical custom".[9]

By the mid 1970s, led by Harvard Business School, Friedman's view had been widely adopted by American management schools as defining the purpose and goal of management. This perspective on the purpose of the corporation was in many ways cemented into the fabric of business education and American business culture with the publication in 1976 of the Jensen and Meckling article entitled "Theory of the Firm: Managerial Behavior, Agency Costs and Ownership Structure" (Jensen and Meckling 1976, pp. 305–360). What this article did was introduce agency theory into the world of management and strategic planning. As Roger Martin points out in his analysis of the roots of recent crises, agency theory is grounded on the view that "the singular goal of a company should be to maximize the return to shareholders" (Martin 2011, p. 11). Further, "(t)o achieve that goal, the company must give executives a compelling reason to place shareholder value maximization ahead of their own nest-feathering" (p. 12). As it turned out, the compelling reason was the granting of stock options.

The Jensen and Meckling article was to have a decisive impact on management and management theory. Its impact on management theory and management education is reflected in the fact that it has become the most widely cited article in the business literature (Martin 2011, p. 11). Its impact on management practices is reflected also in the fact that by the 1990s agency theory and the thesis that the purpose of the firm is to maximize share value had become the dominant view governing management practice throughout North America.[10] One consequence was the emergence of stock-based compensation as a way of aligning "the interests of executives with those of shareholders so that executives" with the goal of ensuring that they would "maximize shareholder value rather than to maximize their own rewards" (Martin 2011, p. 56).

A second striking example is the United Nations Global Compact. Introduced by then Secretary-General, Kofi Annan, the Global Compact advocates ten principles that it proposes should command the allegiance of responsible corporations. The reason most often cited for signing the Global Compact and implementing its principles is corporate self-interest. Thus Tom Campbell (2012, p. 60) observes:

> it is noteworthy that the recurring theme of the UN Global Compact Office in the commentaries given on the ten principles is the strategic advantages to be derived from protecting corporate reputation through respecting the principles to the relative exclusion of anything resembling an affirmation of the moral value of intrinsic CSR.[11]

What this approach to the Global Compact implies is either that the profit maximization model is the appropriate model on which to build an assessment of the moral principles that should guide corporate conduct, or, alternatively, the profit maximization/shareholder primacy model is so deeply entrenched in the corporate world that only a demonstration of the instrumental value of the principles could be expected to persuade corporations to sign on to the Global Compact and fulfill its requirements.

A third striking example can be found in the reports of the Special Representative of the Secretary-General of the United Nations laying the groundwork for the proposed UN framework for identifying the human rights responsibilities of transnational corporations and other business enterprises. A fundamental component of this framework is the principle that corporations have a responsibility to respect human rights in their operations whether or not they are compelled to do so by law or its enforcement. The proposed framework has obvious and significant implications for public policy and the strategic management of corporations doing business in global markets. What is striking, however, is that in advancing his proposals, the Special Representative, John Ruggie, nowhere appeals to or connects his recommendations to ethical values or an ethical framework.[12] Rather, he proposes that the responsibility to respect human rights is based on a social expectation embedded in what his third report (2008) identifies as "a company's social licence to operate." Failure to live up to this social expectation, he points out, may "subject companies to the courts of public opinion … and occasionally to charges in actual courts" (Ruggie 2008, p. 54). To put it otherwise, the failure to respect human rights can create risks that may impact operations and damage a company's reputation and, by implication, a company's bottom line.

What all this evidence serves to highlight is the degree to which the profit maximization model has assumed a dominant role in articulating the role and responsibilities of management and corporate boards of directors in the late twentieth and early twenty-first centuries.

3.4 PROFIT MAXIMIZATION AND ITS CRITICS

The view that profit maximization is the purpose of the firm has been widely criticized by management educators, business ethicists and management theorists. An example is Sumantra Ghoshal's critique entitled "Bad Management Theories Are Destroying Good Management Practices". Both Social Contract and Stakeholder theory are readily interpreted as rejection of the profit maximization mode by prominent business ethicists. Most recently, Roger Martin has argued that the management theories on which the profit maximization model is based are "fatally flawed" (Martin 2011, p. 10). Martin points out that one key result is that between 1980 and 2000 CEO compensation was up eightfold (Martin 2011, p. 62) which he then connects to "three massive, blowout scandals involving hundreds of executives each: the accounting scandals (2001–2002), the options backdating scandal (2005–2006) and the subprime mortgage scandal (2008–2009)" (Martin 2011, p. 93).

One of Martin's conclusions is that the "illegal and unethical behavior of business executives over the past few decades suggests that something is seriously out of whack in the corporate world. Assuming that people would rather be ethical than unethical, how did we wind up with such pervasive unethical and illegal behavior?" (Martin 2011, p. 94). There have been a wide variety of responses to this question. Some have located the answer in human greed. Others have pointed to an absence of government regulation. Martin locates the problem in the profit maximization model that now dominates management theory and practice.

What has not been offered, however, by critics of the shareholder primacy theories is an account that looks quite specifically at the impact of the profit maximization model on the normative logic of both management theory and practice. Is there a normative logic buried in the model? Is there something about the model that undermines or corrodes ethical values in the organizational setting in which it dominates? If there is, what is that impact on the ethical values in play and on the capacity of an organization to sustain trust that is ethically justifiable?

These are the questions to which we now turn.

3.5   THE NORMATIVE IMPLICATIONS OF THE PROFIT MAXIMIZATION MODEL

The profit maximization model assigns ethics two distinct but related roles and, as a consequence, has embedded within it two normative logics. The first and most prominent role this model assigns to ethics is a strategic role, that of a means, or tool, or instrument. That is to say, the normative logic the model assigns to ethics is the logic of instrumental rationality. The logic of instrumental rationality is in turn a consequentialist logic[13] which does give to ethical values and principles, for example human rights or the ten Global Compact principles, a clear but instrumental role in management theory and practice. If the purpose or goal of the shareholder-owned corporation is to maximize profits then, if ethics is to have a role in management, it must be because it can contribute to maximizing profits. The link might be either negative or positive. Ignoring ethics can generate serious risks to corporate profitability and even corporate existence. Alternatively, building an ethical culture or conducting one's business ethically can contribute positively by building trust and enhancing the capacity of the corporation to do business profitably. Both possibilities are plausible. There is no shortage of examples illustrating the pitfalls that can accompany both explicitly unethical but also ethically indifferent strategic planning and day-to-day company operations. Enron and Arthur Andersen illustrate the former. Talisman in Sudan and Shell in Nigeria could be taken to illustrate the latter. In short, it is not difficult to find studies or experiences that illustrate the benefits of ethical business conduct.

In so far as it plays a strategic or instrumental role within business, this role for ethics as a means to enhance profitability is relatively unproblematic. This is not to say that discerning its proper role will always be easy. To the contrary, discerning risks or potential reputational or other benefits may be quite complex. Nonetheless, the skill sets required to embed ethics within the instrumental rationality of strategic management are well-understood in strategic management circles. The logic of strategic management structured by the pursuit of profit maximization is the logic of instrumental rationality. The skills required are closely allied and are best illustrated by cost–benefit analysis. The driver is what is assumed to be the self interest of investors. What this means, however, is that the value of ethics when assigned an instrumental role is the value it can be shown to have in advancing the profit maximizing interests of shareholders.

What is significant about ethics when it is playing this role is that it has a role to play *if and only if* ethics can be shown directly or indirectly to advance the interests of shareholders. The immediate result of assigning ethics this role, however, is that ethics loses all intrinsic or what might be described as categorical normative force. If ethics is only a means to some further end, and if acting ethically is required and indeed is morally legitimate only if acting ethically can be shown to further the end to be achieved, then ethical values can generate only hypothetical imperatives or directives.

As it turns out, however, the profit maximization model also requires that ethics play a second role in management. Buried within the theory is a very important ethical assumption, namely that the primary ethical obligation of boards of directors and the managers they hire is to shareholders as owners of the firms for which they have management responsibilities. It is the interests of shareholders to which corporations owe their primary allegiance. This is a moral obligation, and it is an important moral obligation. Managers and boards of directors are the agents of shareholders. Pursuing profits is not simply something that shareholders want them to do. It is something they have an ethical obligation to do. As we shall see and as Milton Friedman points out, it is also a corporate social responsibility.

In this second role ethics does have intrinsic normative force. In this role, ethics specifies the primary ethical obligation governing those with management and governance roles in the corporation. It requires that those with management and governance roles subordinate their own interests to those of the shareholders they are hired to serve. It follows that the moral logic that defines the responsibilities of management, given this model, cannot be exclusively consequentialist in character. Rather, this second role that the model assigns to ethics has two components. First, it identifies the primary moral obligation of managers as the obligation to serve the interests of shareholders, whose interest in turn is principally maximizing the value of their shares in the company. But second it creates for management a set of side constraints which are entailed by the moral obligation to maximize profits for shareholders. The function of the side constraints is to constrain the pursuit by management and those with governance responsibilities of their own personal interests. That is to say the role of the side constraints is to ensure that managers subordinate the pursuit of their own interests to those of the shareholders whose interests they are hired to advance.

In its role as a side constraint, we can extract from the profit maximization model, three distinct functions for ethics. The first, and for the purposes of the model the most important function of the side constraint role of ethics, is to ensure that the corporation serves the interests of shareholders and not the interests of those elected by the shareholders, the board of directors, or hired by the board of directors, senior management, to carry out the wishes of the shareholders. The model, that is to say, assumes that corporate directors are duty bound to serve the interests of the corporation and thereby to serve the interests of the shareholders. This is a moral obligation which is passed by the board of directors to the CEO and by the CEO to senior management. The moral obligation is captured in corporate law as a legal obligation to serve the interests of the corporation which in turn is in place to serve the interests of shareholders. Milton Friedman, in his well known *New York Times Magazine* article, refers to this moral obligation as a social responsibility.

Built into the model, though in a less prominent role, however, is a second and third side constraint role for ethics. The second side constraint role that is widely assumed to be embedded in the model is an obligation to advance the interests of shareholders *within the framework of the law*. The third side constraint role of ethics on this model is to advance the interests of shareholders within the framework of what is sometimes described as *local ethical custom* and sometimes described as *the rules of the game*.[14]

The second and third side constraints have an explicitly social function. Corporations serve private interests. However, they also serve public or social interests that fall broadly under three headings. The first is to facilitate and encourage economic activity. The second is to ensure that public or social benefits flow from the economic returns that corporate activity generates. The third is to protect public interests. Examples include labour regulations, human rights, safety and environmental regulations.

3.6 THE MORAL HAZARD CONUNDRUM

Built into the logic of the profit maximization model is a basic shareholder conundrum. How can shareholders ensure that the people they elect or appoint to manage their assets put the interests of shareholders first? This conundrum is generated by the fact that the model is built on the assumption that all economic behaviour is self-interested.[15] The purpose of the firm is to advance the interests of shareholders who, the model assumes, are interested only in share value enhancement. Thus, the responsibility of the corporation is to maximize profits for the benefit of the shareholders. But if all economic behaviour is self-interested, how can the shareholders ensure that those who are elected or hired to serve their interests will do so. The model assumes that those elected or hired to serve the interests of the corporation will, like the shareholders, be concerned only to advance their own interests. What, then, is to prevent those directing the affairs of the corporation from shirking their responsibilities with a view to advancing their own personal interests?

The challenge this dominant model generates for shareholders, then, is how to exercise effective control over management with a view to ensuring that shareholder interests are served. The answer to what is in fact a conflict of interest issue is agency theory. Managers, it proposes, are the agents whose responsibility is to act in the interests of shareholders who are described as "principles". The challenge that agency theory is designed to address is the challenge of aligning the interests of the agents (i.e., managers) hired to conduct the affairs of the corporation with those of the shareholders who are the principles. The way in which this is typically done is through the use of "external incentives" typically in the form of financial remuneration (Heath 2009, p. 501). For lower levels of management, staff and employees, the primary tool will be oversight designed to detect and penalize shirking.

Seen from a theoretical perspective, then, the answer to moral hazard is agency theory. What agency theory calls for is the alignment of the interests of those working for the corporation with the interests of shareholders through the manipulation of extrinsic motivators or external incentives, namely rewards and penalties. That is to say, agency theory grounds the solution to the moral hazard problem on external or extrinsic incentives. The result is what appears to be a theoretically persuasive solution to the problem of moral hazard as seen from a shareholder perspective.

An important theoretical and practical consequence of the model, however, is that it renders the first of the three ethical side constraint roles redundant. The goal is to ensure that managers and others with corporate governance roles do their job efficiently because it is in their interest to do so; a sense of moral obligation is redundant.

3.7   MORAL HAZARD: A SOCIETAL PERSPECTIVE

Shareholder primacy theory is focused on the role of the corporation in addressing the financial interests of shareholders. The problem with both the model and the solution, however, is that the model makes moral hazard the central ethical conundrum not just for the corporation but also for society. The model includes the assumption that the goals and objectives of the corporation will be pursued within the constraints laid down by the law and by the rules of the game or alternatively by local ethical custom. The model assumes therefore that management will obey the law. Indeed, it assumes that managers have a moral as well as a legal obligation to obey the law as well as the rules of the game and/or local moral custom, whether or not it is in the interests of shareholders to do so in any particular instance. However, the model also assumes that the interests of the corporation and the interests of society can clash. Otherwise, there would be no need for laws. This possibility creates a second type of moral hazard. This time, however, the hazard is a hazard not for shareholders but for society or what might be described as the public interest.

It is as essential for society to resolve or address this moral hazard as it is for the corporation to address the moral hazard generated by the model for shareholders. However, if we assume that all economic behaviour is self-interested, then we must also accept that the corporation will behave opportunitistically and shirk its societal responsibilities if it can do so. The danger that the corporations will not fulfill its legal obligations if it is not in its interest to do so is for society a significant moral hazard. Similarly, the corporation cannot be assumed to play by the rules of the game which includes not engaging in deception or fraud if breaking those rules can be shown to be in the interests of the maximization of profits.

The bribery of public officials is a concrete illustration of the dilemma. It involves deception. It is against the law in virtually every country in the world. Nonetheless, the temptation to use bribery to gain and retain business in many parts of the world (see, for example, Transparency International indices[16]) is very strong. Why then should the agents of shareholders not bribe public officials if doing so will advance corporate interests, that is to say where bribery is common and the laws prohibiting it are not enforced or not enforced effectively?

The obvious response to this dilemma is to identify societal incentives that make it in the interests of corporations to respect the law, ethical custom and the rules of the game. John Ruggie's attempt to ground the justificatory foundations of his "respect, protect and remedy" framework on "a social licence to operate" illustrates this option. The problem, however, is that it is all too evident that while informal systems of extrinsic incentives like reputational risk can work in some instances, in many instances they will not (Arnold 2010; Richardson 2010; Cragg 2002).

The alternative most often advocated is to fall back on the law accompanied by penalties and punishments designed to counterbalance the benefits to be gained by corporate shirking.

The problem with this second option is that using the law for its capacity to generate extrinsic incentives designed to overcome the moral hazard the economic model of the firm generates for society is that it instrumentalizes the corporate obligation to obey the law and in doing so reconstrues the obligation to obey the law as an obligation to act prudently. The result is that the obligation to obey the law collapses into a calculation of the costs and benefits that can be anticipated to flow from respecting the law on one hand or ignoring or breaking it on the other. The model implies therefore that only external incentives can be trusted. As a consequence the second and third side constraints are also redundant. What started as an obligation to obey the law because both the law and ethics require it becomes a council of prudence: consider your options carefully and then do what is most likely to maximize profits.

It should not come as a surprise, given the dominance of the profit maximization model of the firm, that the view that corporations, in deciding whether to obey the law, should be guided by economic considerations based on an assessment of how most effectively to advance their economic interests, has acquired the status, in the United States and no doubt elsewhere as well, of an influential jurisprudential theory of corporate law.[17]

The problem then is this. Where the theory and practice of management is guided by a profit maximization model, addressing moral hazard becomes a central management responsibility. The ethical response to this problem is to acknowledge the necessity for side constraints in the form of a moral obligation to manage the corporation in the interests of shareholders and to do so within the constraints of the law, the rules of the game and local ethical custom. However, because the model assumes that all economic behaviour is self-interested, it can provide no theoretical or practical reason for managers to allow the pursuit of profits to be constrained by law or ethics where the profit generating benefits of ignoring the constraints outweigh the costs.

The model does have access to a theory, agency theory, which offers a remedy for the problem of moral hazard as seen from a shareholder perspective. What the model does not have access to is a theory that can provide a strategy for resolving the moral hazard created by the model as seen from a social or societal perspective. If self interest is the guiding principle, informal systems of constraint will be not always be effective. This in turn opens the door to substantial risks to public and societal interests. The only alternative system that society has available to align the interests of managers with the public interest is the law. However, the model provides no reason for a corporation or its agents to obey the law where the benefits of breaking the law outweigh the costs.

Cynthia Williams points to the weakness that accompanies a shareholder primacy approach that relies on extrinsic incentives to secure corporate legal compliance. She points out that:

> Under this penalty-driven approach to law, what is of paramount importance about law are the penalties, either because the penalties form the basis for determining whether to obey the law or not (efficient breach), or because they form the basis for determining the law's importance and how much money a corporation should spend on compliance efforts (efficient compliance). Moreover, under the efficient breach theory a corporation may purchase the "right" to violate the law by simply risking paying the penalty. (Williams 1997–1998, p. 1268)

3.8 THE MODEL'S THEORETICAL AND PRACTICAL IMPLICATIONS FOR ETHICS

As previous discussion shows, the profit maximization model assumes a role for ethical and legal side constraints that requires that corporations at a minimum avoid deception and fraud, respect local ethical customs and obey the law independently of issues of profitability. In application, however, these side constraints collapse into a consequentialist logic governed by prudential considerations of risks and costs versus benefits. Under these conditions, the normative force of the side constraints dissolves into the logic of a hypothetical imperative and ethics is absorbed into a framework of strategic considerations governed by an ethical obligation to maximize profits. However, as we have seen, the obligation to maximize profits in turn finds itself dissolving into a system of externally governed incentives under the influence of agency theory.[18]

The model, of course, is just that, a model grounded on a theory or theories that are designed to ensure that the interests of shareholders govern corporate strategy and operations (Martin 2011, p. 63). However, in spite of the absence of empirical evidence that the model has this result, it has been widely adopted. Further, although as a model it appears to require that corporations respect a set of ethical and legal constraints in their pursuit of profits, the model can provide no theoretical backing for respecting these constraints beyond a counsel of prudence.

There can be no question that the constraints the model appears to require are widely respected by many corporations and their leaders. Furthermore, it is clear that no corporation or CEO could publicly admit to a policy of obeying the law or avoiding deception or fraud only when it was to the corporation's advantage. Nonetheless, it is equally hard to ignore the fact that subordinating ethics to the pursuit of profits has become an entrenched reality in a world of globalized markets. The evidence can be found in the world of finance, investment and investment banks, the professions, for example law and accounting, and the world of business and management.

It is ironic that the evidence for the degree to which the profit maximization model has impacted the role of ethics in the contemporary world of business is found most strikingly in the scandals and spectacular failures and bankruptcies that scar recent business history. A striking example in the world of investment is the story of Long Term Capital Management, a story told in detail by Roger Lowenstein (2001) in his book *When Genius Failed*. In many respects, Long Term Capital Management was the canary in the mine shaft. The name communicated a focus on the long term; the trading strategy was however very short term. What is significant about the company is that by virtue of its trading policies it created a situation that very nearly caused the international financial system to collapse (Lowenstein 2001, pp. 189–218). What is interesting about Lowenstein's account is that the word "ethics" appears to enter into management level discussion only once, where it was described as being dismissed by Laurence Hillibrand, who was to become a Long Term Capital partner, because he "couldn't see that an intangible such as Solomon's ethical image was also worth a price" (Lowenstein 2011, p. 18). One of the underlying themes of Lowenstein's analysis of the collapse of Long Term Capital is the gradual legitimiz-ation of business arrangements and investment practices on the part of virtually all the prestigious Wall Street firms through the 1980s and 1990s in which the conflicts of interest were increasingly tolerated. It is exactly the kinds of conflicts that were tolerated that constitute the problem of moral hazard that agency theory is designed to resolve for shareholders but that the model and agency theory ignores and indeed exacerbates seen from a social or societal perspective.

Although a global financial crisis was averted, key elements of the Long Term Capital crisis returned to play a central role in the financial meltdown of 2008 in which virtually all the Wall Street financial institutions implicated in the Long Term Capital collapse were again involved. Analysis of the cause of the financial meltdown has varied widely. Lowenstein in his analysis of "The Rise and Fall of Long-Term Management" ascribes the collapse of Long Term Capital Management to "insatiable greed". Others have pointed to an era of deregulation and offered the hope "that this crisis and new regulations will make Wall Street firms more responsible."[19] Not surprisingly, it is the regulatory path that subsequently has dominated the American response to the crisis. Yet as previous analysis indicates, strengthening the law can serve to resolve irresponsible corporate conduct only if the corporate community accepts a moral responsibility to respect the law. However, as we have seen, when acted on, the profit maximization model corrodes respect for both ethical and legal side constraints by embedding them within a normative logic that gives priority to profit maximization.[20]

Evidence of how the model subordinates ethics to the pursuit of profits can also be found in the Enron saga. The collapse of Enron is widely understood as simply a business failure. However, Eichenwald's analysis (2005) in *Conspiracy of Fools* points to the impact the profit maximiz-ation model has had on the professions. Accountants and lawyers were key players in that scandal. Senior partners in Arthur Andersen, a prestigious global accounting firm, are described as having played a central role in structuring the books of the company so as to conceal the company's true financial position. In "Making Sense of Moral Meltdowns", David Luban (2006) refers to the Powers Report in which an investigator is quoted as recalling that:

> when Enron's lawyers were explaining the details of the elaborate "special purpose entity" deals that siphoned millions of dollars into Andrew Fastow's pockets, they weren't ashamed or embarrassed. They were proud of their handiwork and eager to explain how they did it. (Luban 2006, p. 72)

Kurt Eichenwald reports that when faced with investigations by US federal authorities, company employees engaged in the destruction of electronic records, files and other documents with the apparent involvement of the company's legal department (Eichenwald 2005, pp. 643, 666).

These ethical aberrations cannot be said to be anomalies. Neither can the involvement with Enron be labeled an isolated event for Arthur Andersen, as the company turned out to be the accounting firm that missed the massive accounting fraud at Worldcom, a company whose collapse followed closely on the heels of Enron (Eichenwald 2005, p. 667).

The Enron bankruptcy resulted in criminal charges which revealed that, although Enron had a widely admired ethical code of conduct and had persuaded a wide audience of their commitment to ethical business conduct, ethics had slipped well back as a priority as the company posted huge profits and senior management won huge bonuses. Arthur Andersen's slide was also hidden behind a façade in which ethics played a prominent role. Ironically, in the early 1990s, Arthur Andersen, with the cooperation of top business ethicists in the United States, financed the production of a series of videos extolling the virtues of business ethics. Those tapes are no doubt still in use in North American business ethics classrooms.

The Enron saga illustrates not only the subordination of ethics to profits by professionals in accounting and law and also the firms with which they were associated. It also illustrates the "ethical disintegration" of a business firm that at one point prior to its collapse held 25 per cent of the world's energy trading contracts. The history of business in the first decade of the twenty-first century indicates that Enron had a good deal of company. Many of the scandals point to examples of ethics taking a back seat to profit maximization. The BP oil spill in the Gulf of Mexico would appear to be an example. What legal proceedings will eventually establish is yet to be seen. However, among other things, a commission appointed by the President of the United States to investigate the disaster is reported to have identified eleven choices made by senior BP management that both saved time and increased risks. The *Globe and Mail* (30 March 2011, B10) reports that "decisions (preceding the disaster) included moving ahead with operations without the recommended equipment, failing to run a test to ensure the well's stability, and misreading the results of other tests."A review of the US Congressional hearings suggests a number of concerns regarding the safety of the Deepwater Horizon. There was a previous incident in which 77 people were evacuated from the Deepwater Horizon in 2008 after it listed and began to sink when a section of pipe was removed from the ship's ballast system.[21] In the Deepwater Horizon incident, the rig was running five weeks behind schedule and, according to a number of rig workers, it was understood that workers could get fired for raising safety concerns that might delay drilling.[22] A confidential survey commissioned by Transocean weeks before the explosion revealed that workers were concerned about safety practices and feared reprisals if they reported mistakes or other problems.[23] Investigations have revealed a number of decisions that were made that were found to have simultaneously increased the risk while saving time and therefore money, given the substantial day rate of the rig. These decisions included: "[Halliburton] cement[ing] the well with a mixture [BP] knew to be flawed; BP's apparent failure to center the well properly; BP's decision to use seawater instead of heavy drilling mud to fill the well, leaving it vulnerable to an upsurge in gas; BP's apparent failure to use enough plugs to seal the well; and the failure by BP's and Transocean to pay close attention to pressure tests showing the well to be unstable."[24]

The resulting disaster claimed lives and caused environmental damage that will be felt in the Gulf for untold years into the future (BBC 2010a, 2010b).

Unfortunately, it is not the case, however, that the link between the profit maximization model and unethical decisions can be established empirically. The model is a normative model. It does not purport to describe how business decisions are made. Its purpose is to describe how business decisions should be made. All that empirical studies can do is to point to examples of unethical decision-making that illustrate situations where profit maximizing was clearly in play and where it coincided with the subordination of ethics in ways that are consistent with, and implied by, the normative logic of the profit maximization model. What is also clear is that imposing more complex regulatory systems on business, while perhaps emotionally satisfying, must come up against hard realities. Given the continued dominance of the model, leaders and their professional advisors must inevitably find themselves calculating the costs and benefits of taking risks associated with skirting regulations that inhibit their pursuit of profits. The justification for so doing is built into the model; the primary ethical responsibility of managers is to maximize profits for shareholders. It is an ethical imperative. What is more, the justification for doing so is built into senior management compensation models crafted by Boards guided by agency theory whose use in turn the model has made virtually obligatory.

3.9 REBUILDING THE FOUNDATIONS OF ETHICS AND TRUST

Roger Martin argues in *Fixing the Game* that "(t)he only way we can avoid increasingly frequent stock market meltdowns – and all the pain suffering and economic dislocation they cause – is to explore the theories that underpin American capitalism" (Martin 2011, p. 10). The theory that underpins the theories to which he refers is the theory that the principal obligation of Boards of Directors and senior managers is to maximize profits. Further as the brief history leading into this discussion shows, it is a theory whose dominance is of relatively recent vintage. While there are many ways of critiquing the theory, an analysis of the normative framework governing the application of the theory demonstrates that, both in theory and practice, the theory undermines the ethical foundations of corporate behaviour. The result can have only damaging implications for trust and the capacity of a system governed by this model to contribute to the public good.

While the status quo continues to have influential supporters, it is encouraging to note that some of the most influential management theorists in the history of the discipline have long been of the view that the theory and the model it advocates is both seriously mistaken but also potentially very destructive. Peter Drucker is a case in point. In *The Practice of Management*, he argues that "(p)rofit is not the purpose of business enterprise and business activity, but a limiting factor on it" (Drucker 2001, p. 35). He goes on to propose that the purpose of business "must lie in society since a business enterprise is an organ of society" (p. 37). Further, failure to recognize that this is the case can be expected to undermine not just management's public standing but "the very future of our economic and social system" (p. 383).

More recently, Harry Mintzberg has echoed these sentiments. He points out in an interview undertaken by the *Ivey Business Journal* that the second greatest failing of business organizations in today's world is the doctrine of shareholder value. "Shareholder value," he says, "is an antisocial, disruptive notion that will be bad for business in the long run" (Mintzberg 2000, p. 20). Interestingly, unease with the theories that underpin shareholder primacy theories is also beginning to penetrate the field of socially responsible investment. An example is a recent study by Ethical Funds entitled "Crisis, What Crisis: Executive Compensation in the 21st Century."[25] On page one of this report, Ethics Funds examines "how shareholder primacy – a theoretical construct that drives how executive compensation is designed – is taking us down the wrong path".

All these critiques provide an account of why shareholder primacy theories are not only mistaken but also damaging. What they all have in common is recognition of the negative impacts this cluster of theories can have on corporate behaviour. What the argument of this chapter has been designed to determine is why shareholder primacy theories can be expected to have this impact. Shareholder primacy theories are grounded on a primary ethical assumption, namely that the principal obligation of senior managers is profit maximization. But what our examination demonstrates is that the ethical foundations of the theories underpinning the profit maximization model are inherently unstable.

Inherently unstable ethical environments inevitably erode trust. Trust rests on ethical foundations. To trust is to assume that those with whom one is dealing can be trusted to fulfill their ethical obligations. In complex business environments that dominate free market economies, one such assumption, but only one, recognized by virtually all business leaders, is that corporations and their managers and employees have an obligation to obey the law except under very carefully defined circumstances.[26] More fundamental is the recognition that business in today's world is grounded on contracts, both formal and informal. Contracts themselves are at their root the exchange of promises resulting in an agreement to enter into a business arrangement. The view that a corporation is basically a "nexus of contracts", a view that Jensen and Meckling assume as a fundamental building block of agency theory,[27] is simply one dramatic illustration of this reality.

Promise making and promise keeping is a fundamental moral institution. Its essential ingredient is trust, trust on the part of the parties to the contract that promises made that comprise the contract will be carried out or performed. It is this sense of obligation that is eroded when the pursuit of profit maximization becomes the defining purpose of a business enterprise.

The erosion of trust unavoidably results in a loss of respect. Both are characteristics of the contemporary world of business. If both are to be regained, a new understanding will have to take the place of what has become the dominant view of the purpose of business. In many respects identifying that purpose is relatively easy. The purpose of business is to provide goods and services ethically and profitably. The contours of that understanding have been articulated by theorists like Peter Drucker to take just one example. Drucker (2001) argues that "there is only one valid definition of business purpose: to create a customer" (p. 20). Roger Martin, a half decade later, echoes Drucker's view in arguing that for business, customers should be the focus and the central task of companies is to find ever better ways of serving them" (Martin 2011, p. 31).

Exactly why and how this is the solution to regaining trust, humanity and purpose in the age of crisis, would require a more positive forward looking account of the role of ethics in business than space here allows. What we can safely conclude from what has been argued, however, is that the trajectory of modern management theory is toward crisis and instability to the extent that it is grounded on the thesis that the purpose of business and therefore the purpose of management is to maximize profits.

NOTES

1. See Davis (1905) for an historical account of the history and evolution of the modern corporation from its medieval and early modern roots.
2. See also McLean (1999), and for a more detailed account, Horwitz (1992) and Alexander (1992).
3. It is tangentially interesting to note that eliminating bureaucratic discretion and replacing it with non-discretionary procedures and laws is currently advocated by some as a way of reducing corruption in government administration. It is possible that similar considerations motivated the shift from an approach to incorporation involving the exercise of extensive bureaucratic and political discretion to a largely rule governed system in the nineteenth century.
4. See McLean, op. cit. p. 130, who attributes this view to Horwitz (1992), p. 68.
5. This shift in understanding was undergirded by the thesis that corporations were "natural entities or expressions of the right of freedom of association". For a brief discussion of these theories see the introductory essay in *Corporate Social Responsibility* (Cragg 2009, pp. xv–xix). See also M.J. Horwitz's account of the development of corporate theory (Horwitz 1992), Janet McLean (1999) and Margaret Blair ((1995), reprinted in *The Corporation and its Stakeholders: Classic and Contemporary Readings*, edited by Max Clarkson, Toronto: University of Toronto Press, 1998, pp. 47–71. For a critical analysis of the shift and the two theories that accompanied it, see my chapter "Ethics, Law and Corporate Self-Regulation" in *Ethics Codes, Corporations and the Challenge of Globalization*, edited by Wesley Cragg (Cheltenham, UK and Northampton, MA, USA: Edward Elgar Publishing, 2005).
6. 204 Mich. 459, 170 N.W. 668. (Mich. 1919).
7. See for example Clark (1916). See also Berle and Means (1932) and Dodd (1932). Dodd in his article describes the view that corporations exist for the sole purpose of making money as "the traditional view" of the corporation.
8. See Bowen (1953).
9. Both these formulations are found in Friedman's famous *New York Times Magazine* article.
10. This theme has been taken up by small coterie of management school academics of which Sumantra Ghoshal's (2005) critique entitled "Bad Management Theories Are Destroying Good Management Practices" is a good example.

11. "Intrinsic CSR" is a commitment to corporate social responsibility not for its instrumental value but because of its intrinsic moral value. On this view, a corporation would endorse the principles of the Global Compact because of their status as moral principles and a sense of moral obligation.

12. John Ruggie was appointed by Kofi Annan, who was at the time of the appointment the Secretary-General of the United Nations, to take up questions relating to the human rights responsibilities of corporations with a view to formulating recommendations for consideration and adoption by the United Nations. In pursuit of his mandate, the special representative has prepared a number of reports culminating in a series of recommendations that are now referred to as "the UN Framework".

13. Note it is consequentialist, not utilitarian, since the goal or purpose that the reasoning serves is not pleasure or happiness but rather profit maximization.

14. Milton Friedman (1970) uses both descriptions of this constraint in his famous *New York Times Magazine* article entitled "The Social Responsibility of Business is to Increase its Profits" (Vol. 33, pp. 122–126).

15. Joseph Heath points out (2009, p. 500) that strictly speaking the concept of economic rationality "entails no commitment to such claims". Economic rationality assumes that action is based on preferences that may or may not be egoistical. He goes on to point out, however, that "one can search the economic theory of the firm literature for a very long time before finding an actual example of an agency analysis that ascribes altruistic motives to any of the parties."

16. Transparency International's Corruption Perception Index and Bribe Payers Index can be found at www.transparencyinternational.com.

17. For an exhaustive analysis of the implications that follow from the instrumentalization of the corporate obligation to obey the law, see Cynthia Williams' (1997–1998) article entitled "Corporate Compliance with the Law in an age of Efficiency". She describes the thesis and its implications succinctly by quoting Mel Eisenberg, Chief Reporter for the *ALI Principles* who comments:

> It is sometimes maintained that whether a corporation should adhere to a given legal rule may properly depend on a kind of cost–benefit analysis, in which probable corporate gains are weighed against either probable social costs, measured by the dollar liability imposed for engaging in such conduct, or probable corporate losses, measured by potential dollar liability discounted for likelihood of detection. This argument is premised on a false view of the citizen's duty in a democratic state. With few exceptions, dollar liability is not a "price" that can ethically be paid for the privilege of engaging in legally wrongful conduct. (p. 1271)

18. It is instructive to note as an illustration that in the 1976 Jensen and Meckling discussion of the concept of agency and its implications for management theory and practice, there is no discussion in the body of the theory of a role for ethics or the thought that the conduct of management should be structured by a recognition of a moral obligation to fulfill management responsibilities.

19. See for example Fareed Zakaria's analysis in *Newsweek*, 3 May, 2010 at p. 23.

20. For a critique of recourse to regulation as a solution to the moral hazard problems generated by the profit maximization model, see Martin's discussion of regulative solutions to the moral crisis that the profit maximization model has created in *Fixing the Game* at pp. 8–10.

21. Minerals Management Service (2008).

22. Bronstein and Drash (2010).

23. Urbina (2010).

24. *New York Times* (2010).

25. http://www.neiinvestments.com/neifiles/PDFs/5.4%20Research/Exec_Comp_English_Final.pdf (accessed 13 February 2013).

26. The exception is normally thought to be limited to situations where the law itself is in conflict with fundamental moral principles or values.

27. See their 1976 article for an articulation of this assumption.

REFERENCES

Alexander, G.S. (1992), *Commodity and Propriety*, Chicago: University of Chicago Press.

Arnold, Denis G. (2010), 'Transnational Corporations and the Duty to Respect Basic Human Rights', *Business Ethics Quarterly*, **20** (3), pp. 371–400.

BBC (2010a), 'Gulf oil spill: President's panel says firms complacent', 9 November, retrieved from http://www.bbc.co.uk/news/world-us-canada-11720907 (accessed 12 November 2010).

BBC (2010b), 'Oil spill: BP did not sacrifice safety to save money', 9 November, retrieved from http://www.bbc.co.uk/news/world-us-canada-11714906 (accessed 12 November 2010).

Berle, A.A. and G.C. Means (1932), *The Modern Corporation and Private Property*, New York, NY, USA: Macmillan.

Blair, Margaret M. (1995), 'Whose Interests Should Be Served', in *Ownership and Control: Rethinking Corporate Governance for the Twenty-first Century*, Washington, DC, USA: Brookings Institute, pp. 202–234.

Bowen, H.R. (1953), *The Social Responsibilities of the Businessman*, New York, NY, USA: Harper.

Bronstein, Scott and Wayne Drash (2010), 'Rig survivors: BP ordered shortcut on day of blast', *CNN.com*, retrieved from http://www.cnn.com/2010/US/06/08/oil.rig.warning.signs/index.html (accessed 9 June 2010).

Campbell, Tom (2012), 'Corporate Social Responsibility: Beyond the Business Case to Human Rights', in *Business and Human Rights*, Cheltenham, UK and Northampton MA, USA: Edward Elgar Publishing.

Carroll, Archie (1999), 'Corporate Social Responsibility: Evolution of a Definitional Construct', *Business and Society*, **38** (3), pp. 268–295.

Clark, J.M. (1916), 'The Changing Basis of Economic Responsibility', *The Journal of Political Economy*, **24** (3), pp. 209–229.

Clarkson, Max B.E. (1998), *The Corporation and its Stakeholders: Classic and Contemporary Readings*, Toronto, Canada: University of Toronto Press.

Cragg, Wesley (2002), 'Business Ethics and Stakeholder Theory', *Business Ethics Quarterly*, **12**, pp. 113–142.

Cragg, Wesley (2005), 'Ethics, Law and Corporate Self-Regulation', in *Ethics Codes, Corporations and the Challenge of Globalization*, Cheltenham, UK and Northampton, MA, USA: Edward Elgar Publishing.

Cragg, Wesley (2009), *Corporate Social Responsibility*, Farnham, UK and Burlington, VT, USA: Ashgate Publishing.

Davis, John P. (1905), *Corporations: A Study of the Origin and Development of Great Business Combinations and Their Relation to the Authority of the State*, New York, NY, USA: G.P. Putnam's.

Dodd, E. Merrick (1932), 'For whom are Corporate Managers Trustees?', *Harvard Law Review*, **45**, pp. 1145–1163.

Drucker, Peter F. (2001), *The Essential Drucker*, New York, NY, USA: Harper.

Eichenwald, Kurt (2005), *Conspiracy of Fools*, New York, NY, USA: Broadway Books.

Friedman, Milton (1970), 'The Social Responsibility of Business is to Increase its Profits', *New York Times Magazine*, **33**, pp. 122–126.

Ghoshal, Sumantra (2005), 'Bad Management Theories Are Destroying Good Management Practices', *Academy of Management Learning & Education*, **4** (1), pp. 75–91.

Gillies, James (1992), *Boardroom Renaissance: Power, Morality and Performance in the Modern Corporation*, Toronto, Canada: McGraw-Hill Ryerson.

Globe and Mail (2011), 30 March, Business Section p. 10, Toronto, Canada.

Heath, Joseph (2009), 'The Uses and Abuses of Agency Theory', *Business Ethics Quarterly*, **19** (4), pp. 497–528.

Horwitz, M.J. (1992), *The Transformation of American Law 1870–1960*, Oxford, UK: Oxford University Press.

Jensen, Michael C. and William H. Meckling (1976), 'Theory of the Firm: Managerial Behavior, Agency Costs and Ownership Structure', *Journal of Financial Accounting*, **3** (4), pp. 305–360.

Lowenstein, Roger (2001), *When Genius Failed: the Rise and Fall of Long-Term Management*, London, UK: Fourth Estate.

Luban, David (2006), 'Making Sense of Moral Meltdowns', in *Moral Leadership: The Theory and Practice of Power, Judgment and Policy*, San Francisco, CA, USA: Jossey-Bass, pp. 57–73.

Martin, Roger (2011), *Fixing The Game: Bubbles, Crashes, and What Capitalism Can Learn from the NFL*, Harvard, NY, USA: Harvard Business Review Press.

McLean, Janet (1999), 'Personality and Public Law Doctrine', *University of Toronto Law Journal*, **123**, p. 130.

Minerals Management Service (2008), 'Accident Investigation Report', retrieved from http://www.gomr.mms.gov/homepg/offshore/safety/acc_repo/2008/0805 26a.pdf?q=transocean-deepwater-horizon (accessed 22 April 2010).

Mintzberg, Harry (2000), *Ivey Business Journal*, September/October, p. 20.

Myers, Gustavius (1914), *History of Canadian Wealth*, Chicago, IL, USA: James Lorimer and Company Publishers.

New York Times (2010), Editorial, 'A Culture of Carelessness', 14 November, *New York Times* retrieved from http://www.nytimes.com/2010/11/15/opinion/ 15mon2.html?ref=gulf_of_mexico_2010 (accessed 3 April 2011).

Richardson, Benjamin J. and Wesley Cragg (2010), 'Being Virtuous and Prosperous: SRI's Conflicting Goals', *Journal of Business Ethics*, **92** (1), pp. 21–39.

Ruggie, John (2008), 'Protect, Respect and Remedy: A Framework for Business and Human Rights', Report of the Special Representative of the Secretary-General on the issue of human rights and transnational corporations and other business enterprises, UN Doc A/HRC/8/5 (7 April).

Urbina, Ian (2010), 'Workers on Doomed Rig Voiced Concern About Safety', *The New York Times*, 21 July, retrieved from http://www.nytimes.com/2010/07/ 22/us/22transocean.html (accessed 11 November 2010).

Williams, Cynthia A. (1997–1998), 'Corporate Compliance with the Law in an age of Efficiency', *North Carolina Law Review*, **76**, p. 1265.

Zakaria, Fareed (2010), *Newsweek*, 3 May, p. 23.

4. Business and the greater good as a combination of private and public wealth

Georges Enderle

4.1 INTRODUCTION

Although the literature on "business and society" is vast, it tends to ignore the fact that the economic system mediates between business and society. All too often the analysis jumps from "business" directly to "society" at large as if business organizations weren't embedded and shaped by the economic system as part of the overall system of society.[1] This neglect of the economic system has far-reaching consequences. The purpose of the company, commonly taken for granted, is not articulated and aligned with the purpose of the economy. Since business operates in and focuses on the marketplace, the market is often mistaken for the entire economy. The company's relations to its various stakeholders do not account for systemic issues of the economy. And when corporate relations to "society" are investigated, the targets are simply "people," "citizenship," or the "environment" detached from any economic content.

Therefore, in addressing the question of "business and the greater good," proper attention should be paid to the economic system as mediating between business and society. Consequently, in this chapter, we may focus on the "greater good" that is more than business but less than society. First, business (understood as business organizations) has to be placed in the economic system and conceived as one part but not as the whole of it. Second, it is proposed to define the purpose of the economy – and hence of business – as the creation of wealth in a comprehensive sense, understood as "the greater good." Third, one important feature of this definition determines wealth as a combination of private and public wealth, which excludes both the individualistic notion of wealth as the mere accumulation of private wealth and the collectivistic notion of public wealth. Fourth, the understanding of wealth as a combination of private and public wealth has far-reaching implications for the motivational structures of creating wealth and the roles of markets and collective actors (such as government and other institutions). Fifth, in defining human rights as public goods, some implications for corporate responsibility are explored.

4.2   BUSINESS AS PART OF THE ECONOMIC SYSTEM

As long as the economic system seems by and large to function smoothly, there is little pressure to question the system and scrutinize its essential components and functioning. After all, we breathe air unconsciously and take it for granted as long as we have no problems with our lungs and the supply and quality of air. However, we have good reason to reflect on the system when it seems to be challenged and threatened. This has been the case again and again in the history of capitalism and, to some extent, of socialism as well. After the Second World War, Germany was divided into two very different parts, one with a social market economy and the other with a centrally planned socialist economy. Thus, facing this alternative, German business could not ignore the importance of the economic system. Today, if US corporations want to do business in China, they need to take the Chinese system into account and must learn to operate in a political, economic, and socio-cultural system that starkly contrasts with the American one. Moreover, after the global financial crisis, critical scrutiny has targeted not only individual and corporate failure. Particularly shocked by "systemic risk" and the potential collapse of the financial sector, one has also questioned the legitimacy of the capitalistic system. Given these and similar experiences, it appears imperative to broaden the business perspective and explicitly place and discuss it in the context of the economic system as it actually is and as it ought to be.

There are many different ways of characterizing and evaluating economic systems, explicated in an immense body of literature (see, among others, Argandoña 2008; Hamlin 2001; Heilbroner 1987; Kromphardt 1991 and 1993; Nove 1987; Rich 2006; Witt 2008).[2] For the purpose of this chapter, it might suffice to highlight a few crucial considerations.

In his pertinent analysis of economic systems, Jürgen Kromphardt (1991) criticizes the widespread habit of characterizing an economic system with one single feature, for instance, "capitalism," "socialism," "market economy" or "free enterprise system." He argues that an economic system always consists of three basic components:

1.   Ownership and decision-making: who participates in the process of economic decision-making? Who plans and controls production, distribution, and consumption, for instance, through a high concentration of economic power or a broad participatory economy?
2.   Information and coordination: with the help of which information system are the individual decisions coordinated, for example, by decentralized markets or centralized planning?
3.   Motivation: what objectives motivate the various decision makers: for example, self-interest, the common good or loyalty? Which ways are chosen to implement economic decisions and what type of behavior is expected?

Accordingly, "capitalism" and "free enterprise system" point to the first component and "market economy" to the second. Each term stands as a *pars pro toto*, that is, a part indicating the whole. Hence, the use of terms like these can be misleading. Yet, capitalism is not only about private property rights and free enterprise, but also about decentralized information gathering and coordination through markets and a strong (if not exclusive) emphasis on self-regarding motivations. In addition to stressing the role of the market for gathering information and coordinating actions, the market economy (including its social variants) is also based on private property rights and economic freedom and is driven by self-regarding and, to some extent, also other-regarding motivations. Generally speaking, each economic system contains all three components. However, these components can take on very different forms which shape not only the system as such but also the attitudes and behaviors of individuals and organizations within the system. For this reason, individuals and organizations should not ignore the impact of the system; rather, they need to understand it and take it into account.

Other misleading "shortcuts," which mistake one part for the whole, happen when "business," "the private sector" and "the market" are substituted for the entire economy. Running a business is wrongly considered equivalent to running an economy, and being successful in business does not guarantee success in steering the economy. These shortcuts do not work for several basic reasons. "Business" understood as business organizations and associations are not the only economic actors. Consumers and their organizations as well as government agencies at all levels (by collecting taxes and distributing subsidies, etc.) are indispensable parts of the economy. In addition to including all economic actors, one has to account for all types of goods and services, specifically for both "private" and "public" goods and services (as defined in economics that characterizes public by non-rivalry and non-exclusivity).

This comprehensive notion of goods and services has far-reaching implications for the understanding of the economy, its basic institutions in terms of ownership and decision-making as well as information and coordination, and its necessary motivations of self-regarding and other-regarding nature. These implications will become clearer in the following sections which discuss the purpose of the economy as wealth creation and focus on wealth as a combination of private and public wealth. For the time being, it is noteworthy to point out one important limitation of the market institution. As good economics knows, the market institution is efficient in producing private goods, but fails in generating public goods. Hence, other than market institutions (that means collective actors such as governments) are indispensable as well in order to create wealth in a comprehensive sense. Given this limitation, it goes without saying that the market cannot substitute for the entire economy.

4.3 THE PURPOSE OF THE ECONOMY AND BUSINESS IS TO CREATE WEALTH

As discussed in the previous section, business needs to be explicitly placed into the broader, systemic context of the economy. The fundamental question which then arises concerns the purpose of the economy and consequently about the purpose of business. Not surprisingly, there is a wide variety of answers ranging from making money to maximizing profit or share value, providing goods and services, adding value, creating jobs, overcoming poverty, to name a few. The answer offered in this chapter is to create wealth in a comprehensive sense, drawing from more extensive elaborations elsewhere (Enderle 2009, 2010, 2011).

We may begin with concentrating on the meaning of the wealth of a single nation.[3] Although this approach might seem to be somewhat outmoded in the age of the "decline of the nation-state," it provides some advantages when compared with other approaches. When we ask for the "wealth of a nation," it is difficult to deny that wealth should encompass both private and public goods. Thus two types of assets are involved: those that can be attributed to and controlled by individual actors, be they persons, groups, or organizations, and those from which, in principle, no actor inside the nation can be excluded. Such "public goods" are defined, as already mentioned, by the characteristics of non-rival and non-exclusive consumption. They clearly have a material component, even though it might be difficult to put a price on them. For instance, we may consider as public goods natural resources in a country, basic security, an effectively functioning rule of law, a relatively corruption-free business environment, a business-supportive culture, a decent level of education and health care of the citizens, etc. whereas the lack thereof can be called "public bads." This understanding of wealth as a combination of private and public wealth will be further discussed in the next section.

We may define the wealth of a nation as the total amount of economically relevant private and public assets including not only financial capital, but also physical (i.e., natural and produced), human (in terms of health and education), and "social" capital (as trust relations in Robert Putnam's sense; see Putnam 1993 and 2002, also Bartkus et al. 2010). Wealth is primarily a stock (an economically relevant quantity at a certain point in time); but, in a broader sense, it also includes flows (increasing or decreasing quantities over a certain period of time, for instance, income). Accordingly, we understand wealth as the economically relevant stocks and flows. How then can they be expressed in monetary terms in a proper fashion? As for private goods, monetary indicators are only reliable if the markets function properly (which can hardly be asserted for the recent financial crisis); and as for public goods, the markets fail (by definition) to provide reliable prices. Therefore, sound economic thinking offers serious caveats against equating money with wealth. "Making money" can be destroying wealth while creating wealth can be losing money.

What do we mean by the "creation" of wealth? It seems obvious but nevertheless deserves emphasis that wealth creation is more than both possessing and acquiring wealth; it constitutes a special form of increasing wealth. To create is to make something new and better. It is an innovative activity that is constantly searching for improvement, not only because it is pushed by competition but also, and foremost, for the sake of a better service to people and the environment. Examples can be found in rich and poor countries and in many economic activities, ranging from the Grameen Bank in Bangladesh to environmental pioneers such as Rohner Textil in Switzerland and the medical equipment corporation Medtronic in the United States. Wealth creation is not a short-term affair, but evolves in a long-term horizon. It is "sustainable," fulfilling the demand "to meet the needs of the present without compromising the ability of future generations to meet their own needs" (as defined by the World Commission on Environment and Development, see WCED 1987, 8). The needs can be substantiated in terms of human capabilities or "real freedoms that people enjoy" (Sen 1999, p. 3 and Sen 2009, pp. 248–252). More specifically, Sen distinguishes five types of freedom, which can further substantiate the notion of sustainability: political freedoms, economic facilities, social opportunities (basic health care and essential education), transparency guarantees, and protective security (Sen 1999, p. 10).

Two more features are fundamental for wealth creation. It would be an all too common mistake to conceive the process of creation as merely a process of production, followed by a process of distribution. In other words, "one first has to bake the pie before one can divide it," or less colloquially it is about creating and then distributing wealth. This view is remote from reality and ignores that production actually involves a distributive dimension, permeating all of its stages from the preconditions to the generation process, the outcome, and the use for and allocation within consumption and investment. In fact, the productive and distributive dimensions of wealth creation are intrinsically interrelated.

Moreover, as the example of the Grameen Bank can illustrate, providing poor women with fair microcredits in order to become productive and move out of poverty is not a merely material and financial process but, by strengthening their self-confidence, has a spiritual aspect as well. Or, by offering sophisticated medical equipment to patients, Medtronic not only sells material products but strives to live up to its mission of "alleviating pain, restoring health, and extending life," which clearly also includes a spiritual aspect. Generally speaking, wealth creation has both material and spiritual aspects and is therefore a noble activity.

We can now summarize the features of wealth creation as presented above. Wealth consists of physical, financial, human, and social capital. It encompasses private and public wealth, the creation of which is interdependent. Creating wealth is more than possessing and acquiring wealth. It means making something new and better. It is sustainable in terms of human capabilities, adopting an intergenerational perspective. The creation of wealth includes both a productive and a distributive dimension, which are related to each other. It also involves both material and spiritual aspects, which make wealth creation a noble activity.

In a nutshell, it is proposed to define the purpose of the economy and business as the creation of wealth in a comprehensive sense. With good reasons, it can be understood as "the greater good."

4.4 WEALTH AS A COMBINATION OF PRIVATE AND PUBLIC WEALTH

In crafting a definition of wealth, it is crucial to clearly identify the unit of analysis. As indicated above, we arguably start with a focus on the wealth of a single nation. In adopting this unit of analysis, it is not difficult to understand that wealth is not a mere accumulation of private wealth. A nation's wealth (or lack thereof) consists of more than private wealth, including other types of wealth as well. They may be or originate from public goods or merit goods and can be "goods" (i.e., assets) or "bads" (i.e., liabilities). So, without such a more comprehensive notion of wealth, the wealth of a nation cannot be captured adequately, which may lead to multiple misunderstandings in assessing the wealth or poverty of nations.

Ascertaining such a more comprehensive notion is, however, necessary not only from a nation's perspective. It also matters for many other units of analysis, be they situated at the local, regional, international, continental, or global levels. The prosperity of cities and local communities depends on an appropriate combination of private and public wealth. Public goods are of increasing importance to and often the driving force for transnational regimes and institutions. Without the public good of a reasonably stable financial system, national and international finance cannot flourish and will falter. And if the climate change cannot be contained (at two centigrade according to scientific expertise), large parts of the globe will be struck by environmental disasters.

We may now discuss different types of wealth comprising private, public, and merit goods. In 1954 and 1955, Paul Samuelson (influenced by Richard Musgrave) published two short articles on the theory of public expenditure (Samuelson 1954 and 1955), which were of groundbreaking importance for the development of the modern theory of public economics and contained fundamental implications for market failure. Despite intensive subsequent discussions among economists, the power of his analysis has been widely forgotten, or even repressed over the years (see Enderle 2000).

Samuelson developed an analytical definition of the "public good" that he sharply distinguished from the "private good." If a private good (for instance, a glass of wine) is consumed by an individual, it cannot be consumed at the same time by another individual. In contrast, a public good (for instance, sunshine) does not prevent the simultaneous consumption by others. The distinctive criteria are non-rivalry and non-exclusivity, the first meaning the consumption by one individual does not diminish the consumption by another, and the second meaning that no individual (in reach of the public good) can be excluded. To illustrate the difference, the use of a software program or the enjoyment of a music CD is non-rival; that is, it can be consumed (i.e., "copied") by many people without diminishing the program or the music. On the other hand, the criterion of non-exclusivity concerns the impossibility of excluding anyone from the consumption of the good. So the copyright protection of the software program or the music CD attempts to exclude others from using them.[4] This distinction between private and public goods can be summarized in Table 4.1.

Table 4.1   Distinction between private and public goods

		Rivalry	
		yes	no
Exclusivity	yes	private good	
	no		public good

A third type of goods or wealth, developed in the theory of public finance by Richard Musgrave (Musgrave 1957 and 1958), is "merit goods." While divergent interpretations exist, some basic features are common (Musgrave 1987). A merit good is not defined by characteristics of the good itself (such as rivalry or exclusivity), but by the type of consumer preference from which it is derived. Therefore, it should not be confused with a public good. Instead of individual preferences commonly assumed as the basis of the demand for private and public goods, community values (or preferences) restrain individual choice. They determine the goods the community or the government should supply, for instance, education, vaccination, redistribution or primary distribution of income and wealth. Because community values may diverge from individual preferences, merit goods might be imposed against certain individual preferences (which raises the question of paternalism). Although important in public finance, this type of goods will not be discussed here further, given the purpose of this chapter and the merit goods' specific characteristics.

As stated above, we understand wealth as the economically relevant stocks and flows, following a broader definition of wealth, similarly proposed by the Stiglitz–Sen–Fitoussi Report (Report 2009). By definition, a stock is an economically relevant quantity at a certain point in time (for instance, the value of a house or wealth in a narrow sense), whereas a flow is an increasing or decreasing quantity over a certain period of time (for instance, income). By including both stocks and flows, we account for a long-term perspective of sustainability.

After discussing several aspects of private and public wealth, we finally ask how to understand the wealth of a nation (or another large entity) as "a combination" of private and public wealth. First, wealth as a combination includes both private and public wealth, thus excluding a strictly individualistic as well as a strictly collectivistic notion of wealth. Second, private and public wealth can be combined by way of addition or multiplication, depending on the more specific forms and respective extents of private and public wealth. Third, notwithstanding the immense variety of possible combinations, the mutual dependence of private and public wealth needs to be stressed. The production of private goods depends on public goods and can suffer from public bads. Individuals and companies need public goods in order to be productive. On the other hand, the production of public goods depends on the contributions by individuals and companies through taxes, philanthropy, and expertise in science and technology, arts and the humanities, and in many other fields. Thus, this interdependence of private and public wealth should not be ignored nor underestimated.

4.5 FAR-REACHING IMPLICATIONS OF WEALTH AS A COMBINATION OF PRIVATE AND PUBLIC WEALTH

The understanding of wealth as a combination of private and public wealth has far-reaching implications for the types of institutions and motivations required for creating wealth.

The discussion of public goods in economics has highlighted the strengths and limitations of the market institution. Based on individual preferences and the price system coordinating supply and demand, the market has proven a powerful means for producing private goods in an efficient manner. Prices convey information, provide incentives, guide choices, and allocate resources. The price is "right", if supply meets demand, and more (or less) goods are produced. The basic assumption is that there is a price which properly reflects supply and demand and clears the market.

In contrast, no price can be assigned to public goods, which would coordinate supply and demand. Because their consumption is non-rival (that is, nobody can be excluded), the price system does not work. Public goods can be consumed without paying a price (which is the so-called free-rider problem), and public bads cannot be reduced or avoided by charging a lower price. Thus, by definition, the market institution fails to produce public goods.

Of course, many attempts have been undertaken in order to mitigate this sobering result. One might refer to the approximation to shadow pricing.[5] Another way, indicated above, has been by restraining the assumption of individual preferences and introducing community preferences. Nevertheless, the fundamental difference between private and public goods remains, and the basic limitation of the market institution has to be accepted.

Because the market institution, in principle, fails to produce public goods, we may ask whether there are other institutional arrangements that can achieve this goal. Major collective actors are the states and the governments at different levels. Depending on the kind and reach of public goods, these actors might be in a position to address this public challenge. But often, particularly in the international arena, they do not exist or may fail because of weakness. In the wake of Garret Hardin's challenging article on "the tragedy of the commons" (Hardin 1968), groundbreaking research on the evolution of institutions for collective action has been conducted, displaying a rich institutional diversity of self-organization and self-government. Elinor Ostrom's work (Ostrom 1990 and 2005) is of particular merit. Although her focus is on problems of common-pool resources (not public goods; Ostrom and Ostrom 1977), her insights certainly also help to better explain successful and failed institutions for producing public goods.

Furthermore, not only does the market institution fail to produce public goods, but it also can be understood as a public good itself. It meets the criteria of non-rivalry and non-exclusivity. In a perfect market, the participation by one actor does not diminish the participation of another, and no actor should be excluded. Thus the functioning of the market is truly a public "good" and the dis-functioning thereof a public "bad." An interesting historic example of this "dialectic" can be found in Adam Smith's work and the creation of wealth in eighteenth century Scotland: on the one hand, he advocates free international trade to efficiently produce private goods, and, on the other hand, he silently accepts the property regime of his time (technically speaking, a public good) that thrives on the international slave trade from Africa and the tobacco production in North America (see Marvin Brown's analysis in *Civilizing the Economy*, 2010, Chapter 2).

A third far-reaching implication of wealth conceived as a combination of private and public wealth concerns different types of motivations. In order to produce private goods, the motivation of self-interest, undoubtedly, plays an important though not an exclusive role. One might recall Smith's famous saying that it "is not of the benevolence of the butcher, the brewer, or the baker that we expect our dinner, but from their regard to their own interest" (Smith 1776/1981, pp. 26–27). However, as Amartya Sen (1997, pp. 7–8) points out, this saying focuses only on exchange (not production and distribution) and does not express the whole motivational structure of Smith's theory. After all, Smith published not only the book on the wealth of nations but also *The Theory of Moral Sentiments*.

When it comes to producing public goods, the motivation of self-interest is utterly insufficient. In its extreme form, it is based on the anthropological assumption that the individual person is an autonomous and completely independent person who has to care about himself or herself exclusively. Commitment for others is only acceptable if it helps or at least does not hurt oneself. Any sacrifice for others has to be rejected. This view expresses the ideal of "the self-made person," vigorously defended by philosophers such as Ayn Rand (1957/2005 and 1964). However, it ignores the fundamental fact that humans are relational beings who are shaped by and in turn can shape the relations with other people.

The production of public goods is based on human relatedness and needs other-regarding motivations such as gratitude for the gifts received, entrepreneurial spirit, and service to others. Commitment to public goods does not earn immediate rewards, may offer uncertain personal benefits in the future, and can even demand personal sacrifices. But, not infrequently, it is actually made because the interests of other people count, their rights are to be respected, and the needs of the community and society should be addressed. Therefore, other-regarding motivations are indispensable for creating public wealth.

4.6 CORPORATE RESPONSIBILITY FOR HUMAN RIGHTS DEFINED AS PUBLIC GOODS

So far the concept of the public good characterized by non-rivalry and non-exclusivity has been understood in the descriptive–analytical sense. It clearly contrasts with the concept of the private good and involves no assumptions in the normative–ethical sense. Hence one can speak of public "bads" as well as of public "goods." We now turn to the question about the normative–ethical contents of public goods with a special focus on human rights. Needless to say, the realm of public goods – even in the normative–ethical sense – is much larger than the realm of human rights.

The special focus on human rights is suggested for several reasons. In the process of globalization, economies and businesses have expanded far beyond national borders and increasingly been connected both internationally and globally. Through this process, the realm of not only private but also public goods has been enlarged dramatically. With this expansion comes a growing need for universal normative standards for businesses and economies. Since the Universal Declaration of Human Rights in 1948 the ethical (and legal) framework of human rights has developed to a widely accepted, though not undisputed universal ethical framework that has no comparable alternatives. Moreover, in the new millennium, the global concern for business and human rights has considerably strengthened. In 2008, John Ruggie, the Special Representative of the UN Secretary-General on the issue of human rights and transnational corporations and other business enterprises, declared all human rights relevant for business: civil, political, economic, social and cultural rights, including the right to development; in total 30 human rights (UN 2008).[6] In 2011, the United Nations released the UN Guiding Principles on Business and Human Rights (UN 2011), which since seem to have gathered increasing momentum. An excellent account of the development and up-to-date impact of the UN Framework is Ruggie's book *Just Business* (2013).

The two criteria of public goods can be easily applied to human rights. Non-exclusivity means that no human being *should* be excluded from any human right. In other words, all people should enjoy all human rights. Non-rivalry implies that the enjoyment of any human right by any person *should not* diminish the enjoyment of any other human right by oneself or any other person. In other words, no trade-offs between human rights are acceptable. For example, the right to political life should not impair the right to freedom of thought, conscience and religion, nor vice versa; or the freedom of association should not negatively affect the right to non-discrimination, nor vice versa.

Beyond the exclusion of negative impact, one can argue that the enjoyment of any human right by oneself or any person may be neutral vis-à-vis the enjoyment of other rights. For example, the right to freedom of movement may not affect the right to freedom from torture. Furthermore, the enjoyment of one right may even reinforce the enjoyment of another right. For instance, the right to an adequate standard of living (including food, clothing, and housing) can strengthen the right to work and education, and vice versa.

The definition of human rights as ethically demanded public goods, obviously, has far-reaching implications for the states and inter-governmental organizations because collective actions at multiple levels are required (which is a broad topic area beyond the scope of this chapter). For now, three implications are briefly outlined that pertain to "corporate responsibility" as defined by the UN Guiding Principles (see Enderle 2013). First, transnational corporations and other business enterprises are "responsible to respect human rights" and to help "remedy human rights violations," but not "to protect human rights" which is the "duty" of states. In other words, corporations have to contribute to this kind of public goods, in addition to producing private goods. Second, contributing to public goods necessitates a motivation that transcends the self-interest of corporations and includes other-regarding motives. There is no pre-established harmony that would coordinate exclusively self-regarding behaviors in order to produce public goods in general and the respect for human rights in particular. Third, contributing to public goods is not just a kind of "charitable donation" (or a "supererogatory" work) to society. Rather, a certain set of public goods (such as the rule of law and human rights, social customs, technological knowledge, educational skills, and health conditions) are actually preconditions to producing private goods. Therefore, corporations have a moral obligation to recognize these inputs from society and to "give back to society" their due shares, including respecting human rights and remedying human rights violations. In such a way the understanding of the wealth of a society as a combination of private and public wealth can clarify and reinforce corporate responsibility for human rights (see Enderle 2011a).

4.7 CONCLUDING REMARKS

In exploring the question of "business and the greater good," we have proceeded in several steps. "Business" should not be related simply to "society" at large; but it is part of the economy and, therefore, needs to be placed and understood in the economic system. We propose to define the purpose of the economic system and thus of business as the creation of wealth in a comprehensive sense. Accordingly, one major feature of wealth consists in the combination of private and public wealth, excluding the extreme notions of wealth as a mere accumulation of private wealth as well as the mere sum of public wealth. This feature, combining the private and the public, specifies the three basic components of the economic system that aims at wealth creation: (1) ownership and decision-making is in the hands of both private and public actors; (2) information and coordination of economic transactions are based on both market and governmental institutions; and (3) both self- and other-regarding motivations are required to create wealth. In order to provide some substance to the notion of public goods, we suggest defining human rights as ethically required public goods, exhibiting the characteristics of non-rivalry and non-exclusivity. We then relate this notion to "corporate responsibility" as defined by the UN Guiding Principles on Business and Human Rights. In this light, "business and the greater good" entails respecting human rights and helping to remedy human rights violations.

NOTES

1. An entry on "economic system" is in Becker et al. (2001) and Black et al. (2009), but missing in Eatwell et al. (1987), Kolb (2008), and Werhane and Freeman (2005). "Capitalism" and "socialism" can be found in Eatwell et al. (1987) and Kolb (2008); "Kantian capitalism" in Werhane and Freeman (2005). Moreover, from 1999 to 2012, the journals *Business and Society* and *Business and Society Review* explicitly addressed issues of economic systems in only one book review and two main articles, respectively.
2. See also the definition of an economic system by Black et al. (2009, p. 132): "Economic system: the part of the social system composed of institutions and customs related to the production, distribution, and consumption of goods and services. Important characteristics of an economic system are the property rules and the degree of economic planning; examples are traditional, capitalist, socialist, and mixed systems."
3. Recent studies of the World Bank offer new ways of conceptualizing and measuring the wealth of nations (World Bank 2006 and 2011). James Robinson and Daron Acemoglu (2012) emphasize the importance of inclusive economic institutions for nations to succeed.
4. Later on, this distinction was crucial for Paul Romer's theory of "endogenous technological change." In his famous article he stated right at the beginning: "The distinguishing feature of the technology as an input is that it is neither a conventional good nor a public good; it is a non-rival, partially excludable good" (Romer 1990, S71). While he maintains the feature of non-rivalry (characterizing public goods), he introduces different degrees of excludability (departing from the notion of public goods). By the way, the thought process of this conceptual development is well explained to non-specialist readers by David Warsh (2006) in *Knowledge and the Wealth of Nations. A Story of Economic Discovery* (particularly pp. 276–288).
5. Black et al. (2009, p. 409) define shadow prices as "prices of goods, services, and resources that are proportional to true opportunity costs for the economy, taking account of any externalities. ... In an economy with no market failure, market prices and shadow prices would be equivalent. In an economy with market failure ... actual and shadow prices do not coincide." However, to the extent that this no-coincidence can be estimated, a kind of shadow prices can be approximated.
6. The list of all human rights includes (UN 2008, § 52):
    Labor rights: Freedom of association; right to organize and participate in collective bargaining; right to non-discrimination; abolition of slavery and forced labor; abolition of child labor; right to work; right to equal pay for equal work; right to equality at work; right to just and favorable remuneration; right to a safe work environment; right to rest and leisure; right to family life.
    Non-labor rights: Right to life, liberty and security of the person; freedom from torture or cruel, inhuman or degrading treatment; equal recognition and protection under the law; right to a fair trial; right to self-determination; freedom of movement; right of peaceful assembly; right to marry and form a family; freedom of thought, conscience and religion; right to hold opinions, freedom of information and expression; right to political life; right to privacy; right to an adequate standard of living (including food, clothing, and housing); right to physical and mental health; access to medical services; right to education; right to participate in cultural life, the benefits of scientific progress, and protection of authorial interests; right to social security.

REFERENCES

Argandona, A. (2008), 'Capitalism', in Kolb (2008), **1**, pp. 257–265.

Bartkus, V.O. and H.J. Davis (eds) (2010), *Social Capital: Reaching Out, Reaching In*, Cheltenham, UK and Northampton, MA, USA: Edward Elgar Publishing.

Becker, L.C. and C.B. Becker (eds) (2001), *Encyclopedia of Ethics*, 3 volumes, Second edition. New York, NY, USA: Routledge.

Black, J., N. Hashimzade, and G. Myles (2009), *A Dictionary of Economics*, Third edition. Oxford, UK: Oxford University Press.

Brown, M. (2010), *Civilizing the Economy*, Cambridge, UK: Cambridge University Press.

Eatwell, J., M. Milgate, and P. Newman (eds) (1987), *The New Palgrave: A Dictionary of Economics*, 4 volumes, New York, NY, USA: Stockton.

Enderle, G. (2000), 'Whose Ethos for Public Goods in a Global Economy? An Exploration in International Business Ethics', *Business Ethics Quarterly*, January, pp. 131–144.

Enderle, G. (2009), 'A Rich Concept of Wealth Creation beyond Profit Maximization and Adding Value', *Journal of Business Ethics*, **84**, Supplement 3, pp. 281–295.

Enderle, G. (2010), 'Wealth Creation in China and Some Lessons for Development Ethics', *Journal of Business Ethics*, **96** (1), pp. 1–15.

Enderle, G. (2011), 'What is Long-Term Wealth Creation and Investing?', in A. Tencati and F. Perrini (eds) (2011), *Business Ethics and Corporate Sustainability*, Cheltenham, UK and Northampton, MA, USA: Edward Elgar Publishing, pp. 114–131.

Enderle, G. (2011a), 'Three Major Challenges for Business and Economic Ethics in the Next Ten Years: Wealth Creation, Human Rights, and Active Involvement of the World's Religions', *Business and Professional Ethics Journal*, **30** (3–4), pp. 231–252.

Enderle, G. (2013), 'Some Ethical Explications of the UN-Framework for Business and Human Rights' in Williams (2013), 163–191.

Enderle, G., K. Homann, M. Honecker, W. Kerber, and H. Steinmann (eds) (1993), '*Lexikon der Wirtschaftsethik*', Freiburg: Herder.

Hamlin, A.P. (2001), 'Economic Systems', in Becker et al. (2001), **1**, pp. 439–445.

Hardin, G. (1968), 'The Tragedy of the Commons', *Science*, **162**, pp. 1243–1248.

Heilbroner, R.L. (1987), 'Capitalism', in Eatwell et al. (1987), **1**, pp. 347–353.

Kolb, R.W. (ed.) (2008), *Encyclopedia of Business Ethics and Society*, 5 volumes, Los Angeles, CA, USA: Sage.

Kromphardt, J. (1991), *Konzeptionen und Analysen des Kapitalismus: von seiner Entstehung bis zur Gegenwart*. 3. Auflage. Göttingen: Vandenhoeck und Ruprecht.

Kromphardt, J. (1993), 'Wirtschaftssysteme, Wirschaftsordnungen', in Enderle et al. (1993), pp. 1319–1327.

Musgrave, R.A. (1957), 'A Multiple Theory of Budget Determination', *Finanz Archiv*, New Series, **17** (3), pp. 333–343.

Musgrave, R.A. (1958), *The Theory of Public Finance*, New York, NY, USA: McGraw-Hill.

Musgrave, R. A. (1987), 'Merit Goods', in Eatwell et al. (1987), pp. 452–453.

Nove, A. (1987), 'Socialism', in Eatwell et al. (1987), pp. 398–407.

Ostrom, E. (1990), *Governing the Commons. The Evolution of Institutions for Collective Action* (29th printing 2011), Cambridge, UK: Cambridge University Press.

Ostrom, E. (2005), *Understanding Institutional Diversity*, Princeton, NJ, USA: Princeton University Press.

Ostrom, V. and E. Ostrom (1977), 'Public Goods and Public Choices', in Savas (1977).

Putnam, R.D. (1993), *Making Democracy Work: Civic Traditions in Modern Italy*, with R. Leonardi and R.Y. Nanetti, Princeton, NJ, USA: Princeton University Press.

Putnam, R. D. (ed.) (2002), *Democracy in Flux: The Evolution of Social Capital in Contemporary Society*, New York, NY, USA: Oxford University Press.

Rand, A. (1957/2005), *Atlas Shrugged* (Original edition 1957, New York, NY, USA: Random House). Centennial edition, New York, NY, USA: Plume.

Rand, A. (1964), *The Virtue of Selfishness. A New Concept of Egoism*, with additional articles by Nathaniel Branden, New York, NY, USA: Penguin.

Report on the Measurement of Economic Performance and Social Progress (Report) (2009), under the leadership of J.E. Stiglitz, A. Sen, J.-P. Fitoussi: www.stiglitz-sen-fitoussi.fr.

Rich, A. (2006), *Business and Economic Ethics: The Ethics of Economic Systems*. Leuven: Peeters.

Robinson, J.A. and D. Acemoglu (2012), *Why Nations Fail: The Origins of Power, Prosperity and Poverty*, New York, NY, USA: Crown.

Romer, P. (1990), 'Endogenous Technological Change', *Journal of Political Economy*, **98** (5), S71–S102.

Ruggie, J.G. (2013), *Just Business: Multinational Corporations and Human Rights*, New York, NY, USA: Norton.

Samuelson, P.A. (1954), 'The Pure Theory of Public Expenditure', *Review of Economics and Statistics*, **36**, pp. 387–389.

Samuelson, P.A. (1955), 'Diagrammic Exposition of a Theory of Public Expenditure', *Review of Economics and Statistics*, **37**, pp. 350–356.

Savas, E.S. (ed.) (1977), *Alternatives for Delivering Public Services. Toward Improved Performance*, Boulder, CO, USA: Westview Press.

Sen, A. (1997), 'Economics, Business Principles, and Moral Sentiments', *Business Ethics Quarterly*, **7** (3), pp. 5–15.

Sen, A. (1999), *Development as Freedom*, New York, NY, USA: Knopf.

Sen, A. (2009), *The Idea of Justice*, Cambridge, MA, USA: Belknap.

Smith, A. (1776), *An Inquiry into the Nature and Cause of the Wealth of Nations*, edited by R.H. Campbell and A.S. Skinner (1976), Oxford, UK: Clarendon Press; (1981) Indianapolis: Liberty Press.

United Nations (UN) (2008), *Promotion of All Human Rights, Civil, Political, Economic, Social and Cultural Rights, Including the Right to Development. Protect, Respect and Remedy: A Framework for Business and Human Rights*. Report of the Special Representative of the Secretary-General on the issue of human rights and transnational corporations and other business enterprises, John Ruggie. Human Rights Council. Eighth Session, A/HRC/8/5.

United Nations (UN) (2011), *Guiding Principles on Business and Human Rights: Implementing the United Nations "Protect, Respect and Remedy" Framework*. Report of the Special Representative of the Secretary-General on the issue of human rights and transnational corporations and other business enterprises, John Ruggie. Human Rights Council. Seventeenth Session. A/HRC/17/31.

Warsh, D. (2006), *Knowledge and the Wealth of Nations. A Story of Economic Discovery*, New York, NY, USA: Norton.

Werhane, P.H. and R.E. Freeman (eds) (2005), *The Blackwell Encyclopedia of Management*, Second edition, *Business Ethics*, Malden, MA, USA: Blackwell.

Williams, O.F. (ed.) (2013), *Sustainable Development: The UN Global Contact, The Millennium Development Goals and the Common Good*, Notre Dame, IN, USA: University of Notre Dame.

Witt, A. (2008), 'Socialism', in Kolb (2008), **4**, pp. 1972–1975.

World Bank (2006), *Where Is the Wealth of Nations? Measuring Capital for the 21st Century,* Washington, DC, USA: World Bank.

World Bank (2011), *The Changing Wealth of Nations. Measuring Sustainable Development in the New Millennium*, Washington, DC, USA: World Bank.

World Commission on Environment and Development (WCED) (1987), *Our Common Future*, New York, NY, USA: Oxford University Press.

5. The tortoise and the hare: alternative approaches to capitalism

Eleanor O'Higgins

5.1 INTRODUCTION

On 15 September 2008, Lehman Brothers filed for bankruptcy. This was the shock event that forced the acceptance that the global financial system was in deep trouble, as investment banks had made staggering losses on risky trading activities. The effects of these losses were quickly and intensely felt throughout society as the banking failures infected the global economic system, especially when governments engaged in gigantic bank bailouts. Recovery remains elusive, as governments and supra-government bodies tinker with proposed regulation, whilst financial institutions seem to want to go back to "business as usual" (Banziger 2012).

Trust in financial institutions has plummeted globally (Lex 2012; Tyrie 2012; Edelman 2013). Various deep-rooted factors are blamed, such as the de facto public subsidies given to banks too big to fail by bailouts, high barriers to new entry that stifle competition, lack of price transparency, information asymmetries that have resulted in the sale of inappropriate products to retail and wholesale customers alike, weak corporate governance oversight, and overall short-termism.

Crotty (2009) talks about the "perfect calm" in the 2003 to mid-2007 period before the financial crisis came to a head. The perfect calm period seemed to suggest that gravity had been turned on its head, that high-risk–high-return investments were actually safe. In any case, bailouts by central banks over the previous three decades in the face of systemic banking crises only served to reassure bankers that financial gains of the boom would be private while losses were socialised. This is exactly what happened, with the exception of Lehman Brothers. Crotty also points out that the unsustainable practices of financial institutions were encouraged by academics and governments.

Basically, the perfect calm was a period of rising profits and stock prices, that tended to encourage the practices that eventually led to the crisis – dependence on a faulty theory of efficient capital markets, excessive risk-taking in banks that resulted in systemic risk, perverse incentives and complex opaque securities that could not be priced properly – ticking time bombs (Crotty 2009, p. 4), alongside light touch regulation.

The chapter now analyses the investment value chain to explain how the bubble and bust of the global financial crisis materialised though principal–agent problems. Then the notion of trust and how its absence in a market-based culture facilitated the crisis is examined. The need for trust as an enabler in economic processes is spelled out. The chapter tries to suggest some directions for the future by introducing the fiduciary concept and professional ethics into the investment value chain, with accompanying trust benefits. This would have the effect of slowing down empty trading and enhancing long-term value creation through "slow finance".

5.2 THE INVESTMENT VALUE CHAIN

John Kay (2012), leading an investigation of UK equity markets, observes that the investment chain has expanded by means of "an explosion of intermediation" (Kay 2012, p. 10), so that the relationship between corporate issuers of equity and debt and investors has grown increasingly removed by additional stakeholders not only along the main value chain, but also by additional value chain support functionaries.

An outline of the current investment value chain is seen in Figure 5.1.

Given that each player in the value chain gets a cut out of the final returns, it means increased costs for investors, with a potential for misaligned incentives for the intermediaries, many of whom may focus on the short-term rather than the creation of long term value. Each agent in the value chain employs its own compliance staff, and has to pay for services of auditors and lawyers while still earning sufficient to reward its employees and investors.

The next section provides an overview of some selected players in the value chain, especially key intermediaries.

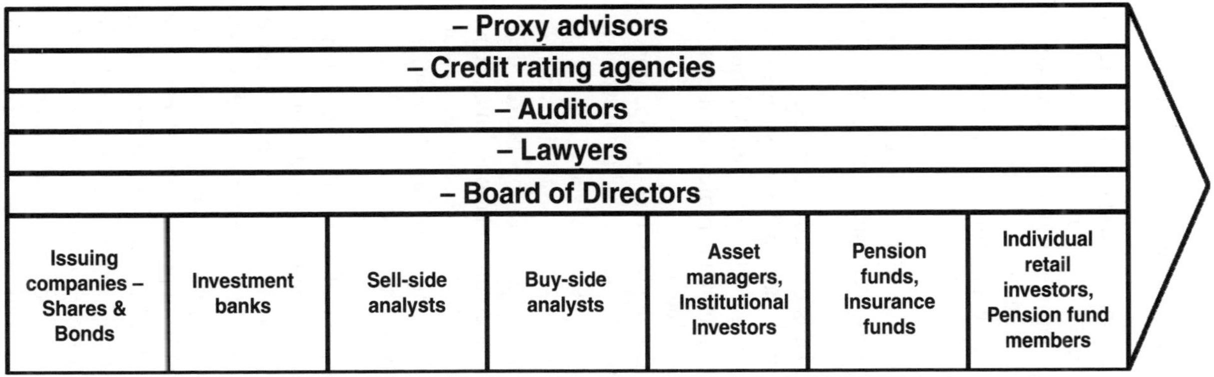

| Issuing companies – Shares & Bonds | Investment banks | Sell-side analysts | Buy-side analysts | Asset managers, Institutional Investors | Pension funds, Insurance funds | Individual retail investors, Pension fund members |

– Proxy advisors
– Credit rating agencies
– Auditors
– Lawyers
– Board of Directors

Note: The figure does not include registrars, nominees, custodians, agents who wrap products, retail platforms, index providers and distributors.

Figure 5.1   The investment value chain

5.2.1 Investment Analysts

Securities analysts are meant to offer knowledgeable opinions to investors on the corporation's future prospects, based on careful analysis of all information that they can gather, including, but certainly not confined to company disclosures. Analysts are of three types:

- Sell-side – analysts who are employed by large integrated financial firms that offer broker dealer and investment bank services. A smaller sell-side group are employed by broker dealers who do not provide investment banking services.
- Buy-side – analysts who are employed by investors to conduct proprietary research.

Coffee (2006) describes some features unique to analysts, in contrast to other professionals, such as accountants or lawyers. These features are:

- Undeveloped standards or methodologies.
- Limited regulation – no compulsory qualification, and limited liability (however, in the UK, as from 1 January 2013 all advisers must hold a higher minimum professional qualification to continue delivering investment advice).
- Competition through duplication – competitors can duplicate each others' services, so any number of analysts can report on any one company, unlike auditors or lawyers.
- The necessity of subsidisation – sell-side analysts are paid by their employing investment banks or by broker dealers from business generated by their recommendations, thus generating conflicts of interest. Reforms in the US to separate research analysts' work from investment banking have simply resulted in less research, since no one wants to pay for it.

In the UK, the introduction of new rules on 1 January 2013 saw the abolition of commission, so the opportunity for an investment adviser to receive commission from a financial product is replaced with what is being called "adviser charging". This means that independent advisers will need to develop their own charging structures, with no influence on the level of remuneration from product providers. Resistance in continental EU countries to this kind of ban on inducements is evident, both by EU officials and investment fund managers, as they claim that investors, unused to paying for advice will simply do without it altogether. The same unwillingness by investors to incur the expense of paying for research is also observed in the UK, according to Mainelli et al. (2009).

The reluctance to pay is not the only reason for the persistence of reliance on apparently conflicted analysts. Retail investors are hesitant to rely on independent analysts who do not have the name recognition of well known investment banks. Moreover, it has been found that independent analysts issue even more optimistic ratings than non-independents in their ratings. Coffee (2006) suggests that this is because independent analysts ultimately depend for their revenues on investors who dislike "sell" recommendations for their holdings. Smaller independent analysts are also more vulnerable to threats from large issuers.

Mainelli et al. (2009) found that sell-side research:

- Misses most major insights or turning points in companies; errs persistently to buy recommendations, supporting current company fads; This may be attributed to the fact that most analysts are experts at financial modeling, but lack any understanding about the way businesses and managers operate. This extends to a lack of understanding of malfeasance as well as ESG issues.
- Allied to this point is the neglect by sell-side analysts of sustainability issues that may affect the company's long-term prospects. Most analysts do not have the ability to operate complex comparative models or conduct in-depth investigations comparing environmental–social–governance (ESG) performance of different companies. This has a permissive effect on companies continuing often unsustainable approaches, which result in failure, e.g., the dot.com bubble.
- Errs persistently to "buy" recommendations. A common reporting standard which does not yet exist would see analysts disclose the percentage of companies in "buy", "hold", "sell" stocks for all companies and for those of investment banking clients.
- Follows consensus forecasts and views.
- Prioritises client marketing over company research.
- Focuses on short or at best medium-term.

Coffee (2006) and Mainelli et al. (2009) mention various sources of conflicts of interest among research analysts in addition to the obvious ones of investment banking whereby analysts push products issued by their investment banks and broker–dealer conflicts whereby analysts generate business by making more "buy" recommendations. "Sell" recommendations may actually cause a loss of confidence that would leave investors in serious losses. Furthermore, personal conflicts among analysts may occur when they own or decide to sell shares which they are following. In the former case, there is an obvious conflict in pushing shares which they own; in the latter case, they are obviously giving advice in which they do not believe. Taken together, various issues around sell-side analysts have driven Kay (2012) to conclude that sell-side analysts are a dispensable link in the chain of intermediation.

Even when an analyst is not beholden to the issuer of shares, s/he still requires access to carry out his/her work, which is often curtailed in the case of "unfriendly" recommendations. Notwithstanding legislation prohibiting lack of access in the US, "freeze-outs" remain the rule rather than the exception (Mainelli et al. 2009). "Sell" recommendations are also unappreciated by institutional investors (who pay brokerage commissions) when they hold substantial positions in stocks which they cannot then sell without a loss. Further, Mainelli et al. (2009) recount regular instances of personal inducements offered to analysts by issuing companies, in the form of job recommendations. Herding itself constitutes a conflict, as analysts suffer less if they are wrong on the basis of following the optimistic herd than they would if they made an individual wrong prediction.

Buy-side analysts are evaluated by investors on the basis of fees excluding brokerage costs, which encourage research costs to both be minimised and/or to find their way into brokerage costs. This necessitates their reliance on the "free" research offered by the sell-side.

5.2.2 Asset Managers

Pension funds and insurance companies outsource their investments to specialist asset managers to make buy and sell decisions. Kay refers to the UK Investment Management Association distinction between asset managers who engage in trading versus those who engage in investing. The former mainly trade shares based on the current flow of buy and sell orders, momentum in the share price and short-term correlations between the prices of different investments, driven by short term trends and a rapid portfolio turnover. They do not analyse underlying company performance. In contrast, investment oriented asset managers focus on the business, strategy and activities of the issuing company in addition to its likely earnings and cash flow. However, trader types predominate, as it has been found that hedge funds, high frequency and proprietary traders were responsible for 72 per cent of market turnover in the UK in 2012.

In addition to increased costs of frequent trading, it is claimed that often the fees charged to clients for services by asset managers are not transparent, with different fee structures for different share classes and different shareholders. In the UK, a study has shown that contrary to claims by asset managers that big fees are worth paying to outperforming managers, a study has shown that asset management and the potential for outperformance are less important than cost, especially for low earners in pension funds, as some schemes carry total expense ratios (TERs) of 3 per cent (Skypala and Kelleher 2012).

Since relative performance as monitored by asset holders and their advisors determines the bonuses of asset managers, it is easy to see why trading for the short-term might be quite a tempting style. It is also easy to see the converse, as to why asset managers do not engage in costly engagement with companies (voice), but instead choose to just sell the shares (exit). Moreover, benefits from the time and effort put into engagement with companies accrue to all potential asset managers, not just the one who exercised "voice", i.e., the free-rider problem. Consistent with the short-term view, like sell-side analysts, asset managers have been found not to pay much attention to sustainability issues, not because they are unaware of them, but because they do not perceive demand from investors and pension funds to be accountable for these issues (Grene 2012).

Generally, it is observed that asset managers are "conspicuous by their absence" in exerting significant influence on the companies they collectively own, overwhelmingly supporting existing boards of directors and management pay plans. Management remuneration is based on short-term rises in share prices. Bogle (2012) claims this passivity by asset managers to discipline management is due to three factors:

- Attracting negative attention and controversy could result in negative marketing value.
- Many fund managers are now owned by publicly owned groups, resulting in a conflict of interest when asset managers feel a duty to serve their own public shareholders.
- Fund managers owe their profitability largely to the giant corporations whose pension funds they manage, another conflict of interest.

5.2.3 Auditors

Statutory audits are a pillar of global financial markets. Auditor independence is paramount, since the role of the auditor is to perform a thorough and reliable audit to endorse the accuracy of the accounts of a company for the benefit of various stakeholders, including actual and potential investors and creditors. When stakeholders do not trust the audited accounts, costs of trade increase and markets may collapse as occurred in the inter-bank lending market when banks no longer trusted the accuracy of each others' published accounts (Max Planck Institute 2012).

Ironically, although the accuracy of a company's accounts is of critical importance to various parties with an interest in that company, it is the company itself which chooses and pays for the auditing services. This in itself produces a conflict of interest when auditors might be tempted to provide comfort to the company, even if it compromises the accuracy of the accounts. The conflict of interest is deemed to be exacerbated when auditing firms are in a position to obtain lucrative consulting work from auditing clients. Further, it has also been pointed out that alumni of the Big Four accountancy firms heavily dominate positions of audit committee chairman (60 per cent) and chief financial officers (66 per cent) of UK companies, making them more favourably disposed to do business with their former firm (Jones 2012a).

Globally, the auditing market is dominated by the "Big Four" firms, which audit the largest international corporations and domestic champions worldwide. This dominance is underpinned by the infrequence with which leading companies change audit firms. To date there is no definitive evidence that this "monogamous nature of the market" has the effect of inflating fees and undermining the independence and quality of audits (Jones 2012b), although auditors are blamed for not "waving red flags" about problems prior to the collapse of banks heading into the global financial crisis (Kelleher 2012). The continued dominance of the Big Four appears to exist as a vicious or virtuous cycle, depending on one's perspective. They can point to a wealth of experience and an impressive established client base when touting for new work. This certainly provides comfort and a propensity to trust in these firms by potential clients. Moreover, some lenders stipulate conditions on borrowers to use a Big Four auditor.

Coffee (2006) points out that auditors depend on reputational capital that comes from professional standards of conduct and on regulation to counteract damaging accusations of compromise, thus reducing the likelihood that auditors would violate their standards to gain any temporary advantage over competitors. While competition might encourage auditors to cut corners to please corporate clients, on the other hand, Coffee (2006) suggests that if there were lower barriers to entry and a greater number of competent global firms of auditors, some could differentiate themselves on the high standards of their audits even if it meant being tougher on clients. In turn, clients could use the reputation of their auditors to attract investors and reassure creditors. This would create a virtuous cycle of reputational enhancement for certain auditing firms and their clients, ironically, something that was enjoyed by Arthur Andersen and its blue-chip clients in the pre-Enron days.

So, what might cause auditing firms to risk their valuable reputational capital? Coffee (2006) puts forward a number of propositions. Whilst firms may attempt to safeguard their reputations, they cannot necessarily control individual agents. Thus, the lead partner on a particular audit may be seduced into compliant behaviour toward a corporate client, especially in the hope of winning more work from that client, as happened spectacularly with Andersen and Enron. Furthermore, reputational schizophrenia means that audit firms want to be perceived as strict monitors to investors, but simultaneously as flexible and problem-solving to clients. The 1980s saw a wave of takeovers of smaller audit firms by the larger established high reputation ones in their intent to become global players to follow transnational corporate clients. This resulted in a blurring of reputations, so investors could not really distinguish among them. Moreover, during bubbles, all that corporate clients require is an auditor to certify their accounts, and do not expect much more, so auditor reputation is not so important in gaining leverage, according to Coffee (2006). This may explain the lack of influence of auditors in preventing both the dot.com bubble and the global financial crisis of 2008.

Auditing firms do not tend to attempt to impugn each others' reputations, since it is a zero-sum game that would invite destructive retaliation and not necessarily win over clients. Therefore, when an audit firm runs into trouble because of a scandal, instead of dancing on its grave, the others look away. There is a "live-and-let-live" attitude. Moreover, competing for auditing work is less in its own right than opening the door to cross-sell other services.

Since the financial crisis, there has been a resurgence of calls to reform the auditing profession, especially in the EU and the UK, in particular (Kelleher 2012; Max Planck Institute 2012). Much of this concentrates on rotation of auditing firms after a number of years. This would not only prevent the auditors from "going native", it would also avoid auditors being influenced by their historical judgements, thereby reducing risk. The suggestions for limited terms range from 5 years to 25 years, so the issue remains uncertain. Alongside the ideas for limiting auditing firm engagements externally, are proposals to rotate the engagement staff on any particular audit, even if the firm stays on. Of course, no company is forced to retain its auditors anyway. Another area for suggested reform is to limit the proportion of fees that auditing firms may receive from audit clients from non-audit work, alongside disclosure of fees earned by auditing firms from their clients.

5.2.4 Proxy Voting Services

Proxy voting services provide information and advice, usually to institutional shareholders about corporate governance events around companies whose shares are held by the fund. In particular, proxy voting services help shareholders to decide whether or not they will vote for the board members proposed by the company, and increasingly, whether shareholders should support proposed executive remuneration packages.

Opinion over the role of proxy voting services is mixed. Some, such as Robert Monks, a corporate governance guru, and founder of the world's biggest proxy services agency, see them as the vanguard of promoting the best of corporate governance practices in companies (Sullivan 2012). However, others bemoan proxy voting services as yet another unnecessary intermediary, that actually distances fund managers from their fiduciary and stewardship duties. They are concerned that proxy voting firms sell formulaic voting policies, based on a "one size fits all" notion of what constitutes good corporate governance, often applied in ways that do not take account of specific companies' circumstances and prospects. In 2012, BlackRock, the US fund manager announced that it would take a direct interest in the companies in which it invests, preferring to engage directly with the companies to address corporate governance issues. BlackRock emphasised that it did not depend on proxy voting agencies' advice, but reached its own conclusions on voting intentions based on its own internal criteria (Wachtell et al. 2012). The advantage of this approach is that this type of engagement suggests a long term approach. While it obviously entails an intense psychological and time commitment by institutional investors, it means that institutional investors are likely to invest in fewer companies, but to know them better, and influence them more.

5.2.5 Credit Rating Agencies

Although credit rating agencies have been condemned for their part in perpetrating recent damaging financial bubbles, like the dot.com bubble, and the events leading to the current financial crisis, their power continues unabated. For the rating agencies, it is as if their part in the economic collapse had not occurred. A potential downgrade by a credit rating agency remains a cause of vital concern for companies, issuers of structured products and sovereign governments alike. In its 2012 annual report, the US Securities and Exchange Commission (SEC) found that rating agencies still breached internal processes aimed at keeping business considerations from interfering with credit research (Foley 2013).

This is notwithstanding a $6 billion lawsuit against Standard & Poors by the US Department of Justice, alleging fraud in its rating of mortgage backed securities, alongside several smaller lawsuits by investors against rating agencies.

In effect, there is little competition within the industry, with control by a duopoly, Standard & Poors and Moodys or at best, a triumvirate, if Fitch is added. For over a century, rating agencies have been providing standardised information about creditworthiness, rating sovereign and corporate debt and special purpose vehicles. Their ratings are distilled into an alphabetical symbol, ranging from AAA to D, with below BBB deemed non-investment grade. The information is meant to help investors in fixed income investments. However, credit rating agencies are paid not by investors, but directly by the issuers of debt. Whilst this sets up a classical conflict of interest, the industry structure mitigates this to some extent by low competition. However, the lack of competition can lead to lax standards. Moreover, credit rating agencies do compete for extra consulting work from clients, much as auditing firms compete for lucrative consulting work.

Further, ratings agency practices are procyclical. In the boom, complex products get excessively optimistic ratings that reinforce the boom's momentum. But then, when the crisis hits, agencies are widely criticised by investors and regulators for rosy ratings that eventuate in large losses. In response, agencies drastically cut ratings, and this reinforces the dynamics of collapse.

There is little regulatory oversight of credit rating agencies. The US SEC established nationally recognised NRSRO has only four members – the big three and one other small Canadian organisation, Dominion Bond Rating Service. Agencies take no responsibility for the use of their ratings and are not liable if their ratings fail to identify the high risk of some debts. Since changes in credit ratings can have intense consequences, benefiting or harming investors in fixed income securities and taxpayers through costs of sovereign debt, there are calls for greater regulation of the agencies. This includes more monitoring of the agencies and making them more liable for their mistakes. Outside the US, organisations complain that the US-based agencies do not understand local financial structures and US benchmarks are therefore not appropriate, leading to an overweighting of US investments by fund managers (Mainelli 2003). It is suggested that accreditation should be opened to more agencies to increase competition, and that greater transparency in fees paid to credit rating agencies should be effected by organisations filing such payments clearly in their accounts. However, competition could kick-start the conflict of interest problem. Another suggestion is for the users of rating agencies' information, i.e., investors, to pay for their services, restoring the principal–agent relationship. However, the non-excludability of non-paying users would induce a free-rider problem (Coffee 2006).

Apart from the potential conflicts of interest, Mainelli et al. (2009) identifies other issues. One is the question of the competence of rating agencies. Although the agencies provide evidence of poor ratings with later default, these may be self-fulfilling prophecies, and in many instances, the problems were well known by the market before the rating agencies issued downgrades. An example is Enron which was downgraded only at a late stage in its decline. Moreover critics point to instances of poor prediction, and especially for exotic financial instruments, the rating system developed a century ago may not be fit for purpose. Rating agencies have been compared with protection rackets by some critics when they have gratuitously taken it upon themselves to supply credit ratings for organisations "in the public interest", upgrading the ratings subsequent to being paid by the organisation.

5.3 FAST FINANCE

Woolley (2010) shows how the intermediation within the value chain creates bubbles and destroys value, since bubbles, crashes and rent capture are caused by principal/agent problems. Agents have access to more and better information than the investors who appoint them, and the interests and objectives of agents frequently differ from those of their principals. For their part, principals cannot be certain of the competence or diligence of the agents. This is manifested when fund managers shirk by relying excessively on rating agencies instead of doing their own due diligence. Moreover, there are no sanctions against agents when things go wrong, whether through incompetence or suspect motives, which introduces moral hazard that characterises finance at every level.

The principal–agent problems in the investment value chain give rise to a bias for action, as traders earn returns closely related to the volume of activity in their dealt securities (Kay 2012). Analysts are rewarded on the basis of buy and sell recommendations arising out of their narratives, whilst investment bankers and advisors depend on transactions for their earnings. Advisors have been rewarded by commissions, and Kay (2012) suggests that even after commissions are no longer allowed, clients will be more likely to be willing to pay for advice to do something rather than nothing. Pension funds, driven to take excessive risk in the face of rising payout demands, along with insurance companies, also contributed to the buildup of risk in the system. The fact that the agencies rated 80 per cent of risky mortgage backed products AAA, and that regulators and financial analysts acted as if these ratings were as solid as the AAA ratings given to the safest corporate bonds, also contributed to the ensuing bubble.

After a period of consistently high profits, asset managers become overconfident. They are tempted to shirk and it becomes correspondingly harder to induce them to exert continuing effort. This introduces momentum giving rise to bubbles, whereby the price of securities is more likely to keep moving in the same direction than to change direction. Once a momentum trader sees acceleration in a stock's price, earnings or revenues, the trader will often take a position in the stock in the hope that its momentum will continue in either an upward or downward direction. This strategy relies on short-term movements in a stock's price rather than fundamental value. Once momentum becomes embedded in markets, agents then logically respond by adopting strategies that are likely to reinforce the trends. Those who are impatient for results or who have no ability or desire to undertake the hard work of fundamental analysis to find cheap stocks, will use momentum. Further, short-term incentives, such as annual performance fees, cause fund managers and others to concentrate on high-turnover. These strategies add to the distortions in markets (Woolley 2010). Kay asserts that the norms of behaviour in the City of London copied the example of apparently successful US investment banks which involved transactions and trading over relationships.

Woolley (2010) reports that short-termism has come to dominate capital markets over the past couple of decades, with average holding periods of only eight months. The growth in trading of derivatives, most of which have maturities of less than a year, is also symptomatic of shortening horizons. High turnover comes at a heavy cost to long-term investors through management fees and associated trading costs. This pessimistic view does not even take into account the phenomenon of "high frequency trading", which covers more than half of all US stock trading. High frequency trading is defined as "the automated use of sophisticated computer programmes or algorithms to take advantage of miniscule price discrepancies in fractions of a second" (Massoudi and MacKenzie 2013, p. 11).

5.4 TRUST IN FINANCIAL MARKETS

The issue of the loss of trust is a depressing outcome of the global financial crisis, and a perplexing one to resolve. Tyrie (2012) suggests that the question of whether financial institutions are too big to trust is a fundamental existential one. Much of the loss of trust in financial institutions is blamed on their culture of concentration on profits and pursuit of excessive remuneration, whilst deceiving customers.

Very occasionally, a banker breaks rank to confirm the worst of what the public already suspected about the unethical cultures of financial institutions. A spectacular example was Greg Smith, a trader who resigned from Goldman Sachs in March 2012 after a 12 year career there. Mr Smith had served as a Goldman Sachs executive director and head of its US equity derivatives business in Europe, the Middle East and Africa. Castigating Goldman Sachs's culture, people and identity in a *New York Times* op-ed piece on the day he resigned from Goldman Sachs, Mr Smith wrote:

> I can honestly say that the environment now is as toxic and destructive as I have ever seen it. To put the problem in the simplest terms, the interests of the client continue to be sidelined in the way the firm operates and thinks about making money … culture was always a vital part of Goldman Sachs's success. It revolved around teamwork, integrity, a spirit of humility, and always doing right by our clients. The culture was the secret sauce that made this place great and allowed us to earn our clients' trust for 143 years. It wasn't just about making money; … this decline in the firm's moral fiber represents the single most serious threat to its long-run survival … . It makes me ill how callously people talk about ripping their clients off. Over the last 12 months I have seen five different managing directors refer to their own clients as "muppets," sometimes over internal e-mail … . It astounds me how little senior management gets a basic truth: If clients don't trust you they will eventually stop doing business with you. It doesn't matter how smart you are. (Smith 2012)

No doubt, there is good reason to lose trust in financial markets, as the moral malaise described by Mr Smith is not seen as an anomaly, but as a systemic problem. In fact, the issue is not only loss of trust, but downright mistrust, which adds another layer to the problem (Lewicki et al. 1998).

First, let us examine what is meant by trust, is it really lost, and does it matter? The concept of trust is an important one in many disciplines, ranging across psychology, sociology, economics and management (Rousseau et al. 1998). Bhattacharya et al. (1998) stipulate that, by definition, trust exists in an uncertain and risky environment, and reflects an aspect of expectancy about outcomes. In this respect it is situation and person specific, so that it could vary even for Mother Teresa, subject to the situation she was facing, and with whom she was dealing. Trust can vary in importance and degree.

Rousseau and her colleagues define trust as "a psychological state comprising the intention to accept vulnerability based upon positive expectations of the intentions or behaviour of another" (Rousseau et al. 1998, p. 395). However, there may be myriad differing assumptions embedded in this definition. The definition may cover trust as a deterrent, which suggests that the truster believes the trustee will behave in a certain way because costly sanctions in place for breach of trust exceeds any potential benefits from opportunistic behaviour. This is akin to Barney and Hansen's (1994) concept of a semi-strong form of trust-worthiness, based on mechanisms such as regulation or contracts, rather than on personal characteristics of the trustee or positive qualities of the trusting relationship. There are those who would dispute whether this is trust at all, if trustees will behave benevolently simply because of sanctions (Williamson 1993; Rousseau et al. 1998) state that the need for strict controls in itself is indicative of mistrust, demonstrating a paradox. The next step up is calculus based trust, where perceived positive intentions by the trustee on the part of the truster is based not only on deterrence, but also on credible, verifiable information, such as from certification or reputation, regarding the intentions and competence of the trustee, at least as far as a particular transaction is concerned. Williamson (1993) would also disregard calculus based trust as real trust, since it is not based on norms, but on the costs and benefits of trusting another and an assessment that gives rise to a calculated prediction about the way another will behave, rather than on anything to do with the qualities of the trustee.

Beyond calculus based trust is relational trust derived from repeated interactions, so trust has been built up within a relationship. This trust has an emotional component, based on the formation of attachments. Lewicki et al. (1998) suggest that deep relational trust has the effect of enhancing the fruition of new mutual opportunities, while simultaneously eliminating negativity in the form of mistrust. Moreover, relational trust can be subject to a virtuous cycle of development through being tested successfully again and again.

Repeated experiences with the same partners may not always result in increased relational trust. Game theory scholars, studying cooperation and competition in the course of trust related interactions between partners have found that relational trust and emotional bonding increases in the context of reciprocity, but spirals downward in the face of any defections (Eberl 2004; Sitkin and Roth 1993).

Institutional trust is also mentioned as another form whereby reputation or other signals open the door to relationships that turn out to be either calculus or relational, depending on how they develop. Thus, institutional trust may act as a control (e.g., avoiding loss of reputation), and similar to deterrence controls, may end up undermining deeper trust.

Another prominent perspective on trust is provided by Mayer et al. (1995). In their framework, trust is based on an interrelated number of factors, notably the truster's propensity to trust, the perceived trustworthiness of the trustee and the risk involved in trusting the trustee. The assessment of trustworthiness is itself a function of three necessary factors – ability, benevolence and integrity. Ability refers to perceived competence or expertise within a specific domain, germane to the trusting relationship. Benevolence is the perception that the trustee has intrinsic positive intentions toward the truster, beyond extrinsic reward for carrying out his/her duties and can only develop in the context of the experience of the relatonship. Integrity is the perception by the truster that the trustee adheres to a set of principles that the truster finds acceptable. This is what has been deemed by some to be "principled" trust, and occurs with or without external constraints or coercion (Colombo 2010). Perceived trustworthiness will wax and wane during the course of a relationship as actual positive and negative occurrences of the ability, benevolence and integrity of the trustee are experienced. As defined by Mayer et al., trust may be cognitive and/or affective.

Colombo (2010) discriminates among the different types of trust by dividing them between cognitive trust, which is situation specific and involves calculative reasoning, versus affective trust, which is more generalised with respect to various trustees. Sitkin and Roth (1993) make roughly the same dichotomy of types of trust, between task specific reliability and value congruence, based on expectations of outcomes. The latter refers to expectations by the truster of the compatibility of the trustee's beliefs and values with his/her own. They make the point that when value congruence is challenged, it goes beyond mere disappointment that the trustee has not fulfilled expectations in a particular situation, i.e., has been unreliable. It engenders active mistrust that cannot be easily reversed. This kind of mistrust cannot be remedied by regulatory or legalistic devices.

In sum, many scholars have separated different aspects of trust. There are some situations where there are no vulnerabilities, so trust does not matter and is not present; Barney and Hansen's (1994) weak form trust. However, when trust counts, and is present, there would appear to be two types. One is based on control of some type. This may constitute regulatory, governance or legalistic contract measures which have the effect of restraining the would-be trustee. This kind of control may also occur when the would-be trustee has something at stake and would suffer some kind of loss if s/he were to defect. This can be a material loss or a loss that has material consequences, i.e., loss of reputation that would result in being struck off, or at least losing custom. Barney and Hansen's semi-strong form trust corresponds to this type. Not only is such trust likely to be costly to all sides, since it involves a great deal of checking, it can be counter-productive as trust breaks down in the face of monitoring (Colombo 2010; Rousseau et al. 1998). However, calling this trust of any kind may be a misnomer, since it is basically dependent on the truster knowing that the trustee stands to suffer some kind of penalty if s/he does not fulfil the expectations of the truster. It suggests that as soon as this insurance is removed, the trust will disappear.

The other type of trust, Barney and Hansen's (1994) strong-form trust, or "hard-core" trustworthiness is akin to relational or principled or generalised trust (Colombo 2010; Sitkin and Roth 1993; Lewicki et al. 1998; Rousseau et al. 1998). Unlike calculative trust it has a moral dimension, in that it expects that the trustee acts not on the basis of consequential reward or punishment, but because it is the right thing to do, consistent with the principles and moral values held by the trustee. Thus, the truster knows that the trustee would not "defect", because s/he just wouldn't do it, as a matter of personal honour. It is suggested that trusters "care about the shadow of the past", in contrast to calculative trust which looks to "the shadow of the future" (Stout 2009, p. 11). To behave in a trustworthy fashion is part of the trustee's identity. It is simply not in his or her repertoire to behave in an untrustworthy manner. The importance of identified personal qualities of integrity of the trustee is critical here.

How do we know when an actor is fulfilling our positive expectations out of integrity or out of calculativeness? Barney and Hansen (1994) suggest that strong-form trustworthiness is path-dependent, socially complex and causally ambiguous. They assert that strong-form trustworthy partners are only too happy to make themselves open to audit, since they know they would not behave opportunistically. Also, strong-form trust agents might make unilateral transaction specific investments before an exchange is finalised. Stout (2009) discusses that trustworthy individuals may be identified not only through own repeated experience with those individuals, but also through indirect observation of their actions with other trusters, and importantly, when their trustworthiness is endorsed by trusted others with whom they have dealt.

5.4.1 Does Trust Really Matter?

When trader Greg Smith resigned from Goldman Sachs over its mistreatment of clients, one of those very clients declared that it was well known that the firm traded against its clients for years, but that he continued to do business with them because they are "good traders" (Craig and Thomas Jr. 2012). This suggests that trust does not matter. However, perhaps the reflections of this anonymous client demonstrate all that is wrong with financial markets and why the global financial system is in disarray.

Most observers of trust in business see it as a good thing, for various reasons. We assume that trust entails the expectation of positive, not negative outcomes, according to Bhattacharya et al. (1998). Further, the positive side of trust is seen to emanate from strong-form, relational trustworthiness, rather than through trust based merely on control or restraint of the trustee. Barney and Hansen (1994) show how strong-form trust confers a sustainable competitive advantage, since it incurs fewer costs than other forms, and is difficult for competitors to imitate, as it emerges over a long history. Studying value chains in manufacturing, Dyer and Chu (2003) show how trust not only minimises transaction costs, but also has a mutually causal relationship with information sharing, which, in turn creates value in the exchange relationship. Capaldo and Giannoccaro (2012) found similar results in an experiment, whereby trust had a positive influence on supply chain performance. Stout (2009) shows that trust reciprocated by trustworthy behaviour results in benefits to all in game experiments.

If information sharing is so important in the manufacturing value chain, it is even more important in finance, where accurate, timely and transparent information is the critical ingredient that ultimately creates value. In fact, Lynn Stout (2009) considers trust a *sine qua non* for the functioning of securities markets. Notwithstanding that her paper was written after the start of the global financial crisis, she is of the belief that investors still fundamentally trust in the US securities markets as a system. The evidence for this is that "they are willing to buy trillions of dollars of securities, even when they are not quite sure what they are buying or whom they are buying from" (Stout 2009, p. 14). Surely, many of these investors are misguided or have no choice since the information costs in investigating the trustworthiness of agents in the finance value chain are simply too burdensome. As seen in the analysis of the various gatekeepers and monitors, depending on these only moves the problem back a step. Just because investors do not engage in elaborate monitoring of agents along the investment value chain, this is not evidence of trust. Rather it shows just how difficult such monitoring is, and how helpful it would be if investors could rely on value chain agents through earned trust, rather than through no alternative.

5.4.2   Trust and the Investment Value Chain

By its nature, interdependencies occur in any supply chain, as each player depends on the others, even those who are not adjacent to them in the chain. In this sense, the value chain is a collective (Capaldo and Giannoccaro 2012). However, the players in the value chain experience a tension between acting out of self-interest and the interests of the broader collective community of the value chain, and in particular, the end client (Rousseau et al. 1998). In true trust, there is no "them and us", only "us". This corresponds very well to the nature of relational trust.

How then does the notion of trust relate to the investment value chain? First of all, the plethora of intermediaries between the market users, i.e., the originator of securities and the final customers (investors, savers) means there is no direct contact between them. Thus, how can relational trust, which is based on personal experiences and direct assessment of the trustworthiness of the trustee based on these experiences occur in the context of the investment value chain as it is constituted at present? Not only is there distance between the final client and others in the value chain, there are conflicts of interest everywhere along the chain, and moreover, among those who are meant to be protecting its integrity, i.e., the monitors and gatekeepers.

5.5   WHERE DO WE GO FROM HERE?

5.5.1   The Role of Fiduciary Duty: A Proposal

The notion of fiduciary duty to clients is not as apparent as is necessary to invite trust as a governing principle in the investment value chain. According to Kay (2012), all value chain participants should observe fiduciary standards in their relationships with clients, so clients' interests are put first, whilst costs of services should be reasonable and transparent. Conflicts of interest should be avoided, and overall, "standards of decent behaviour" should be observed. In the absence of direct relationships and the presence of conflicts of interest within the value chain, Kay's (2012) suggestion of invoking fiduciary duty rather than market based mechanisms could engender the trust that is necessary along the value chain to benefit the collective, and create value for the end user, and society in general.

Let us look more closely at what is meant by a fiduciary. The word fiduciary derives from the Latin, "to trust". It means that a person has been entrusted in some way to act on behalf of someone else rather than themselves, and precludes behaviours such as conflicts of interest and self-dealing at the expense of the party on whose behalf the fiduciary is supposed to be engaged. The difficulty at present is how to introduce a sense of fiduciary duty among each and every player in the investment value chain, since the chain is only as strong as its weakest link.

Fiduciary duty as envisaged by Kay would involve information sharing and genuine engagement between the company invested in and the investor, through fund managers acting in a fiduciary manner. It means a concentration on the long-term rather than on current stock prices, so that a real appreciation of current performance and future prospects of each investee company is paramount. By definition, this is a stewardship rather than a transaction based orientation.

While some professions are liable for fiduciary duties by law, this is a coercive type of control which is not the same as the type of relational, principled trust that is necessary for sustainability. A fiduciary would embrace the letter and spirit of professional ethics, with internalised values. This entails:

- a common body of knowledge;
- a certification system;
- use of specialised knowledge for the public good, and
- a code of ethics.

The meaning of acting in the public good should be taken seriously. In particular, it means public good via client welfare as a primary focus and renunciation of self-interest; placing professional values and standards ahead of individual advantage, not profit maximisation. In contrast to a contractual market exchange, the professional has to go further in understanding client needs. This is in contrast to strict contract relationships, which are impersonal, incomplete and restrict professional discretion, and where the inequality between professional and client is not acknowledged.

The professional code of ethics should embrace integrity as a foundation, recognising that professionals are held to a higher standard of integrity. Unlike legal instruments, it depends on individual conscience, whereby moral error is considered highly egregious. There is a distinctive moral commitment to serve a client good, acting as a fiduciary. Professional member bodies act as a major referent for personal values, beliefs, and identity.

At present, there are already professionals, such as auditors and lawyers who supposedly adhere to professional standards present in the investment value chain. However, Coffee (2006) and the Enron debacle have shown that some of these professionals have not always adhered to the highest professional standards. Generally, the existing professionals should be returned to their ethical roots. Meanwhile, those value chain players who are not already liable to observe the hallmarks of a profession should be organised in that way. Perhaps it should start on a statutory basis, in the hope that it will become internalised through practice within serious professional organisations.

Fiduciary attention among the investment value chain agents would necessarily slow down the trading of securities as, instead of frantic short-term fast trading for immediate if ephemeral rewards, professionals would be acting on behalf of clients and their long term interests.

5.5.2 Slow Finance

Gervais Williams (2011), a successful fund manager, has converted the wisdom of his experience into a philosophy, which he calls "slow finance", emulating the "slow food" movement, to return finance to its basic role of supporting value creation in the economy. While Williams' advice is geared toward individual retail investors, his slow finance philosophy can be invoked by institutional investors too. However, the groundwork for slow finance has to be laid along the investment chain, with each player adopting a fiduciary approach. In fact, if such an approach is adopted, some players can be eliminated altogether. For example, fund managers doing their own due diligence will rely less on analysts and rating agencies, whilst feeling assured that auditors' reports are competent and truthful. Such intermediary eliminations will bring investors and companies closer together and perhaps engender relational trust.

Williams claims that the wake-up call of the financial crisis of 2008 has been largely disregarded as artificial measures to keep interest rates low and money circulating give a false sense of security. The cornerstones of slow finance consist of a renewed interest in the connection between investor and investment. Fast strategies geared towards making quick returns should be replaced by an emphasis on compounding returns over time. Overall, Williams recommends investing in value, in smaller domestic companies, in high dividend, not necessarily high growth companies whose share prices may fall as spectacularly as they rise. Investors are advised to go for companies with good and growing income. Such investment strategies have historically delivered in the long term. Investors, dazzled by the prospect of quick growth, had lost touch with these fundamental truths about long term value, that returns from value investing have outstripped those from growth strategies by a significant margin.

Williams' views on slow finance are consistent with recommendations in the Kay (2012) report. Foremost is the exhortation to understand company fundamentals as opposed to a short-term concentration on share price movements, and the adoption of a stewardship rather than a transaction stance, similar to the practices adopted by Warren Buffett, whose Berkshire Hathaway fund has produced notably successful returns over the decades. This should result in the selection of a relatively small portfolio of businesses, based on the characteristics of the company, with long holding periods, and stakes of sufficient size to be capable of some influence on the management succession and strategy. Kay also points out the alignment of interests between Buffett as fund manager, with his own stake in the investments and the other investors.

5.6 CONCLUSIONS

The boom and bust that gave way to the global economic crisis was facilitated by "fast finance" which was itself made possible by the configuration and behavioural processes of the investment value chain, consisting of the main value chain and support processes. In all cases, conflicts of interest and perverse incentives supported short term trading over long-term value creation. Therefore, the investment value chain was characterised by a lack of trust and fiduciary responsibility. Such trust is necessary for securities markets to function and itself would be enhanced through a fiduciary orientation among the players in the investment value chain, embracing the principles inherent in professional ethics. This could give rise to "slow finance" that enables long-term value creation in the economy through healthy companies.

REFERENCES

Banziger, H. (2012), 'Towards a sustainable business model: How financial institutions have to change to win back society's trust', Special Paper, LSE Financial Markets Group Paper Series.
Barney, J.B. and M.H. Hansen (1994), 'Trustworthiness as a source of competitive advantage', *Strategic Management Journal*, **15**, pp. 175–190.
Bhattacharya, R., T.M. Devinney and M.M. Pillutla (1998), 'A formal model of trust based on outcomes', *Academy of Management Review*, **23** (3), pp. 459–472.
Bogle, J.C. (2012), 'Fund managers must break their silence on governance', *Financial Times*, 20 September, p. 32.

Capaldo, A. and I. Giannoccaro (2012), 'How trust affects supply chain performances: The moderating role of interdependence structure', *International Journal of Production Economics*, **104**, pp. 1–12.

Coffee Jr., J.C. (2006), *Gatekeepers: The professions and corporate governance*, Oxford, UK: Oxford University Press.

Colombo, R.J. (2010), 'Trust and the reform of securities regulation', *Delaware Journal of Corporate Law*, **35** (3), pp. 829–877.

Craig, S. and L. Thomas Jr. (2012), 'Public rebuke of culture at Goldman Sachs opens debate', *New York Times Dealbook* (dealbook.nytimes.com), 14 March.

Crotty, J. (2009), 'Structural causes of the global financial crisis: A critical assessment of the "new financial architecture"', *Cambridge Journal of Economics*, **33**, pp. 563–580.

Dyer, J.H. and W. Chu (2003), 'The role of trustworthiness in reducing transaction costs and improving performance: Empirical evidence from the United States, Japan and Korea', *Organization Science*, **14** (1), pp. 57–68.

Eberl, P. (2004), 'The development of trust and implications for organizational design: A game- and attributional theory framework', *Schmalenbach Business Review*, **56**, pp. 258–273.

Edelman (2013), *Edelman Trust Barometer*, retrieved from http://trust.edelman.com (accessed 20 October 2014).

Foley, S. (2013), 'Ratings from credit crisis return to haunt agencies', *Financial Times*, 6 February, p. 18.

Grene, S. (2012), 'Industry players slow to act on climate issues', *Financial Times, FTfm*, 8 October, p. 3.

Jones, A. (2012a), 'Warning on auditors' alumni', *Financial Times*, 8 October, p. 19.

Jones, A. (2012b), 'Big Four criticized for auditing monogamy', *Financial Times*, 8 October, p. 24.

Kay, J. (2012), *The Kay review of UK equity markets and long-term decision making*, London: UK Department of Business, Innovation and Skills.

Kelleher, E. (2012), 'Investors push hard for audit reforms', *Financial Times, FTfm*, 1 October, p. 3.

Lewicki, R.J., D.J. McAllister and R.J. Bies (1998), 'Trust and distrust: New relationships and realities', *Academy of Management Review*, **23** (3), pp. 438–458.

Lex (2012), 'Financial services', *Financial Times*, 1 October, p. 20.

Mainelli, M. (2003), 'Assessing credit rating agencies: Quis aestimat ispsos aestimatores?', *Balance Sheet*, **11** (3), pp. 55–59.

Mainelli, M., J. Stevenson and R. Thamotheram (2009), 'Sell-side research: Three modest reforms', *Z/Yen Paper*.

Massoudi, A. and M. MacKenzie (2013), 'In search of a fast buck', *Financial Times*, 20 February, p. 11.

Max Planck Institute Working Group on Auditor Independence (2012), 'Auditor independence at the crossroads – Regulation and incentives', *Max Planck Institute*, Max Planck Private Law Research Paper No.12/1.

Mayer, R.C., J.H. Davis and F.D. Schoorman (1995), 'An integrative model of organizational trust', *Academy of Management Review*, **20** (3), pp. 703–734.

Rousseau, D.M., S.B. Sitkin, R.S. Burt and C. Camerer (1998), 'Not so different after all: A cross discipline view of trust', *Academy of Management Review*, **23** (3), pp. 393–404.

Sitkin, S.B. and N.I. Roth (1993), 'Explaining the limited effectiveness of legalistic "remedies" for trust/distrust', *Organization Science*, **4** (3), pp. 367–392.

Skypala, P. and E. Kelleher (2012), 'Charges key to pension outcomes', *Financial Times, FTfm*, 1 October, p. 1.

Smith, G. (2012), 'Why I am leaving Goldman Sachs', *New York Times*, 14 March.

Stout, L.A. (2009), 'Trust behavior: The essential foundations of securities markets', UCLA School of Law, Law & Economics Research paper Series Research Paper No. 09-15.

Sullivan, R. (2012), '"Regulators are wrong" over proxy advisors', *Financial Times, FTfm*, 8 October, p. 1.

Tyrie, A. (2012), 'A mandate to tackle the deep-rooted failures of banks', *Financial Times*, 2 October, p. 13.

Wachtell, Lipton, Rosen and Katz (2012), 'Disintermediating the proxy advisory firms', *WLRK Memo*, 19 January.

Williams, G. (2011), *Slow finance: Why investment miles matter*, London, UK: Bloomsbury Publishing.

Williamson, O.E. (1993), 'Calculativeness, trust and economic organization', *The Journal of Law & Economics*, **36** (1), pp. 453-486.

Woolley, P. (2010), 'Why are financial markets so inefficient and exploitative – and a suggested remedy' In Adair Turner and others. *The Future of Finance: The LSE Report*. London, UK: London School of Economics and Political Science.

PART II

From the technical–materialistic to the
ecological–spiritual

6. Materialistic versus non-materialistic value-orientation in management[1]

Laszlo Zsolnai

Occupy Wall Street and other anti-globalization movements indicate a dramatic loss of confidence in mainstream business. Big business has lost credibility and trust worldwide. The basic assumptions of business management have become questionable.

6.1 THE MATERIALISTIC MANAGEMENT MODEL

The dominant management model of modern business is based on a materialistic conception of man. Human beings are considered as body–mind encapsulated egos with only materialistic desires and motivation. This kind of creature is modeled as "Homo Oeconomicus" in economics and business.

Homo Oeconomicus represents an individual being which seeks to maximize his or her self-interest. He or she is interested only in material utility defined in terms of money.

The Materialistic Management Model assumes money-driven extrinsic motivation and measures success according to profits generated. The economic and financial crisis of 2008–2009 has deepened our understanding of the problems of mainstream businesses which base their activities on unlimited greed and the "enrich yourself" mentality.

There are two distinct but interrelated problems with the underlying assumptions of the materialistic management model. One relates to profit as the sole measure of success of economic activities, while the other deals with money as the main motivation for economic activities (Zsolnai 2011).

6.1.1 Profit as Measure of Success

Profit is inadequate for being used as the sole measure of the success of economic activities. Profit provides an incomplete and not unbiased

107

evaluation of economic activities. It reflects the values of the strongest stakeholders, favors preferences in the here and now and presupposes that all kinds of values can be reduced to monetary value.

The market as a mechanism of evaluation has its inherent deficiencies. First of all, there are *stakeholders* that are simply *non-represented* in the determination of market values. Natural beings and future generations do not have the opportunity to vote on the marketplace. Second, the preferences of human individuals count rather unequally; that is, in proportion to their purchasing power. Accordingly, the interests of the poor and disadvantaged are necessarily *underrepresented* in free market settings. Third, the actual preferences of the market players are rather *self-centered* and *myopic*; that is, economic agents make their own decisions only regarding short-term consequences.

To use the profit that can be generated as the sole criterion for judging the success of economic activities implies *strong commensurability* which means that there must exist a common measure of different values based on a cardinal scale of measurement. Mainstream economics suggests that values external to the market should be calculated by using shadow prices and other market-based evaluation techniques. In this way externalities can be "internalized" and full cost pricing of activities can be undertaken.

However, ecological economists have demonstrated that the strong comparability of values is not possible in economics. The value of natural assets cannot adequately be expressed in monetary terms (McDaniel and Gowdy 2000). Similar arguments can be developed for important human and social values such as health and safety, ethics and aesthetics.

Profit is an indicator of the *financial viability* of economic projects but cannot be used as an exclusive criterion for the success of economic activities. To judge the overall value of economic activities we should use a number of non-financial value-criteria in addition to profit.

6.1.2 Money as Motivation

Considering money to be the main motivation for economic activities is dangerous. It decreases the intrinsic motivation of economic actors which leads to decreases in the quality of their output. Also, it cultivates a self-centered value orientation which results in socially insensitive and ethically irresponsible behavior.

Bruno Frey's "crowding out" theory shows why profit motivation may be counter-productive. A monetary reward offered or expected tends to crowd out an agent's willingness to perform the task for its own sake (i.e., based on intrinsic motivation) if the agent's sense of recognition, fairness, or self-determination are thereby negatively affected. The *crowding-out effect* of pricing may also spill over into sectors where no pricing is applied ("spillover effect") if the persons affected find it costly to distinguish their motivations according to sectors. Motivation crowding-out and spillover narrow the scope for successfully applying monetary rewards (Frey 1997).

In his book *What Money Can't Buy*, Harvard philosopher *Michael Sandel* argues that monetizing certain activities usually *degrades* their *moral standing* and *corrupts* them (Sandel 2012).

Social psychologist *Gian-Vittorio Caprara* and his colleagues show empirically that cultivating greed leads to the manipulation of others and oneself. They start with the observation that a division between thought and action takes place when people break the rules or get involved in dirty business. What is most surprising in rule violation and misconduct is that people are not bothered by their consciences, do not fear any sanction and do not feel obliged to make reparations (Caprara and Campana 2006).

Stanford psychologist *Albert Bandura* discovered the *mechanisms* of *moral disengagement*; the psychosocial maneuvers by which moral self-sanctions become disengaged, giving way to a variety of freely undertaken misbehaviors carried out without moral concern. Self-sanction can be disengaged by reconstructing conduct, obscuring personal causal agency, misrepresenting or disregarding the injurious consequences of one's actions or/and by vilifying the recipients of maltreatment by blaming and devaluing them (Bandura 1990).

Caprara and his team developed a scale to assess civic moral dis-engagement (CMD). Their empirical findings suggest that the more people are concerned with *self-enhancement goals*, the more they are inclined to resort to mechanisms that permit them to *disengage* from the duties and obligations of civic life and to justify transgressions when their self-interest is at stake (Camprara and Campana 2006).

This finding has significant consequences for the naive belief in the beneficial impact of the "Invisible Hand" of the market. If economic agents become self-concerned, then it is likely that – by employing moral disengagement mechanisms – their self-exonerative maneuvers will do *harm* to *others*.

6.2 MATERIALISTIC VERSUS SPIRITUAL VALUE ORIENTATION

American psychologist *Tim Kasser* states that a *materialistic value orientation* reflects the priority that individuals give to goals such as money, possessions, image, and status. Confirming the concerns of many spiritual traditions, empirical research supports the idea that materialistic and spiritual value orientations are relatively incompatible. Psychological research shows that the more people focus on materialistic goals, the less they tend to care about spiritual goals. Further, while most spiritual traditions aim to reduce personal suffering and to encourage compassionate behaviors, numerous studies document that the more people prioritize materialistic goals, the *lower their personal well-being* and the more likely they are to engage in manipulative, competitive, and ecologically degrading behaviors (Kasser 2011).

Spirituality can be defined as people's multiform search for meaning that connects them with all living beings and to God or Ultimate Reality (European SPES Forum 2012).

Spiritual value orientation has two interrelated but irreducible characteristics: *interconnectedness* and *transcendence* (Yin 2009). Spirituality is the recognition of the interconnectedness and the pursuit of transcendence. Therefore, it is universal. Spirituality has profound value implications because a spiritual person is one who is genuinely aware of the interconnectedness of all living beings and is therefore able to surpass egoistic boundary to experience deeper love and compassion toward others. Spirituality is indeed moral in nature, and it is a key component of ethical behavior. Yin suggests understanding spirituality as a person's recognition that the ultimate meaning and purpose in life is transcendence. It reflects a person's innate capability to transcend himself or herself to a higher level of consciousness where a boundary-less existence can be genuinely experienced by recognizing the interconnectedness of self and others and the universe (Yin 2009).

Copenhagen Business School scholar *Peter Pruzan* states that spiritual-based leadership is emerging as an inclusive, holistic and yet highly personal approach to leadership that integrates a leader's inner perspectives about identity, purpose, responsibility and success with his or her decisions and actions in the outer world of business. The emergence of spiritual-based leadership can also be seen as an overarching perspective which may incorporate other approaches to leadership that are characterized by a focus on concepts such as "business ethics," "values-leadership," "corporate social responsibility" and "sustainability". However, spiritually based leadership considers ethics, social responsibility and sustainability not as instruments to protect and promote the classical business rationale, but as fundamental goals in their own right.

While traditional managerial leadership aims to optimize economic performance subject to both self-imposed and societal constraints that mandate paying attention to the well-being of the organization's stakeholders, spiritual-based leadership essentially reverses the means and the ends. The "why" of organizational existence is no longer economic growth but the spiritual fulfillment of all those affected by the organization, although a major restriction is the requirement that the organization maintains and develops its economic capacity to serve its stakeholders. In other words, spirituality provides a framework for leadership that can serve as the very source of an organization's values, ethics and responsibility (Pruzan 2011).

6.3 NON-MATERIALISTIC MANAGEMENT

The non-materialistic management model is based on a spiritual conception of man. Human beings are considered spiritual beings embodied in the physical world who have both materialistic and non-materialistic desires and motivations. For them, materialistic desires and outcomes are embedded in and evaluated against spiritual convictions and experiences.

Luk Bouckaert writes that the *Homo Spiritualis* is not characterized by preferences for and striving after maximum utility but by the awareness of being related to others. This inter-existence of the self and the other cannot be reduced to a shared group interest or a collective welfare function. We are interconnected on a level of being, prior to our acting within and making the world. The spirit in each of us is the point of awareness where we feel related to all other beings and to the Being itself. This spiritual self-understanding is not a matter of abstract philosophical thinking but a feeling of universal love and compassion that gives our lives and actions an inner purpose and drive. It transforms our materialistic ego into a responsible and compassionate self (Bouckaert 2011a).

Bouckaert formulated priority statements expressing the primacy of the spiritual in business (Bouckaert 2011b).

1. *The priority of basic needs over subjective preferences.* Preferences are individual and social constructions which express, intensify and transform basic needs, and in certain cases suppress and obstruct them. Basic needs, on the other hand, are the necessary preconditions for a humane existence in a historically and culturally determined community. One can translate basic needs into rights that one can claim on the basis of one's human dignity.

    The classical objection to the basic needs approach is that there is no consensus about the content of basic needs. What people experience as a basic need, according to this argument, depends precisely on their individual preferences. This is partially true. One cannot consider basic needs to be separate from an individual's subjective aspirations, but that does not mean that basic needs should be reduced to those aspirations.

2. *The priority of commitment over self-interest.* Experimental economics and economic psychology gives empirical support to the claim that social commitment has a moral priority over selfish behavior. Genuine commitment has its own logic. One who selflessly devotes one's life to promoting justice is aiming at something other than the pleasure of satisfying his/her own altruistic preferences. He or she does it for the sake of justice itself, not (at least not primarily) as a means to an extrinsic end, such as personal happiness or prestige. There is an essential difference between the instrumental function of a preference and the noninstrumental function of a commitment. While commitment is directed to bringing about an identity, a way of being, preference satisfaction aims at bringing about an advantage or a pleasure.

3. *The priority of mutual trust over mutual advantage in the market.* A well-functioning market requires cooperation and mutual trust. The market instrumentalizes all values in the function of individual, subjective preferences. When everyone determines their own values, a lack of moral cohesion can open the way to far-reaching opportunistic behavior, which is in the long term a threat to the functioning of the market. Hence, there is the growing awareness that moral self-regulation and "social capital" in the form of mutual trust are constitutive of a well-functioning market.

4. *The priority of economic democracy over shareholder capitalism.* Economic democracy is an alternative to bourgeois capitalism and to Marxist collectivism. Stakeholder management and co-creative entrepreneurship are highly valued in today's capitalism. Business ethics criticizes shareholder capitalism and promotes the stakeholder theory of the firm. The strong version of stakeholder theory empowers stakeholders and makes them full partners of the firm. They receive the rights and claims of partners and form a community of co-responsible persons. In principle, an economic democracy is broader than a workers' democracy, while it aims at fostering the balanced participation of all stakeholders.

6.4 EXAMPLES OF NON-MATERIALISTIC MANAGEMENT

A prime example of non-materialistic management is the social business model advocated by Nobel prize winning *Mohamed Yunnus*, the founder of *Grameen Bank* in Bangladesh.

Solidarity lending is a cornerstone of Grameen Bank. Although each borrower must belong to a five-member group, the group is not required to provide guarantees to obtain a loan for a member. Repayment responsibility solely rests on the individual borrower, while the group and the center oversee that everyone behaves in a responsible way and none have repayment problems. There is no form of joint liability; i.e., group members are not obliged to pay on behalf of a member that defaults. However, in practice the group members often contribute to repaying debts with the intention of collecting the money from the responsible member at a later time. Such behavior is facilitated by Grameen's policy of not extending any further credit to a group in which a member defaults.

There is no written contract between Grameen Bank and its borrowers; the system works based on trust. To supplement the lending, Grameen Bank also requires that borrowing members regularly save very small amounts in a number of funds (like emergency funds, group funds, etc.). These savings help serve as insurance against contingencies.

When the social and ethical elements are severed from the microcredit business model it fails tragically, as recent examples in India show. In the Indian state of Andhra Pradesh where microfinance has made the deepest inroads, public authorities have held microlenders responsible for the suicides of 57 people. A pressing problem is over-indebtedness, fuelled by rapid growth in a sector with no formal credit bureaus (*The Economist* 2010a).

In their study into microfinance *Abhijit Banerjee* and *Esther Duflo* conclude that when it works well, microfinance can be a win–win situation. "The poor can borrow money at rates that may look high, but are much lower than those offered by moneylenders; and banks can make a sustainable business in lending to the poor. All this rests as much on a social contract as on a legal contract. Microfinance institutions need to be more diligent in their lending and screen borrowers better – if too many borrowers can't repay their loans, the social obligation will start to fall apart" (*The Economist* 2010b).

Another example of non-materialistic management is the *Triodos Bank* in the Netherlands which also has branches in Belgium, Germany, United

Kingdom and Spain. Triodos is a pioneer in ethical and sustainable banking. It finances projects which add cultural value and benefit both people and the environment. The name, Triodos – "tri hodos" – is from the Greek and means "three-way approach". Triodos only lends to businesses and charities judged to be of social or ecological benefit. This "positive screening" means that the scope of its policies extends beyond those employed by banks which solely avoid investing in companies judged to be doing harm ("negative screening"). Triodos uses money deposited by hundreds of thousands of savers and lends it to several thousands of organizations, such as fair trade initiatives, organic farms, cultural and arts initiatives, renewable energy projects, and social enterprises.

Triodos' mission is to:

- Help create a society that protects and promotes the quality of life of all its members and that has human dignity at its core.
- Enable individuals, organizations and businesses to use their money in ways that benefit people and the environment, and promote sustainable development.
- Provide customers with innovative financial products and high quality service.

Triodos was founded as an anthroposophical initiative. The term "anthroposophy" refers to the ideas of the Austrian spiritual thinker *Rudolf Steiner* (1861–1925) whose interests included education, biodynamic agriculture, organic architecture, eurythmy (movement as art) and therapeutic medicine. Triodos Bank's statutes committed it to anthroposophical principles until 1999 when this formal link was dropped and in recent years the bank, under its current head Peter Blom, has embarked on a policy of reaching out beyond Steiner adherents to broaden its appeal to a wider humanistic framework. Nevertheless, Triodos's origins are reflected in the fact that most of the Dutch directors come from the anthroposophy movement, and Triodos continues to be the banker for many Steiner-inspired projects.

In 2011 Triodos' total assets under management amounted to EUR 6,786 million with EUR 17.3 million net profit (Triodos Bank 2011). The critical growth factor for Triodos is not getting new depositors but finding promising new projects which satisfy the ecological, social and financial criteria of the bank. Under the current conditions Triodos cannot grow faster without compromising its core values. However, unlimited growth is not the goal of a sustainable bank such as Triodos.

6.5 CONCLUSION

The materialistic management model does not produce true well-being for people but actually undermines it. By advocating economic action on the basis of money-making, and by justifying success in terms of profits made, the materialistic management model encourages the irresponsible behavior of economic actors, contributes to ecological destruction and disregards the interests of future generations. The presupposed "rational management model" is in fact highly irrational if it produces non-rational outcomes for society, nature and future generations.

Acknowledging the primacy of the spiritual, the non-materialistic management model activates the intrinsic motivation of economic actors to serve the common good and promotes multidimensional ways of measuring success. According to this model, profit and growth are not final ends but only elements of a broader set of goals. Similarly, cost–benefit calculations are not the only means by which to make managerial decisions but are integrated into a more comprehensive scheme of wisdom-based management (Bouckaert and Zsolnai 2012). Spirituality and rationality are not antagonists in good management, but materialism and rationality are.

NOTE

1. The chapter was completed when the author was Visiting International Scholar at the *Jepson School of Leadership Studies, University of Richmond*, Virginia, USA in February–May 2013.

REFERENCES

Bandura, A. (1990), 'Mechanisms of Moral Disengagement', in W. Reich (ed.), *Origins of Terrorism: Psychology, Ideologies, States of Mind*, Cambridge, UK: Cambridge University Press. pp. 45–103.

Bouckaert, L. (2011a), 'Spirituality and Rationality', in Luk Bouckaert and Laszlo Zsolnai (eds), *The Palgrave Handbook of Spirituality and Business* (2011), London: Palgrave Macmillan, pp. 18–25.

Bouckaert, L. (2011b), 'Personalism', in Luk Bouckaert and Laszlo Zsolnai (eds), *The Palgrave Handbook of Spirituality and Business* (2011), London: Palgrave Macmillan, pp. 155–162.

Bouckaert, L. and L. Zsolnai (eds) (2012), *The Palgrave Handbook of Spirituality and Business*, London: Palgrave Macmillan.

Caprara, G-V. and C. Campana (2006), 'Moral Disengagement in Exercise of Civic-ness', in Laszlo Zsolnai (ed.), *Interdisciplinary Yearbook of Business Ethics*, Oxford: Peter Lang Publishers, pp. 87–98.

Economist, The (2010a), 'Discredited: A string of suicides puts microlending under the spotlight', *The Economist*, November 4.

Economist, The (2010b), 'Big trouble for microfinance', *The Economist*, December 2.

European SPES Forum (2012), *Definition of spirituality*, retrieved from http://www.eurospes.be/page.php?LAN=N&FILE=subject&ID=323&PAGE=1 (accessed October 6, 1012).

Frey, B. (1997), *Not Just for the Money*, Cheltenham, UK and Lyme, NH, USA: Edward Elgar Publishing.

Grameen Bank (2012), 'Grameen Bank', retrieved from http://en.wikipedia.org/wiki/Grameen_Bank (accessed March 5, 2012).

Kasser, T. (2011), 'Materialistic Value Orientation', in Luk Bouckaert and Laszlo Zsolnai (eds), *The Palgrave Handbook of Spirituality and Business* (2011), London: Palgrave Macmillan. pp. 204–211.

McDaniel, C. and J. Gowdy (2000), *Paradise for Sale: Regaining Sustainability – A Parable of Nature*, Berkeley, CA: University of California Press.

Pruzan, P. (2011), 'Spiritually-Based Leadership', in Luk Bouckaert and Laszlo Zsolnai (eds), *The Palgrave Handbook of Spirituality and Business* (2011), London: Palgrave Macmillan, pp. 287–294.

Sandel. M. (2012), *What Money Can't Buy: The Moral Limits of Markets*, New York, NY, USA: Farrar, Straus and Giroux.

Triodos Bank (2011), *Annual Report 2011*, retrieved from http://report.triodos.com/en/2011/servicepages/welcome.html (accessed February 27, 2013).

Yin, E. (2009), *Workplace Spirituality: Definition, Measurement and Managerial Implications*. Cambridge, Judge Business School (Manuscript).

Zsolnai, L. (2011), 'Redefining Economic Reason', in Hendrik Opdebeeck and Laszlo Zsolnai (eds), *Spiritual Humanism and Economic Wisdom*, Antwerp/Apeldoom: Garant, pp. 187–200.

7. The source of ethical competency: Eastern perspectives provided by a Westerner[1]

Peter Pruzan

7.1 A PREAMBLE AND SOME PROVISOS

As will soon be clear, the concept of "ethical competency" I refer to in this chapter is one that is different from more traditional and down-to-earth, skill-based perspectives, for example those referring to sensitivity to ethical issues, problem-solving skills when facing moral dilemmas – or even the ability of leaders to justify an ethical position in connection with a decision that can affect different stakeholders. Although I will argue that ethical competency is a self-referential form of knowing, I will not provide an operational definition as that would be counter-productive; the focus of the chapter is on the very essence of what it means to be ethical – as well on how such a state of being can be realized and the relevance of ethical competency for organizational leaders.

Before developing the major theme, to wit that the primary source of human ethical competency and our promptings to act in accord with this competency is our inherent divine nature and not external stimuli in the form of tradition and moral prescriptions, some additional personal comments are in order. It required a lengthy dialogue with myself before I accepted the invitation to write this chapter. At this point of my life (I am now closer to 80 than 75), I place far greater emphasis on peace of mind and living in harmony with my inner promptings than earlier. Therefore I have significantly reduced activities such as writing articles, attending conferences, giving guest lectures and the like, and prefer to beat out and follow my spiritual path rather than to engage others in my thinking about that path. Furthermore, and perhaps more important here, I reflected on my ability to present a chapter that is both academically acceptable and yet is based on personal spiritual experiences as well as on a metaphysical starting point, viz.: we are all "divine" and the purpose of human life is to realize and to live in accordance with this divine nature.[2]

Earlier in my life I approached the concept of ethics from a more traditional intellectual point of view (what do we mean by "ethics"?, how does it relate to other concepts such as "values" and "responsibility"?) as well as from an operational, management point of view (how can these concepts/convictions be operationalized so that they can contribute to the "good life" of an individual leader and the "good life" of an organization?). For example, in the late 1980s and early 1990s, together with a colleague, I developed the concept of Ethical Accounting and wrote extensively on this as well as on the relationship between organizational ethics and decision-making processes. I even became an academic entrepreneur, contributing in the 1990s and early 2000s to the establishment of several educational and institutional initiatives that promoted these perspectives on leadership.[3] However, the last roughly 25 years of my life have been characterized by intellectual reflection and personal experiences that seriously challenged my earlier thinking and that led to my seeking to integrate spirituality as an overall framework for understanding and operationalizing concepts such as ethics, values, responsibility and sustainability. In (Pruzan 2009) I provide a series of reflections on my path from rationality to morality to spirituality and to their wellspring.

Therefore I felt humble when contemplating the invitation to write this chapter, not only due to the aforementioned reservations regarding my ability to present an academically acceptable chapter that is based on personal spiritual experiences and a significant metaphysical presupposition (that is, however, corroborated by those experiences), but also as to my ability to express my thoughts in a way that can contribute to the well-being and personal development of those who read this chapter. Central to this doubt was the realization that although words are necessary for communication (to and with oneself and others), they can also be inadequate to express what we really experience/think/feel when we have experiences that transcend the potentials provided by language and by cognition in general. This is particularly significant here since some powerful personal experiences of a non-sensory nature played a major role in shaping my conscious awareness of what I will attempt to express in this chapter – and these experiences do not readily lend themselves to verbal expression. I will return to this theme in more detail in the sequel.

Finally in this preamble, I note that the reflections I develop regarding the source of our propensity to behave ethically are inspired by an

"Eastern" perspective. In so doing I primarily draw upon the spiritual wisdom from the Indian ethos[4] that since the late 1980s has exerted a profound influence on my thinking and supplemented my otherwise highly rational approach to life and, in particular, to decision-making, which was the focus of much of my earlier professional career as an operations researcher and economist.

In particular, I will draw on the magnificent expression of several great Indian thinkers of the last roughly 100 years as well as on ancient spiritual texts that originated in what we now refer to as India. I note in this connection that India has been my wife's and my "second home" for many years and that its spiritual heritage has been a major source of inspiration to me on my spiritual path. I have also had the privilege of being invited to lecture at a number of India's premier institutions of higher learning, including five of its most prestigious Indian Institutes of Management. Furthermore, together with my wife, I have travelled and sought inspiration from leading thinkers and spiritual centers in many parts of India as well as in neighboring countries to the north-east; Bhutan, Nepal and Tibet.

7.2　INTRODUCTION

In (Pruzan 2004) I presented a series of reflections on spirituality as the context for leadership in what I referred to as the "East" (primarily India) and the "West" (primarily Scandinavia). I referred to an expansion of the focus in Western organizations on purpose and success to include "deeper existential questions as to the identity and responsibility of both corporations and their leaders, questions very similar in nature to those faced by the person with a spiritual quest." And I argued that in the East, there is often "an emphasis on the virtues a leader must possess to be a 'good' leader, both in a moral and an operational sense. ... Here the connection between the leader and his/her spirituality is more direct and explicit" (Pruzan 2004, p. 15).

The present chapter builds upon that earlier paper but its aims and methods are substantially different. It reflects on the ontological basis for human virtuous behavior and is motivated by the observation that while over the ages philosophers have developed a plethora of ethical perspectives regarding the justification of various norms as to right conduct, little appears to be available on the fundamental metaphysical question: *What is the the source of our competency as human beings to behave virtuously and wisely?*

It is conjectured that attention to such a fundamental question can contribute to our ability as human beings to better appreciate, emancipate and empower our propensity as humans to be empathetic, altruistic and to promote the common good. The chapter focuses on this general question and concludes with reflections as to the relevance of these observations to the specific field of "business ethics", in particular as regards the individual leader's development, the integration of programs to promote ethical competency in an organization, and the teaching of business ethics.[5]

Before proceeding to consider the question as to the source of ethical competency, let us commence with brief reflections on the related but different, question: *why* be ethical. My starting point here is the metaphysical assumption that as humans we *all* have an inherent propensity, *ceteris paribus*, to make intentional choices so as to achieve what we consider to be good or acceptable or just results, however the reader chooses to understand these terms. In other words, such choices are not simply the result of the pursuit of rational self-interest, of norms based on tradition, or even of cultural and biological processes that may have led humans to develop mutually supportive behavior.[6]

Although moral philosophy in the West provides various perspectives on the *why* question, it tends to deny justifications based on universal principles or on religious dogma regarding norms. Such justifications typically refer to an external, divine source and thereby are based on a dualistic foundation. It will be seen that the "Eastern" (Indian/Vedantic) perspective to be developed is essentially non-dual and does not refer to either an external source, to a philosophical first principle, to autonomous normative, practical principles (such as provided e.g., by a Kantian perspective) or to a social constructivist perspective whereby historical, social and economic forces determine what we find to be "good" or "bad", "right" or "wrong".[7]

The present chapter presents a very different position, one that has its roots primarily in Eastern (primarily Indian/Vedantic) existential ontological perspectives on the very nature of reality whereby ethical competence is and always has been embodied in all humans, is so to speak, part of everyone's DNA, and therefore does not require justification.[8] However, as will be emphasized later, the access to this awareness is not equally developed in all individuals. It follows that while there can be different moral intuitions that have the same source, this perspective does not challenge the position that rational discourse and a search for consensus are necessary in our post-modern times, characterized by a pluralism of traditions that can lead to different moral intuitions.[9] Nor do I challenge the position that although particular morals, the specific content, cannot be justified from a universal perspective, the phenomenon of moral norms can be universally justified; such norms are required at all levels of human organization – an individual, a family, an organization, a community, a society cannot *be*, cannot have an identity that enables coherence, without shared values and norms.

7.3 SPONTANEOUS ETHICAL BEHAVIOR

However, before reaching such heights, let us introduce more down to earth reflections and consider that in most typical day-to-day activities we experience that we make "ethically acceptable" decisions with confidence and without rational reflection – and that this confidence is based on an inner guidance. This observation deals primarily with routine matters (e.g., not telling a lie, spontaneously assisting an elderly person who has stumbled or avoiding stepping on a frog).

In other words, in most daily situations we tend to deal with whatever confronts us in a more or less spontaneous manner, drawing upon what I will refer to as our "embodied knowledge" in contrast to more deliberate and willed action that is the result of logical generalizations and prescriptive principles. I note that after I began to develop this chapter I was inspired by the lectures delivered by Varela (1999), who draws upon both cognitive science and what he refers to as "non-Western", particularly Tibetan Buddhist (Mahayana) approaches to the concept of "ethical knowing." According to Varela, "Ethics is closer to wisdom than to reason, to understanding than to adjudicating particular situations ... a wise (or virtuous) person is *one who knows what is good and spontaneously does it*." And, referring to actions in what I just spoke of as "daily situations", he writes: "Actions such as these do not spring from judgment and reasoning, but from an *immediate coping* with what is confronting us. And yet these are true ethical actions, in fact, in our daily, normal life they represent the most common kind of ethical behavior" (Varela 1999, pp. 3–5, Varela's italics).

If one accepts the above, then the question one faces is, how do we "know what is good", so that we may spontaneously do it, that is, so that we may develop what Varela refers to as "nonegocentric compassion" (Varela 1999, p. 71)? In other words, what is the underlying, impersonal source of our spontaneous ethicalness? This will be the major focus of this chapter.

In contrast to such spontaneous and "embodied knowing", most modern approaches to ethics, at least in the West, have been formulated within a logical, rational, axiomatic and prescriptive frame of reference.

It is interesting to note here that the field of "business ethics" may be considered as representing an exception to this reliance on a philosophically based prescriptive framework. Teaching is often based on case studies and common sense arguments – but, just as with the more philosophical approaches, does not in general augment these by reference to potential underlying/inherent sources of one's responses to a specific moral dilemma.

But, and this is a central theme here, our "knowing" what to do in a specific situation is not just some combination of intuition, personal experience and rational reflection as to what is the "right" thing to do. In other words, it is not just a balance between: (a) more-or-less spontaneous behavior (which e.g., may be a result of cultural tradition), (b) rational evaluation, supported perhaps by principles from moral philosophy, and (c) utility calculations as to "what's in it for me?" I contend that such "knowing" at a very foundational level is in fact independent of cultural tradition, logical reasoning and reflection on individual (as well as group) benefit, and that *all* human beings have an inherent capacity to know what is the "right" thing to do in a given situation, no matter how complex and characterized by uncertainties and moral dilemmas that situation may be. Which is not the same thing as saying that this inherent capacity is, in general, readily available or that we can rely on it alone. It will be argued that the ability to draw upon this intrinsic capability is related to the degree to which an individual has developed what I here will refer to as a higher level of consciousness, a higher level of self-awareness and self-knowledge, what in a more spiritually oriented vocabulary is often referred to as self-realization or enlightenment.[10]

Finally, in these reflections on "spontaneous ethical behavior" and on "knowing what to do", I feel a sense of obligation to emphasize that I in no way argue that we should simply rely on our spontaneous feelings when making important decisions that can affect one's own well-being as well as that of others. Unless an individual has achieved such a level of self-knowledge and spiritual awareness whereby he or she is continually aware of his or her core essence or "Self" and thereby is free of the ego's self-reflective powerful influence on one's thoughts, words and deeds, a reflective practitioner who is motivated to behave "ethically" will experience a need to balance spontaneous action with rational reflection. Mahatma Gandhi, Martin Luther King, Nelson Mandela, the Dalai Lama and Aung San Suu Kyi are perhaps examples of individuals who personify, who embody, a high level of self-knowledge and manifest it via what we observers consider to be a high level of ethical competence.

The need to supplement spontaneous knowing and action with rational reflection will particularly be the case when facing complex decision situations/moral dilemmas where no single act can meet the demands of differing norms or obligations – that is, where "circumstances are such that an obligation to do *x* cannot be fulfilled without violating an obligation to do *y*" (Matilal 1992, p. 6).

In endnote 9 I referred to the concept of moral dilemmas within a framework of the Indian epic tale, the *Mahabharata*. I note in this context that Matilal (1992) presents an in-depth analysis of the epic as a major source of Indian/Hindu perspectives on the concept of ethics as well as of its relevance for modern ethical analyses. In addition, Nussbaum (2000) provides an analysis of the "costs of tragedy" that opens with a discussion of a class of moral dilemmas that she refers to as "tragic questions" in the *Mahabharata*: "The tragic question registers not the difficulty of solving the obvious question (what the warrior Arjuna should do; my comment) but a distinct difficulty: the fact that all possible answers to the obvious question, including the best one, are bad, involving serious moral wrongdoing. In that sense, there is no 'right answer'"(Nussbaum 2000, p. 1007). Finally in this connection I refer to the inspiring *tour de force* humanistic and secular analysis of the *Mahabharata* (Das 2012). This scholarly and yet highly personal book relates the moral dilemmas that permeate and characterize the epic tale not only to their specific historical contexts, but also to significant, and often painful and ambiguous contemporary public as well as personal issues.

7.4 THE WELLSPRING OF ETHICS

So far I have referred to traditional characterizations of ethical behavior as a potential result of cultural tradition, intuition and rational reflection on individual (as well as group) utility and I have only briefly referred to possible metaphysical sources. While the members of many different religions, particularly the major monotheistic Semitic religions, Judaism, Christianity and Islam with their belief in God and in the constant conflict between forces of good and evil, tend to accept moral injunctions as a matter of faith, philosophers and scientists as well as most secularly oriented thinkers in the West tend to shun any such reference. In courts of law, in scientific laboratories and in business headquarters, rational think-ing is tightly coupled to the idea of empirical verification and justification. However, what both the religious and the rational approaches to ethics share, in spite of their apparent different epistemological bases, is their reliance on external sources of ethical competency (God, first principles, empirical observation). The present chapter presents a distinctly different frame of reference whereby reliance on such external sources can be, and in fact often is, a barrier to progress on one's path to the wellspring of ethical competence.

To pave the way for such a perspective, I will start by reflecting on the concept of "consciousness" that has fascinated scientists and philosophers for hundreds of years and that is fundamental to an investigation of the source of ethical competency. Following this, we will consider the closely related concepts of dualism, non-dualism and unity – which will provide the final stepping stone on the path to the investigation of the source of ethical competency.

7.4.1 Consciousness

Since ethics typically refers to the justification of willed action, it is reasonable in our search for the source of our ethical competency, of our innate ethicalness, to ask the fundamental question: where do thoughts come from? This query can be extended to other areas such as: where do preferences come from? love? conscience? compassion? self-awareness? Can these various aspects or manifestations of consciousness be observed and explained by science – perhaps reduced to molecular/genetic/chemical/quantum-mechanical phenomena? (Pruzan 2013, pp. 303–307).

Such questions become even more challenging when conscious manifestations include non-sensory experiences often referred to as "mystical", characterized by pure consciousness or awareness per se without cognitive/intentional content, that is, content *about* things, events and states of affairs (Forman 1999, Chapter 7).

In his often-cited paper "Facing Up to the Problem of Consciousness" (Chalmers 1997, p. 9, 10, 18), philosopher and cognitive scientist David Chalmers raises fundamental questions as to how we can understand the emergence and existence of consciousness and whether a physical system, no matter how complex it may be, can give rise to experience. "Consciousness poses the most baffling problems in the science of the mind. There is nothing that we know more intimately than conscious experience, but there is nothing that is harder to explain. ... The really hard problem of consciousness is the problem of *experience*. When we think and perceive, there is a whir of information-processing, but there is also a subjective aspect. ... This subjective aspect is experience. ... For any physical process we specify there will be an unanswered question: Why should this process give rise to experience? ... The emergence of experience goes beyond what can be derived from physical theory."

Similar arguments are provided from the field of cognitive psychology by (Kelly et al. 2007) in their in-depth presentation of "the problem of relations between the inherently private, subjective 'first-person' world of human mental life and the publicly observable, objective, 'third-person' world of physiological events and processes in the body and brain" (Kelly et al. 2007, p. xvii). They develop a theoretical framework based on extensive empirical evidence that the mind is an entity independent of the brain or body and, like Chalmers, they provide a powerful critique of contemporary scientific thought regarding consciousness:

> [T]o the extent that any provisional consensus has been achieved by con-temporary mainstream scientists, psychologists and neuroscientists in particu-lar … human beings are nothing but extremely complicated biological machines. Everything we are and do is in principle causally explainable from the bottom up in terms of our biology, chemistry and physics. … Some of what we know, and the substrate of our general capacities to learn additional things, are built in genetically as complex resultants of biological evolution. Everything else comes to us directly or indirectly by way of our sensory systems, through energetic exchanges with the environment of types already largely understood. *Mind and consciousness are entirely generated by – or perhaps in some mysterious way identical with – neurophysiological events and process in the brain.* Mental causation, volition, and the "self" do not really exist; they are mere illusions, by-products of the grinding of our neural machinery. (Kelly et al. 2007, pp. xx–xxi; my italics)

The book provides a powerful challenge to this consensus and argues that the mind cannot be understood adequately as the product of simple physiological sensations or processes and that it is itself a "fundamental elementary and causal principle in nature" (Kelly et al. 2007, p. 56). With respect to the topic of ethical competency, they note that "If human beings are products of deterministic processes, how can they be held accountable for their actions under any social or ethical codes?" (p. 54).

The above reflections regarding consciousness do not just challenge philosophers, psychologists and neuroscientists but also tend to interest laypeople whose reflections on reality are not exclusively or primarily based on a faith in science as the provider of truth, but also include a spiritual dimension. In fact, it is my observation that perhaps the single concept that fascinates most of those who reflect on the nature of spirituality is "consciousness". As will be argued, since science has *not* been able to demonstrate that consciousness has a material source it is reasonable to hypothesize that its basis is not exclusively physical but also includes a source that transcends the material world.

An awareness of the potentials of investigating and understanding reality via a study of consciousness has led to great interest in this phenomenon by neuroscientists, particularly by so-called cognitive neuroscientists, and by laymen as well. See for example www.noetic.org/ research which describes the mission and research activities performed by the Institute of Noetic Sciences in the USA as follows: "Exploring the frontiers of consciousness to advance individual, social and global transformation." Another example, with specific reference to virtuous behavior, is provided by the following excerpt from an announcement of Metanexus' Institute's 2009 conference: 'Cosmos, Nature, Culture: A Transdisciplinary Conference' (http://www.metanexus.net/conference 2009/): "There is something inescapably 'first person' about consciousness. What accounts for this? Can third-person, objective science give a complete analysis of first-person, subjective experience? And can it tell us how to live our lives, how to seek virtue, or how to live together?"

However, the major public awareness of consciousness research is not from such "progressive" sources that reflect a spiritual awakening in the West, but from mainstream science itself. Amongst neuroscientists who focus on the nature and the origin of consciousness there is a strong tendency to start from the fundamental assumption that its source is purely physical. For example, the main theme of the February 12, 2007 issue of the international magazine *Time* was "The Brain – a user's guide", and its cover story was "The mystery of consciousness" with a caption: "You exist, right? Prove it. How 100 billion jabbering neurons create the knowledge – or illusion – that you're here." It should be added that virtually all the reputed scientists who are quoted in the article embrace the position that "our thoughts, sensations, joys and aches consist entirely of physiological activity in the tissues of our brains ... consciousness *is* the activity of the brain" (Kelly et al. 2007, p. 40).

Using highly advanced instruments, neuroscientists appear to be able to locate specific sections of the brain that correspond to particular sensations and behaviors, including such matters as near-death experiences, the sense of self, of transcendence sometimes experienced in meditation or prayer, and the like. For example, researchers at the Center for Spirituality and the Mind at the University of Pennsylvania, established in 2006, have used brain imaging technology to examine people in prayer, meditation and participating in rituals in an attempt to answer questions such as: "Does God exist outside the human mind, or is God a creation of our brains?"[11] The neuro-scientific study of religious and spiritual experiences is frequently being referred to as *neurotheology*.

In this connection I can also note that there are other scientists who hypothesize that consciousness simply emerges once a system's complexity grows beyond a certain point. However, this hypothesis can be strongly challenged by referring to the existence of apparently very complex systems, such as computer networks or the human heart, that do not manifest evidence of consciousness. Furthermore, a non-functional complex system may be just as complex as a functional complex system and yet be useless; for example, a software system with a simple single error cannot function yet it may be just as complex as the "same" system where the error is corrected.

What is noteworthy about the neuro-scientific approaches based on a materialist, reductionist perspective is that they do not appear to consider the possibility that the brain is *not* the source of consciousness but is a human receptor of it whereby thoughts and sensations are recorded there, but do not necessarily originate there – that their origin may be non-physical. I do not hereby imply that there is well-documented scientific evidence underlying this conjecture (which would require an expansion of traditional scientific methodology to investigate phenomena that transcend the physical world!).[12] However, this possibility does appear to be gaining support amongst some leading spiritually oriented thinkers as well as a small but growing minority of hard-core scientists.

For example, according to Stephan Tokan Hagen, leading Zen Buddhist teacher in the US (Hagen 2003, pp. 227–229): "it's not mind or consciousness that's abstract, but matter. ... Our problems with matter stem from the fact that, unlike consciousness, which is directly experienced, matter is always secondary – that is, experienced indirectly via mind. This is our actual, immediate, direct experience – it's purely mental, not physical. In short, physical reality cannot be fully accounted for apart from consciousness. Yet it's not at all clear that matter is necessary to account for consciousness."

Spiritually oriented physicist and computer scientist Peter Russell considers whether there is a causal relationship between matter and consciousness. He refers to the attempts by scientists from various disciplines to explain consciousness in terms of relationships involving brain chemistry, quantum physics, computing theory, and chaos theory, and challenges their meager results: "whatever idea is put forward, one thorny question remains unanswered: How can something as immaterial as consciousness ever arise from something as unconscious as matter? ... (Such approaches) are all based on the assumption that consciousness emerges from, or is dependent upon, the physical world of space, time, and matter. In one way or another, they are attempting to accommodate the anomaly of consciousness within a worldview that is intrinsically materialist" (Russell 2003, pp. 28–29). He concludes by suggesting, similar to Hagen, that "rather than trying to explain consciousness in terms of the material world, we should be developing a new worldview in which consciousness is a fundamental component of reality."

This perspective is also provided by the Nobel Laureate in Physiology/ Medicine, biologist George Wald (1906–1997), who as a "hard" scientist found himself compelled by empirical evidence and his own reflections to accept perspectives on science, physical reality and consciousness that "shocked my scientific sensibilities" (Wald 1984, pp. 1–2):

> Consciousness seems to me to be wholly impervious to science. It does not lie as an indigestible element within science, but just the opposite: Science is the highly digestible element within consciousness, which includes science as a limited but beautifully definable territory within the much wider reality of whose existence we are conscious ... mind, rather than emerging as a late outgrowth in the evolution of life, has existed always, as the matrix, the source and condition of physical reality – the stuff of which physical reality is composed is mind-stuff. It is mind that has composed a physical universe that breeds life, and so eventually evolves creatures that know and create: science-, art-, and technology-making animals. In them the universe begins to know itself.

To this statement I could add on that it evolves creatures that have an inherent ethical competency.

Wald's thinking shares much with the Vedantic concept of Universal Consciousness. Vedanta is often referred to as the "end" of the Vedic texts called the Upanishads, where "end" can be understood both as a goal and as its being the culmination of the Vedas. According to Sri Aurobindo (1872–1950), leading Indian freedom fighter, philosopher, poet and spiritual leader, in the introduction to his translation of the Upanishads (Aurobindo 1985, cited in Abrahams 1995, p. 70): "The idea of transcendental unity, Oneness, and stability behind all the flux and variety of phenomenal life is the basic idea of the Upanishads; this is the pivot of all Indian metaphysics, the sum and goal of our spiritual experience." The great sage Swami Vivekananda (1863–1902), a leading figure in the introduction of Indian philosophy to the West in the late nineteenth century, refers to Vedanta as "the culmination of knowledge, the sacred wisdom of the Hindu sages, the transcendental experience of the seers of Truth ... the essence or conclusion of the Vedas, so it is called Vedanta. Literally, *Veda* means knowledge and *anta* means end" (Vivekananda 1987, editor's note, p. 16).[13]

According to Vedanta, this Universal Consciousness is manifest in all of creation and independent of scientific concepts of matter, time and space such that all physical and social reality, the subject matter of scientific investigation, has its source in a timeless, omnipresent Source, the Universal Consciousness. Although omnipresent, the highest manifestation of that consciousness in sentient beings is in humans; we are embodiments of this Universal Consciousness and are endowed with the capability of self-reference and thereby eventually of self-realization – of realizing the unity of the individual consciousness with all consciousness and the Universal Consciousness; the unity of the individual self with the ultimate source, the Self.[14]

In other words, there appears to be two conflicting metaphysical assumptions regarding the nature of consciousness: (1) The materialist position taken by neuroscientists that human consciousness can be reduced to and be explained by the biological and physical/molecular properties of our nervous systems, and (2) the spiritual position that although there is an interplay between consciousness and the body whereby the experience of consciousness is actualized in the brain via physical processes, its source is in fact independent of our physical forms. To this latter perspective can be added the logical extension that the interplay between consciousness and the body terminates when the body dies while the consciousness, which does not have a material source and is not dependent on the physical frame, continues to exist (which is a metaphysical assumption underlying concepts of reincarnation). A poetic expression of this from a Western writer is provided by Walt Whitman in his celebrated *Leaves of Grass* (1947, section 7, p. 29): "I pass death with the dying, and birth with the new-wash'd babe, and am not contain'd between my hat and boots."

7.4.2 Dualism, Unity, and Ethics from an "Eastern" Perspective

Just as the concept of consciousness is fundamental to reflection on the source of ethical competency, so too is the notion of a subjective "I" relating to an objective "other", no matter whether that "other" is living or not-living (e.g., mountains) or existing or not-existing (e.g., future generations of sentient beings). The natural sciences rest upon a metaphysical assumption, apparently justified by our senses and cognition-based experience as well as our "common sense", that the distinction between a subjective observer and an objective reality is meaningful and justified. As will be clear shortly, such an apparently obvious and self-evident assumption can be challenged when we delve more deeply into the very source of conscious awareness and thereby of ethical competency as well. In fact we will see that the greatest barrier to being able to tap this source is the ego-mind's distinctions between, and judgments regarding, oneself and the rest of what we consider to be an objective, independently existing reality.

Yet another aspect of the concept of duality deals with the ontological distinction formulated by Descartes between the mind as non-physical pure thought, although related to the brain, and the body/world as extended and material. This distinction has been touched on in the previous section on consciousness and has often been referred to in philosophy as the "mind–body problem". According to Descartes (1641, republished 1951; Meditation VI, pp. 69–70):

> I have a body with which I am very closely united, nevertheless, since on the one hand I have a clear and distinct idea of myself in so far as I am only a thinking and not an extended being, and since on the other hand I have a distinct idea of the body in so far as it is only an extended being which does not think, it is certain that this "I" (– that is to say, my soul, by virtue of which I am what I am –) is entirely (and truly) distinct from my body and that it can (be or) exist without it.

In spite of this distinction, Descartes argues that the non-extended immaterial mind and the extended material body causally interact. In other words, a central theme in what is often referred to as Cartesian dualism is that while they are ontologically distinct, the immaterial mind can cause material events and the material body can cause mental events.

While central to the position I will shortly develop, Cartesian dualism has been discarded by most Western philosophical and scientific thought because it tends to reject the monist materialist position whereby mind is essentially and innately material, a position that is, for example, at the heart of most cognitive and behavioral neuroscience.

I note that Descartes concludes his sixth and final Meditation as follows: "But because the exigencies of action frequently (oblige us to make decisions and) do not always allow us the leisure to examine these things with sufficient care, we must admit that human life is very subject to error in particular matters; and we must in the end recognize the infirmity (and weakness) of our nature." (ibid., p. 80). As will be seen, I provide a different explanation whereby the underlying cause of apparent differences in ethical reasoning is not just "exigencies of action" that limit our ability to draw on rational thought. Rather, it is primarily our different levels of conscious awareness, our differing abilities to transcend the ego-mind so as to gain access to our true nature, our higher consciousness, to what I earlier referred to as the "Atman" or "Self"; see endnote 10.

Although students of religion identify significant distinctions between Hinduism and Buddhism as regards the concept of soul and Self, for our purposes, this is primarily one of terminology. Buddhist perspectives regarding the source of ethical competency may be considered as being an interpretation rather than a repudiation of Hinduism. In both cases there is fundamental agreement on the importance of the individual consciousness transcending the mental distinctions between opposites, particularly as regards the experience of "I" as being different from both "you" and "it" and thereby transcending as well the ego-mind.

For example, according to Kriger and Seng (2005, pp. 782–783): "Central to the teachings of Buddhism is the idea that the personal self or 'I' is fundamentally empty of reality and created as a thought in the mind out of delusional thinking and habits." Instead, the notion of selflessness or "no self" (*anatta*) is emphasized as central to Buddhist thinking.[15] This concept of *anatta* is contrasted with Western thinking: "In western psychology much effort is spent trying to discover ways to develop the 'self' and 'to make it whole' or, at a minimum, to free it from neuroses and dysfunctional states. ... The leader, in the Buddhist paradigm, thinks, feels, senses and observes the changing aspects of the world and the inner contents of the mind along with feelings and sensations; however there is no 'self' that is directing the experiencing of the world. For Buddhists, the ego, and its attendant desires, are posited to be the fundamental causes of unhappiness ... selflessness or 'no self' (*anatta*) ... is not the denial of the 'self' but rather the absence of essential distinctions between ourselves and everyone else. In this view everyone and everything in the world is intimately interconnected."

In other words, Buddhism provides a perspective on dualism and consciousness whereby there is a continuum of consciousness but no physical basis in that continuum for an individual, permanent and autonomous self. We are only aware of the consciousness we attribute to a self inasmuch as it is qualified by an object, and only contemplative practice – not scientific investigation – enables us to see the nature of the mind (Revel and Ricard 1998, pp. 29–35).

In Hinduism, non-dual teachings regarding the nature of ultimate reality and the "absence of essential distinctions between ourselves and everyone else" can be considered within the framework of Vedanta. Swami Vivekananda (1987, pp. 58–59) provides the following reflections on the Vedantic concept of *advaita*, the essential unity of all that is with a divine Source or Universal Being:[16]

Vedanta claims that man is divine, that all this which we see around us is the outcome of that consciousness of the divine. Everything that is strong and good and powerful in human nature is the outcome of that divinity, and though potential in many, there is no difference between man and man essentially, all being alike divine. There is, as it were, an infinite ocean behind, and you and I are so many waves coming out of that infinite ocean. And each one of us is trying his best to manifest that infinite outside. So potentially, each one of us has that infinite ocean of Existence, Knowledge and Bliss as our birthright, our real nature, and the difference between us is caused by greater or lesser power to manifest that divinity. Therefore Vedanta lays down that each man should be treated, not as what he manifests, but as what he stands for. Each human being stands for the divine, and therefore every teacher should be helpful, not by condemning man, but by helping him to call forth that divinity that is within him.

And all that we call ethics and morality and doing good to others is also but the manifestation of this oneness. There are moments when every man feels that he is one with the universe, and he rushes forth to express it, whether he knows it or not. This expression of oneness is what we call love and sympathy, and it is the basis of all our ethics and morality. This is summed up in the Vedanta philosophy by the celebrated aphorism, *Tat tvam asi*, 'Thou art That.' ... Thou art one with this Universal Being, and as such, every soul that exists is your soul, and every body that exists is your body. And in hurting anyone you hurt yourself. In loving anyone you love yourself. ... And if love comes out from you, it is bound to come back to you. For I am the universe. This universe is my body. I am the infinite, only I am not conscious of it now. But I am struggling to get this consciousness of the Infinite, and perfection will be reached when full consciousness of the Infinite comes.

A similar profound and articulate expression of the unity that underlies reality and its relation to the apparent dualism between a subjective observer and objective reality is provided by Sri Aurobindo whose prolific writing includes a major focus on the inevitable evolution of human life into divine life. In Aurobindo (1970, pp. 136–137) he refers to:

> [a] truth on which the sages have always agreed, although by the intellectual thinker it may be constantly disputed. It is the truth that all active being is a seeking for God, a seeking for some highest self and deepest Reality secret within, behind and above ourselves and things, a seeking for the hidden Divinity; the truth which we glimpse through religion, lies concealed behind all life; it is the great secret of life, that which it is in labour to discover and to make real to its self-knowledge. ... It is the seeking for a Reality which the appearances of life conceal because they only partially express it or because they express it behind veils and figures, by oppositions and contraries, often by what seem to be perversions and opposites of the Real. ... A One there is in which all the entangled discords of this multiplicity of separated, conflicting, intertwining, colliding ideas, forces, tendencies, instincts, impulses, aspects, appearances which we call life, can find the unity of their diversity, the harmony of their divergences, the justification of their claims, the correction of their perversions and aberrations, the solution of their problems and disputes.[17]

I note that this concept of "the Real" is expressed daily by millions of Hindus in their prayers when they start to recite the famous refrain from a Vedic prayer in the Brihadaranyaka Upanishad (1.2.28) from roughly 800 BCE (Easwaran 1987, pp. 33): *Lead me from the unreal to the Real.*[18]

Perhaps the most poetic expression of the characteristics of a human being that has realized such a non-dual oneness or unity is provided by the description of a *sthitaprajna* in the *Bhagavad Gita*. The *Gita*, as it is often called, provides an exposition of Vedanta philosophy within the framework of the *Mahabharata* and is often referred to as the Gospel of Hinduism.[19] Sthitaprajna is a Sanskrit term[20] for a person who has mastered his or her mind, is released from attachment to the outside world, and realizes unity with all that is. Thus he/she performs all deeds selflessly as an instrument of the Divine, what is referred to in Hindu cosmology as Brahman, the Divine Ground within which all reality as we know it via our senses and mind have their origin. In other words, a sthitaprajna is a person for whom no ethical dilemmas exist or can arise. The poetic translation from Sanskrit of the *Gita* by Swami Prabhavananda and Christopher Isherwood (1954) provides a description of such an active realized human being (pp. 41–44); below I provide a brief excerpt, where the scene for the dialogue is a no-man's land between two huge armies, prepared to start a great fratricidal war. A prince, Arjuna, seeks guidance from his charioteer, Krishna, who is in reality an *Avatar*, an embodiment of the Divine.

Arjuna: "Krishna, how can one identify a man who is firmly established and absorbed in Brahman? In what manner does an illumined soul speak? How does he sit? How does he walk?"

Sri Krishna: "He knows bliss in the Atman
And wants nothing else.
Cravings torment the heart;
He renounces cravings.
I call him illumined.

Not shaken by adversity,
Not hankering after happiness:
Free from fear, free from anger,
Free from the things of desire.
I call him a seer, and illumined.

The bonds of his flesh are broken.
He is lucky, and does not rejoice:
He is unlucky, and does not weep.
I call him illumined.

The tortoise can draw in his legs;
The seer can draw in his senses.
I call him illumined.

The abstinent run away from what they desire
But carry their desires with them:

When a man enters Reality,
He leaves his desires behind him.

…

Water flows continually into the ocean
But the ocean is never disturbed:
Desire flows into the mind of the seer
But he is never disturbed.
The seer knows peace:
The man who stirs up his own lusts
Can never know peace.
He knows peace who has forgotten desire.
He lives without craving:
Free from ego, free from pride.

This is the state of enlightenment in Brahman:
A man does not fall back from it
Into delusion.
Even at the moment of death
He is alive in that enlightenment:
Brahman and he are one."

The Buddhist and Hindu teachings referred to here provide a non-dual perspective on reality whereby our true core essence is neither a non-extended immaterial mind nor an extended material body referred to earlier in connection with Descartes and the "mind–body problem"; we are simply one with an underlying Reality, what Hinduism refers to as Brahman and what Buddhism refers to as *Nirvana*, the state of extinguishidness.[21] In common parlance, both encourage us in our daily lives to seek and see unity in the diversity we perceive in the outer world.

In the sequel I will employ the Sanskrit term *advaita*, briefly introduced earlier, to refer to this aspect of the term non-duality. A Sanskrit saying (originating in the Chandogya Upanishad, ca. 600 BCE[22]) encapsulates the above: "Tat tvam asi", often translated as "Thou art that" or "That thou art". This famous saying is widely interpreted to mean that the Self is one with ultimate Reality – that there is identity between "Tat", the Absolute, commonly written in English as simply "That", and "tvam", literally "thou" but here referring also to the Self.[23] According to the wisdom of the East, the greatest obstacle to being able to realize this identity, to what I elsewhere refer to as self-realization or enlightenment, is the ego mind that continually experiences a distinction between self and all other aspects of reality and thereby inhibits the realization that "thou" and "That" are one. Only when the ego is transcended can unity or union with the very source of ethical competency, the Divine Ground, the Universal Consciousness, be achieved.

In *On the Basis of Morality* (1840, translation from German to English 1903, p. 275), Arthur Schopenhauer (1788–1860) reflects on this "Eastern" insight as to unity as the basis for our ethical competency: "My true inmost being subsists in every living thing, just as really, as directly as in my own consciousness it is evidenced only to myself. This is the higher knowledge: for which there is in Sanskrit the standing formula, tat tvam asi, 'that art thou'. Out of the depths of human nature it wells up in the shape of Compassion, and is therefore the source of all genuine, that is, disinterested virtue, being, so to say, incarnate in every good deed."

At this point it is appropriate to consider whether these reflections that imply that the realized self, being one with the Self (the Absolute/Divine Ground/Brahman) that constitutes the wellspring of ethics, is only relevant for human beings. Since I hitherto have only explicitly referred to humans in the discussions on consciousness and duality and ethics it is relevant to pose the question whether human beings with less-developed mental capabilities (e.g., the senile, infants), non-human sentient beings (e.g., animals), or even non-living matter also possess such a fundamental ethical competency. Referring in particular to advaita Vedanta whereby every being and everything has divinity as its core, the answer is clearly that this competency is latent in all that exists, sentient or not, but that the level of consciousness required to realize it is not identically distributed. So while all of reality has this competency latently, it is only meaningful here to speak of humans as having the capability to fully realize and manifest this competency – and that the extent to which this competency is available depends on the level of conscious awareness possessed by an individual. According to Vivekananda (1987, p. 140): "In speaking of the soul, to say that man is superior to the animal or the plant has no meaning. The whole universe is one. In plants the obstacle to soul-manifestation is very great, in animals, a little less; and in man, still less; in cultured, spiritual men, still less; and in perfect men it has vanished altogether."[24]

It also follows that since all of reality is a reflection of an underlying Reality, ethical behavior does not just concern the relationships between humans but between humans and all of reality, including not-yet-born beings (future generations), lower forms of life, as well as all of nature. With increasing levels of consciousness follow increasing ethical responsibilities – and the awareness of these responsibilities – to respect and to help emancipate and empower the divinity that is inherent in all of reality. This, for me, is the most fundamental expression of ethical behavior!

However, an important additional reflection is also called for here. The assertion that we are all inherently divine should not be made when attempting to justify the ethicality of one's actions. It is only when an individual lives in a state corresponding to a sthitaprajna that such a justification can be relevant – while in that state it would not be made! Otherwise hubris can result, with the feeling that one cannot do wrong, cannot be unethical since "my ethical intuition is from the Source".[25]

A final reflection here deals with the relationship between duality, language and the source of ethical competency. Throughout history societies have developed linguistic capabilities in order to enable communication regarding this world, this observable reality with its living and non-living entities, all considered to be separate and individual. But it is just this implicit assumption regarding the dualistic nature of reality that constitutes a major barrier for the realization of and communication about the Universal Consciousness, the Divine Ground, the Godhead,[26] and therefore about the underlying Source of ethical competency, which is different in kind from the reality that traditional language – as well as mathematics, the "language of science"[27] – enable. This is also the reason why those who have transcended the barrier between "Tat" and "tvam", between "That" and "thou" are inhibited, or at least limited, in communicating their experiences regarding the Universal Consciousness and its manifestation in the transitory reality we experience with our senses and mind. I will return to this shortly when referring to the sages and saints who have transcended this barrier, as well as to my own more limited experience of pure consciousness.

7.5 MEANS TO REALIZE AND TO BE ONE WITH THE SOURCE OF ETHICS

Until now the focus has been on identifying and characterizing the source of ethical competency. I have proposed that it is only when one has attained a heightened state of self-knowledge – of self-realization/ enlightenment – that behavior can be truly ethical, in the sense "spontaneous, impersonal knowing" introduced earlier. But realizing one's ethical competence is not the goal of life. According to insights of spiritual leaders from the East, and my own deepest conviction, that goal is to identify one's "self" (the individual soul or jivatma) with the Self (the Supreme Soul, Paramatma; see endnote 10), to *be* the unity in all this diversity – to achieve "knowledge of the immanent and transcendent Ground of all being" (Huxley 1985, p. 9). It is only then that all one's actions have the immediate, spontaneous quality of being ethical whereby they are in harmony with our inherent nature as divine. However, and this is most significant here, conscious attention to one's inner promptings when acting in the outer, external reality is a vital, perhaps necessary means to develop such a higher state of consciousness, a transcendental knowing, that emancipates and empowers the embodied and latent ethical competency.

In his classic exposition, *The Perennial Philosophy*, Huxley (1985, p. 12) presents a "metaphysic that recognizes a divine Reality substantial to the world of things and lives and minds; the psychology that finds in the soul something similar to, or even identical with, divine Reality; the ethic that places man's final end in the knowledge of the immanent and transcendent divine Reality". Huxley's empirical basis for this universal and immemorial theology is the words of those saints, prophets, sages or enlightened ones from every major religious tradition who have left accounts of the Reality they were "enabled to apprehend and have tried to relate, in one comprehensive system of thought, the given facts of this (first hand; my comment) experience with the given facts of their other experiences". And Huxley adds (p. 14): "If one is not oneself a sage or saint, the best thing one can do, in the field of metaphysics, is to study the works of those who were, and who, because they had modified their merely human mode of being, were capable of a more than merely human kind and amount of knowledge."

As should be clear by now, this is a method I have followed on my own spiritual path. However, my boldness in attempting to write about such matters is not simply due to reading and being inspired by the words of learned people and great sages and saints. It is also in great part due to personal experiences that have convinced me of the veracity and universality of what Huxley referred to as the Perennial Philosophy. It would be outside of the realm of this chapter – and most likely be considered far too subjective and personal – to attempt to relate the nature of these experiences in detail. It should suffice here to refer to them as transcendental and expansive whereby I have experienced levels of peace, awareness and love that are beyond my ability to describe. In both advaita Vedanta and Buddhism, such experiences are referred to as *samadhi*, a Sanskrit term that describes a non-dual consciousness with an absence of all personal identification, as well as, for shorter or longer periods of time, an experience of wholeness, integrity, unity with all that is, with Reality. By this I do not imply that I have experienced the stage of samadhi, referred to as sahaja samadhi (Forman 1999, p. 5) that is experienced by a *sthitaprajna* who simultaneously lives and acts in this phenomenal world while being one with the Reality – only that I am convinced via direct experience that such a state of being is achievable.[28]

7.5.1   The Importance of a Spiritual Teacher

Three factors have had a mutually supportive relationship on my own spiritual path: (1) my academic and personal interest in concepts of virtue, ethics, values and responsibility; (2) my personal experiences; and (3) my living in an ashram – a place of spiritual retreat – in India where I experienced, directly and indirectly, the guidance of a spiritual Teacher/ Master. It is to this third factor I now briefly turn.

In connection with my work on the concept of Ethical Accounting in the late 1980s I met two persons who told me that it would be of great value for my development, both personally and professionally, to visit the ashram of one of India's great holy men, Sathya Sai Baba (1926–2011). At the time, I had no conscious awareness whatsoever of an interest in spirituality and was certainly not motivated to visit a guru. However, and to make a long story short, in August 1989 I followed their prompting and visited Prasanthi Nilayam, the ashram of Sathya Sai Baba, located north of the major city and IT-hub of India, Bangalore in southern India. That visit was a turning point in my life and led to significant changes in my thinking and behavior. Since then, together with my spiritual partner, my wife, I have been in India more than 40 times, always visiting the ashram as well as other spiritual retreats and often lecturing at some of India's most highly regarded universities and business schools. In particular, during the last 10 years since my retirement from the Department of Management, Politics & Philosophy at the Copenhagen Business School I have spent roughly half a year each year as Visiting Professor at the university Sai Baba founded, Sri Sathya Sai Institute of Higher Learning.[29] Some of the powerful and life-changing personal experiences I referred to earlier took place while I was in the ashram together with my wife, particularly in the early and mid-1990s. In any case, I have no doubt whatsoever as to the immense and positive influence of the time spent with like-minded people at the ashram, in particular with respect to the interrelationship between my attempts to conceptualize and operationalize concepts of ethics, to behave in accord with these developing conceptualizations, and my ability to develop the state of mind whereby I could begin to emancipate and empower what I have referred to as our embodied ethicality.

Sai Baba has in his writings and discourses – and in pithy aphorisms such as "Love all, Serve all", "Help ever, Hurt never" and "Hands that serve are holier than lips that pray" – provided guidance at the mental level. However, his greatest influence has been at what I best can refer to as the supra-mental level and I continue to feel this guidance, even though he no longer is present in his physical form. I maintain my focus on this spiritual path via simple means, including meditation, walks in peace-inspiring nature, a focus on being present and removing the chatter and vagaries of my mind, reading elevating literature, prayer and seeking the company of wise and compassionate people. All these "positive" activities have been accompanied by a focus on the avoidance of negative states of mind, including greed, anger, hate, pride, jealousy, fear, violence and attachment to my deeds and their fruits.

A result has been the experience that living and working in accordance with one's values and a deep sense of interconnectedness with others and with Reality can lead to a gradual transcendence of the lower, ego-dominated self. Detached involvement frees one, for shorter or longer periods of time, from the chains of personal desires and ambitions so that the mind becomes "free of and above the dualistic see-saw of daily experiences" (Chakraborty 1991, p. 163). I now know that it is possible to perform action in this spirit – that it is possible to be free from the bondage of the ego-mind such that one's efforts can become acts of selfless service on the path to realizing the Reality that is embodied in our physical form, and to thereby gain access to and be one with the Source of ethical competency.

7.6 CONCLUDING REMARKS – THE RELEVANCE FOR "BUSINESS ETHICS"

Until now I have reflected on the concept of ethical competency, independent of any specific field or focus, and related this competency to fundamental aspects of the human condition and of our inherent divine nature. It is now appropriate to relate these reflections specifically to the field of *business ethics*.

The chapter has developed a perspective on ethical behavior that challenges and transcends more traditional concepts of and approaches to business ethics. It delivers a message that ethical competency is not just a matter of skill or of being able to draw on tradition, or even on philosophical reflection and rational utility calculation; in a given situation it may involve all of these, but if it does not simultaneously draw upon the most fundamental source of our ethical competency, the inner guidance provided by the Self, it will not be in tune with and contribute to the decision maker's spiritual development or to the spiritual development and well-being of those affected by one's actions. It follows from the above reflections that such development, with the concomitant goal of self-realization, is primary to any specific personal goal or organizational goal.

Evidence that the world of business can provide a fertile context for such spiritual development and thereby the ability to integrate and balance rational actions in the outer world of business with one's inner source of ethical competence is provided in *Leading with Wisdom: Spiritual-based Leadership in Business* (Pruzan and Pruzan Mikkelsen 2007/10). The book provides stories about and reflections of 31 business leaders from 15 countries and six continents who lead from a spiritual basis. The following are just three of the many different perspectives provided by these leaders as to the relationship between spirituality, leadership and ethics:

> Spiritual-based leaders respect others and are guided by the fundamental ethic: service to others comes before servings one's self. From an existential perspective, the *raison d'être* of organizations is to serve human needs. Really, there is no other reason for their existence. Individuals and organizations grow when they give themselves to others. Relationships improve when there is a focus on serving the other, be it at the level of the individual, the family, the organization, the community, the society, or all of humanity. (Stephen Covey 1932–2012, Co-founder, FranklinCovey, USA; p. 52)

> As an auditor of large multi-national companies, I have been confronted on almost a daily basis with situations where I have to pass transactions through my internal "ethics" system and see if they pass my litmus test: the Lakshman Rekha.[30] This is the imaginary boundary line that every individual has that he will not cross. I think the current boundary line that has been dictated by ethics is driven largely by human knowledge, meaning that somebody tells you this is not right or that is not right. This is something you usually get from your childhood. When I refer to the *Lakshman Rekha*, I am talking about the invisible line that is within everyone's system that is driven by consciousness. This is a consciousness that has its own existence. It comes into the mind; it is not a product of the mind or societal influences. … It is like a direct knowing, rather than a belief system. (V.V. Ranganathan, Sr. Partner, Ernst & Young, India; p. 297)

> Values such as justice, truth, respect for others, honesty and integrity are the core values that became very strong for me when I went into business. These are more on the ethical side, rather than on the spiritual side. Somewhere along the line however, these two kinds of values began to link. Now I think of ethical values as nothing but a reflection of my spiritual values. When we talk about self-respect in an ethical sense, we are talking about being respectful to your colleagues, shareholders and customers because it is a good business practice. But when you go a little deeper and look at it from a spiritual point of view, you realize that it is really about respecting the inner Self. (Ananth Raman, Chairman, Graphtex, USA; p. 296)

A focus on the source of our ethical competence by business leaders can inspire them to re-consider how they and their organizations formulate the core-meaning, the *raison d'être* of their existence and, in particular, their programs dealing with business ethics, CSR, sustainability and related issues. The epistemological challenge here is imposing. On the one hand the need to provide more existentially and deeply founded bases for ethical behavior. On the other hand the potential difficulty of communicating such messages, particularly to audiences that may consider such expression as both difficult to comprehend and as foreign to the context they work in, often dominated by economic rationality and an emphasis on effectiveness and short-term gain. Consider for example the following excerpts from (Pruzan and Pruzan Mikkelsen 2007):

> When we try to define spirituality we are actually attempting to articulate something that cannot be articulated. We are trying to do our best, but we are trying to define the Infinite, which by definition is a contradiction. Yet we need to try. (Ricardo Levy, Chairman, Catalytica, USA; p. 298)

> I don't openly talk with people about my spirituality, but I think they respect me as someone who is ethical, someone they can trust, and someone who works hard in a selfless way. I don't have to talk about it. I just live it and people appreciate it. (Parantha Narendran, Strategy Director, Eurotel Telecom, Czech Republic; p. 298)

> Today a major share of managers in both private and public organisations would not admit if they were managing their organisation from a background of spirituality – although many would in fact do so unconsciously. (Niels Due Jensen, Group Chairman, Grundfos, Denmark; p. 299)

> The minute I put spirituality as the explicit part, people will look at me as an organizational priest and they will focus on the deviation of what I do as compared to the "textbook", rather than looking at my good deeds as a business leader. Then you will have to start defending spirituality. I want to stay implicit, because this is how spirituality will survive. I used to be more explicit in how I led by my spirituality. I did that through company values and mission statements and through education and development programs. However, looking back, I gradually became more implicit: less program-oriented and more doing-oriented. (Magnus Vrethammar, President Finess, Switzerland and Pergo, UK; p. 300)

> Spirituality in the work place and business success go hand in hand. There is certainly no conflict here at Plantersbank. Spirituality is a way of life for us because it is deeply embedded in our culture and structure, and emanates from our personal convictions. (Floy Aguenza, President & COO, Plantersbank, the Philippines; p. 107)

I conclude with a brief reflection on the relevance of this perspective on the source of ethical competence for education and training programs in leadership. First of all, I have my sincere doubts as to the direct relevance of the thoughts presented here for such programs in the West since they have evolved from a very different mindset than that provided by the East, in particular by advaita Vedanta. In addition, there is a widespread lack of appreciation in the West, with its emphasis on the material empiricism that characterizes economic and scientific rationality, of a *spiritual empiricism* founded on the documented spiritual experiences of individuals.

On the other hand, it is also my optimistic observation that there is an awakening awareness in the West that an underlying context, a precondition for long-term successful, purposeful, organized mercantile activity, is in fact spiritual-based leadership (although the term is not yet part of the management vernacular), and not just the pursuit of material gain. A major, and certainly a long-term, challenge to business schools in the West will be to how best to design and integrate such a perspective in their educational programs – including how to develop research and teaching environments that invite and support the integration of spiritual-based leadership into the curricula.

With respect to the East, it is my observation that it is far easier to integrate such perspectives as have been presented here into educational and training programs, and I refer once again mainly to India which is where I have my primary experience. In spite of a plethora of differing cultural traditions, there exists a widely articulated tradition for drawing upon a shared spiritual ethos. In addition, there is an evolving tradition at some of India's leading business schools, including several of the highly regarded IIMs (Indian Institutes of Management), for offering courses and programs in business ethics that include readings on spirituality and spiritual-based leadership as part of the curriculum as well as teachers who openly are committed to their spiritual paths. This development is reflected as well in the increasing number of major international conferences being organized in India – with many participants from the West – that focus on spirituality as the basis for leadership. However, it is also my observation that in spite of this potential for drawing upon the shared spiritual ethos, mainstream Indian schools of management by and large tend to follow the more "hard core" approaches to management/ leadership education that are promoted in the West.

So a major challenge to business schools in the East will be how best to build upon the rich Indian ethos while at the same time integrating the best of the approaches from the West. In other words, a challenge of how to promote those aspects of their identity, integrity and strengths which are rooted in Indian culture, traditions and spiritual mindsets while preparing their students to compete with firms having a dominating Western materialistic focus.

NOTES

1. I express my thanks to G.S. Srirangarajan, Controller of Examinations at Sri Sathya Sai Institute of Higher Learning, India; Professor Gerrit De Vylder, Department of International Business and Economics, Leuven University, Belgium; and George Bebedelis, Director, Institute of Sathya Sai Education, South Europe for their constructive comments, in particular for their reflections on the chapter's treatment of advaita Vedanta.

2. Since this comment on metaphysics may challenge more positivist-oriented readers, I note that *any* scientific statement draws upon at least the following sources: (1) empirical evidence, (2) rational/logical analysis, (3) personal values and experience, and (4) metaphysical belief. In general, the third and fourth of these, although necessary in order to even choose the topic being discussed, to design the research and its presentation, and to be able to make fundamental, widely accepted, and most often implicit ontological and epistemological assumptions, are offered minimal attention (Pruzan 2013, pp. 3, 45–49). In the sequel, these last two sources, personal values and experience, and metaphysical belief play a central role.

3. I was active in designing educational programs that integrated philosophy and leadership at the Copenhagen Business School (CBS) and was a "founding father" of organizations such as the think tank *AccountAbility* (based in London but with offices in many parts of the world), *EABIS*, European Academy of Business in Society (based in Brussels) and *cbsCSR*, the Center for CSR at CBS – as well as the department, Management, Politics & Philosophy, the largest department at CBS.

4. In the sequel, when I refer to "Indian ethos", my intention will be to refer to a concept that is both broader and more inclusive than the more narrow "Hinduism" (religion) and more homogeneous than "Indian culture", which, in particular in the modern context, is extremely diverse. (Chakraborty 1995, pp. 3–4) distinguishes between Indian *culture* and Indian *ethos*. "Because of the existence of so many religions in this country, along with endless diversity of local customs and deities within the fold of Hinduism itself, it is untrue ... to speak of any single homogeneous Indian culture. ... But Indian ethos, which is essentially and at its best Vedantic is quite different from, though complementary to, Indian culture. If the latter is the ornate, colorful outward superstructure, the former is the deep and unseen foundation supporting that superstructure." I note that the "foundation" Chakraborty speaks of is often referred to in Sanskrit as "Sanathana Sanskruti/Dharma", literally meaning "eternal and imperishable culture/heritage/law". In this connection I note that the Sanskrit words in this chapter are written in Latin characters corresponding to their phonetic pronunciation.

5. It could seem natural to extend the above question to include not only the source of an individual's competency to behave ethically but also the source of the competency of collectivities of individuals, in particular organizations and institutions, to behave ethically. Nevertheless, I have chosen not to include reflections on such an expanded theme as this would lead to a far longer chapter as well as to a major shift in its epistemological basis. I note however that in Pruzan (2001) I have provided a series of reflections on this theme from the perspectives of "systems science".

6. Drawing upon biological approaches to sociology, experimental evidence based on games, and economic models of cooperation (Bowles and Gintis 2011) investigate the cultural and biological processes that have led humans to evolve into what they argue is a cooperative species whose members are genuinely concerned about the well-being of others. Their findings include that the propensity to mutually beneficial activity and altruistic cooperation is the result of evolutionary processes where groups of individuals who were (somehow) predisposed to cooperate tended to survive and expand relative to other groups. Grassie (2010, pp. 81–85) presents several other potential explanations for the existence of other-regarding behavior within an evolutionary paradigm, in particular referring to research within evolutionary psychology.

7. A post-modern perspective argues that all moral norms are without a firm foundation; any chain of justifications must have a first link that cannot be justified, just as intuition and

reference to a moral sense cannot be justified. So from such a perspective the question "why ethics" cannot be answered.

8.　I emphasize here that my drawing upon such an Eastern perspective should not be interpreted as a dismissal of the rich Western perspectives on such matters, e.g., those provided by the Christian mystics or in Platonic and Neoplatonic philosophy; I have simply chosen to draw upon sources of inspiration that have been decisive in my own personal development and that are central to the theme of the chapter. Abrahams (1995) provides a comparative survey of Hindu, Christian and Jewish mysticism.

9.　In this connection I can refer to Manikutty (2012) who presents "Eastern" reflections on the question: "Why should I be ethical?" via analyses of moral dilemmas faced by major protagonists in the famous Sanskrit epic, the *Mahabharata* (the longest version consists of more than 100,000 couplets as well as long sections of prose). He concludes (p. 32): "The only reason to teach or discuss ethics is not to show what is the *right* action, but to help one to find *your own* right action … understanding ethics is a continuing and never ending education, and not a destination and our duty regarding being ethical is to make sure we continue in this journey."

10.　A colleague suggested that I equate this inherent capacity with "conscience". The reason I have not done so is that even though it is not uncommon for people in everyday conversation to justify their actions by referring to their conscience, the ability of an individual to distinguish between the promptings of the desire-oriented ego and those of the inherent ethical capacity referred to here depends on how highly developed the person's sense of discrimination is. I note as well that the concept of "ego" we are familiar with in the vernacular, essentially referring to a person's sense of self-importance, whereby it distinguishes itself from the selves of others, has a complex counterpart in Eastern wisdom. In Sanskrit, it is referred to as Ahamkara which can be split into two terms: "Aham" (meaning "I") and "kara" which means "doing" or "acting"; http://www.advaita. org.uk/discourses/definitions/ahaMkAra.htm. Ahamkara can also be split into "Aham" and "akaram" (meaning "features of the body"); http://vedabase.net/a/akaram. Thus Ahamkara refers to an "acting I" and to the (feeling of) "I am the body". I note this so as to emphasize the importance in advaita Vedanta philosophical thinking of "Self-realization", i.e., the realization that "I" am not the body–mind complex, "I" am not the individual soul (jivatma in Sanskrit) but am the *Self* (Atma in Sanskrit) which is one with the Supreme Soul (Paramatma) – the Universal Consciousness/God/Source.

11.　See　http://www.msnbc.msn.com/id/16842848/ns/technology_and_science-science/t/ scientists-bridging-spirituality-gap/#.UPOYOPKtopw.

12.　The methodological challenge is how to supplement existing demands of "scientific method", which emphasize objectivity and replicability of observations, with subjective and non-replicable observations. An example of the latter is provided by Alexander (2012). While clearly subjective and personal, it provides a powerful documentation by a reputed neurosurgeon as to the existence of consciousness independent of the brain, where the brain essentially performs a filtering function that enables us to limit the amount of information to be processed, which would otherwise be overwhelming, thereby facilitating a normal, conscious daily existence. Clearly this would not be accepted as valid evidence in a traditional scientific investigation, in spite of the details provided by a respected member of the scientific community.

13.　Reference must also be made here to the renowned philosopher statesman Sarvepalli Radhakrishnan (1888–1975; India's second President 1962–1967) who is recognized as a bridge-builder between Indian and Western philosophical and religious thinking, including his interpretation of advaita Vedanta so as to be more accessible to contemporary understanding. His birthday, September 5, is celebrated throughout India as "Teachers' Day".

14.　I note that the concept of time is quite different within a Western and Eastern understanding of "salvation". Westerners/Christians tend to conceive of salvation as life everlasting while Eastern mystics tend to express it as the state of being that does not last at all since time itself is transcended.

15. *Anatta* is the Pali word; a*natman* is the Sanskrit word. The doctrine of anatta/anatman is that there is no "self", there is no atman in the sense of a permanent, autonomous being or soul within an individual existence. I note that atman here refers to the "small" self; in Sanskrit texts, *atma* is not always understood to refer to the divine, *Atma*, just as in English *self* does not in general refer to the divine *Self*.

16. Although *advaita* (monism/non-duality – the Self/Atman and Brahman are identical) is the dominant school of thought in Vedantic philosophy, there are two other major schools: *visistadvaita* (qualified monism – God/Brahman has created the world but we are not entirely separate from God), and *dvaita* (duality – there exist two separate realities/ existences, God and the world).

17. Elsewhere, Aurobindo relates this unawareness of the "One there is", of non-dual oneness, to our unawareness of the source of our ethical competency. He argues that our experience of "conventional reality (is) one of the chief of the forces that hold back human life from progressing to a *true ethical order*. If humanity has made any lasting and true advance, it has been not through the virtue created by reward and punishment or any of the sanctions powerful on the little vital ego, but by an insistence from the higher mind on the lower, an insistence on right for its own sake, on imperative moral values, on an absolute law and truth of ethical being and ethical conduct that must be obeyed whatever the recalcitrance of the lower mind, whatever the pains of the vital problem, whatever the external result" (Aurobindo 1978, p. 154).

18. The complete Sanskrit prayer reads: "*Om, Asatoma sadgamaya, Tamasoma jyotir gamaya, Mrityorma amritam gamaya, Om, Shanti, shanti, shanti*", which means (my comments are in parentheses):

   Lead us from the unreal (ephemeral existence) to the Real (Universal Consciousness, Brahman),
   Lead us from darkness (ignorance) to light (spiritual awareness),
   Lead us from death (mortal finiteness) to immortality (transcendence of finiteness),
   Peace, Peace, Peace.

   I note that for the first time in history, on July 12, 2007, the United States Senate began its day with this Vedic prayer; see e.g., http://newsweek.washingtonpost.com/onfaith/ guestvoices/2007/08/post_7.html.

19. The *Bhagavad Gita* has played a powerful role in my own spiritual development. I have read roughly 15 English and Danish translations and together with my wife have translated an annotated version from English to Danish: *Bhagavad Gita: Herrens Sang* (2005) Copenhagen: Sathya Sai Baba Forlag.

20. The word is composed of two parts, *sthita* and *prajna*: one "standing" (*sthita*) in "wisdom" (*prajna*); understood as a person of steadiness and calm, firm in judgment, contented; from the *Dictionary of common Sanskrit spiritual words* (http://www.advaita.org.uk/sanskrit/ terms_rs.htm).

21. According to Buddhist philosophy, this state of realization of oneness and unchanging reality is in contrast to *samsara*, the endless round of existence of sentient beings, where existence involves suffering.

22. See for example the (for a Western audience) highly readable translations of the most renowned Upanishads: (Shearer and Russell 1989, pp. 61–70) and (Easwaran 1987, pp. 173–204).

23. A more recent Hindu sage, teacher and philosopher of advaita, Sri Nisargadatta Maharaj (1897–1981), presents a lucid personal expression of this ancient wisdom in the book *I AM THAT*, consisting of translated talks by the sage from the original Marathi (third edition, 1981, Bombay: Chetana). The book commences with a quote from the famous sage Sankaracharya (788–820): "That which permeates all, which nothing transcends and which, like the universal space around us, fills everything completely from within and without, that Supreme and non-dual Brahman – that thou art".

24. The "obstacle" is often referred to in advaita Vedanta as *maya*, a veil of illusion, a "cosmic force that presents the infinite Brahman (the supreme being) as the finite phenomenal

world", that needs to be uncovered in order to progress from "the unreal to the Real"; http://www.britannica.com/EBchecked/topic/370816/maya.

25. A similar comment was made earlier with respect to the concept of "conscience". A highly developed sense of discrimination is required in order to distinguish between the promptings of one's "higher self" and those of the ego, the body–mind complex that frames awareness in terms of "I" and "me" and "my" and "mine".

26. I note that this is the first time I have introduced the term "Godhead", often attributed to the great Christian mystic Meister Eckhart (1260–1327) whose teachings are sometimes compared with those of advaita. According to (King 1998, pp. 103–104), "Meister Eckhart's teachings are at one level deeply dualistic while ultimately celebrating the highest unity. … God is revealed to us as a person, but behind this revelation, this manifestation, there is the unrevealed Godhead, the 'ground' of God, undifferentiated and above all distinction, an eternal unity of which nothing can be said, the 'Nameless Nothing', the unoriginated purity of Being, the *puritas essendi*, the Eternal Now."

27. In Pruzan (2010) I reflect on the relationships between mathematics, reality and ethics, including the fundamental question as to whether mathematics is embedded in physical reality such that it is "discovered" or whether it is an artifact created by human beings in their search to "crack the cosmic code".

28. According to Huxley (1985, p. 54), "there is a hierarchy of the real. The manifold world of our everyday experience is real with a relative reality that is, on its own level, unquestionable; but this relative reality has its being within and because of the absolute Reality, which, on account of the incommensurable otherness of its eternal nature, we can never hope to describe, even though it is possible for us directly to apprehend it." This has, on occasion, been my direct experience.

29. Sathya Sai Baba founded one of the world's largest nonsectarian humanitarian aid organizations based exclusively on private donations. It provides services primarily in the fields of health, education and the provision of drinking water.

30. My comment: In the great Hindu epic *Ramayana*, Lakshman Rekha refers to a line drawn by Prince Lakshmana around the hut he shares with his brother Rama and Rama's wife Sita so as to protect Sita while he leaves in search of Rama.

REFERENCES

Abrahams, E. (1995), *A Comparative Survey of Hindu, Christian and Jewish Mysticism*, Delhi: Satguru Publications.

Alexander, E. (2012), *Proof of Heaven: A Neurosurgeon's Journey into the Afterlife*, New York, NY, USA: Simon & Schuster.

Aurobindo, S. (1970), *The Human Cycle; The Ideal of Human Unity; War and Self-determination*, Second edition, Pondicherry, Tamil Nadu, India: Sri Aurobindo Ashram, Publication Department.

Aurobindo, S. (1978), *The Problem of Rebirth*, Third edition, Pondicherry, Tamil Nadu, India: Sri Aurobindo Ashram, Publication Department.

Aurobindo, S. (1985), *The Upanishads*, Pondicherry, Tamil Nadu, India: Sri Aurobindo Ashram, Publication Department.

Bowles, S. and H. Gintis (2011), *A Cooperative Species: Human Reciprocity and Its Evolution*, Princeton, NJ, USA: Princeton University Press.

Chakraborty, S.K. (1991), *Management by Values: Towards Cultural Congruence*, Delhi: Oxford University Press.

Chakraborty, S.K. (1995), *Ethics in Management: Vedantic Perspectives*, Delhi: Oxford University Press.

Chalmers, D. (1997), 'Facing Up to the Problem of Consciousness' in J. Shear, (ed.), *Explaining Consciousness – The 'Hard Problem'*, Cambridge, MA, USA: The MIT Press (originally published in the *Journal of Consciousness Studies*, vol. 2, pp. 200–219, 1995).

Das, G. (2012), *The Difficulty of Being Good: On the Subtle Art of Dharma*, London, UK: Penguin.

Descartes, R. (1641, republished 1951), *Meditations*, translated with an introduction by L. Lafleur, New York, NY, USA: The Liberal Arts Press.

Easwaran, E. (1987), *The Upanishads*, Tomales, CA, USA: Nilgiri Press.

Forman, R.K.C. (1999), *Mysticism, Mind, Consciousness*, Albany, NY, USA: State University of New York Press.

Grassie, W. (2010), *The New Sciences of Religion: Exploring Spirituality from the Outside In and Bottom Up*, New York, NY, USA: Palgrave Macmillan.

Hagen, S. (2003), *Buddhism is Not What You Think: Finding Freedom Beyond Beliefs*, New York, NY, USA: HarperCollins.

Huxley, A. (1985), *The Perennial Philosophy*, London, UK: Triad, Grafton Books.

Kelly, E., E.W. Kelly and A. Crabtree (2007), *Irreducible Mind – Towards a Psychology for the 21st Century*, Lanham, MD, USA: Rowman & Littlefield.

King, U. (1998), *Christian Mystics: The Spiritual Heart of the Christian Tradition*, New York, NY, USA: Simon & Schuster.

Kriger, M.P. and Y. Seng (2005), 'Leadership with Inner Meaning: A Theory of Leadership Based on the Worldviews of Five Religions', *The Leadership Quarterly*, **16**, pp. 771–806.

Manikutty, S. (2012), 'Why Should I be Ethical? Some Answers from the Mahabharata', *Journal of Human Values*, **18** (1), pp. 19–32.

Matilal, B.K. (1992), 'Moral Dilemmas: Insights from Indian Epics' in B.K. Matilal (ed.), *Moral Dilemmas in the Mahabharata*, Delhi: Motilal Banarsidass, pp. 1–19.

Nussbaum, M.C. (2000), 'The Costs of Tragedy: Some Moral Limits of Cost–Benefit Analysis', *The Journal of Legal Studies*, **29** (S2), pp. 1005–1036.

Prabhavananda, S. and C. Isherwood (translators) (1954), *Bhagavad-Gita: The Song of God*, New York, NY, USA: Mentor.

Pruzan P. (2001), 'The Question of Organizational Consciousness: Can Organizations have Values, Virtues and Visions?', *Journal of Business Ethics*, **29**, pp. 271–284.

Pruzan, P. (2004), 'Spirituality as the Context for Leadership' in L. Zsolnai (ed.), *Spirituality and Ethics in Management*, London, UK: Kluwer Academic Publishers, pp. 15–31; also available in revised form in L. Zsolnai (ed.) *Spirituality and Ethics in Management* (Second edition, 2011), Dordrecht, Germany: Springer, Issues in Business Ethics, **19**, pp. 3–22.

Pruzan, P. (2009), *Rational, Ethical and Spiritual Perspectives on Leadership: Selected writings by Peter Pruzan*, Oxford, UK: Peter Lang.

Pruzan, P. (2010), 'Matematik, virkelighed og moral' ('Mathematics, reality and morality') in Jørgensen et al. (eds), *Maskinen skabt i menneskes billede*, Copenhagen: Nyt Nordisk Forlag, pp. 31–42.

Pruzan, P. (2013), *Perspectives on Research: Teaching Notes in Research Methodology* (unpublished teaching notes, submitted for publication in 2014), Prasanthi Nilayam, Andhra Pradesh, India: Sri Sathya Sai Institute of Higher Learning.

Pruzan, P. and K. Pruzan Mikkelsen (2007), *Leading with Wisdom: Spiritual-Based Leadership in Business*, Sheffield, UK: Greenleaf Publishing and Delhi: Sage Publications/Response Books (rights for South Asia only). Also available as *Ledelse med visdom: Spirituelt baseret lederskab i virksomheder*, revised edition, translated into Danish (2010), Copenhagen: Gyldendal Business.

Revel, J.-F. and M. Ricard (1998), *The Monk and the Philosopher*, translated from the French by J. Canti, New York, NY, USA: Schocken Books.

Russell, P. (2003), *From Science to God: The Mystery of Consciousness and the Meaning of Light*, Novato, CA, USA: New World Library.

Schopenhauer, A. (original 1840; translation from German by A.B. Bullock 1903), *On The Basis of Morality*, London, UK: Swan Sonnensenschein.

Shearer, A. and P. Russell (1989), *The Upanishads*, London, UK: Unwin Paperbacks.

Varela, F.J. (1999), *Ethical Know-How: Action, Wisdom, and Cognition*, Stanford, CA, USA: Stanford University Press.

Vivekananda, S. (1987), *Vedanta: Voice of Freedom*, Calcutta: Advaita Ashrama.

Wald, G. (1984), 'Life and Mind in the Universe', *International Journal of Quantum Chemistry; Proceedings of International Symposium on Quantum Biology and Quantum Pharmacology*, vol. **26**.

Whitman, W. (1947), 'Song of Myself', poem in *Leaves of Grass*, London, UK: J.M. Dent and Sons.

8. Aesthetics, human rights and economic life: temporal perspectives

Kevin T. Jackson

8.1 INTRODUCTION

Taking an existential, non-scientistic[1] approach, this chapter explores some philosophical and practical aspects of *time* concerning: (1) *aesthetics* (temporal relationships between economic value and moral values), (2) *human rights* (time's impact on our capacity for well-being), and (3) *economic life* (comprehending business as a temporal art).

If we take human beings to be a substantial unity of body and spirit,[2] how are we to understand a state of human existence in "good temporal order"? Assuming that there is such a thing as temporal soundness, I will argue that we all have a basic human right to the enjoyment of it, and that living with such time-balance is in fact a vital existential need – a prerequisite for flourishing in a state of physical and mental health.

Following an intellectual path begun in a recent book (Jackson 2012a), I shall enlist music as a dialogue partner, helping us grasp the sense in which business (like music itself) is a complex, pulsating temporal art that engages our whole being in multiple layers of time cycles. Such temporal patterns are everywhere; they are intricate and overlapping, ranging from our brain waves, heartbeats, and other physiological patterns to natural rhythms such as seasonal change, to cultural trends, fashion fluctuations, and economic rhythms such as stock market dynamics and technology "hype cycles."

Music is about making and receiving sounds *in time*. Flowing in rhythm, the sounds of music have aesthetic, economic, and spiritual value. Further, as Plato recognized, the process of creating, performing, and receiving music is of immense value to our physical and mental well-being, and even plays a role in the cultivation of moral virtue. For Socrates, of all the images of art, music remained the most influential. Thus he opines that "[m]usical training is a more potent instrument than any other, because rhythm and harmony find their way into the inward places of the soul, on which they mightily fasten, imparting grace, and making the soul of him who is rightly educated graceful, or of him who is ill-educated ungraceful" (Plato 1888). Music builds magnetism for the truth that philosophy pursues. The exquisiteness in music reveals to the soul the realm of the beautiful and the intelligible. With its charm and the natural delight attending it, music nurtures an enduring predilection for ordered beauty. And this is precisely what the philosopher is yearning for. As Socrates states in Plato's *Republic*, the philosopher associates with the divine and orderly in the universe.

Business, too, fundamentally involves making and receiving things of value (goods, services, information) through relationships of exchange that occur in peculiar temporal arrangements – the "rhythm of business." Important issues of moral value are bound up in how business decision-making privileges some time orientations over others (short- versus long-term goals and their consequences; satisfying present as opposed to the future interests implied by sustainability; degree of attention paid to pursuit of prospective ends as compared with satisfaction of past delicts). There are many examples of our actions producing negative long-term effects that cancel out their intended positive short-term effects (e.g., DDT spraying, disposal of nuclear waste).

Yet little attention has been paid in moral philosophy to the criteria according to which value should be allocated as between the past, the present, and the future. Instead temporal assumptions tend to be made and used as a basis for judgment without critical reflection or justificatory support. For instance, in the discourse of sustainability it is assumed outright that obligations toward future generations are always more important than present (or past-oriented) obligations. But on what rational basis is this so?

Just how far out does responsibility extend into the future? What is the moral significance we ought to attribute to remote human beings living, say, more than 5,000 years from now? It is pretty difficult to gets one's mind around anything beyond about two generations hence. And how far back does responsibility extend in the past? Surely at some point so much time passes by that we forgive and forget? But why shouldn't we just forgive earlier instead of waiting it out so long? Finally, how much moral weight should we, or better, the disciples of Eckhart Tolle (2004), assign to the present, as compared with the future and the past?

Extending our time-directed reflections further, we may ask: insofar as our technocratic and materialistic culture is caught up in a kind of temporal malaise, including but not limited to disturbances such as "busy-ness" and acute time pressurization, how much is business responsible for this dis-ease, and are there avenues we might pursue for getting ourselves into a healthier relationship to time? In the spirit of Augustine's treatment of *distentio animi*,[3] I will introduce the notion of *chronopathy*[4] to characterize a modern condition of temporal discordance – a species of "invisible" human rights deprivation (partially self-inflicted, and in part the result of institutional and cultural influences) that inhibits one's healthy in-dwelling within the dimension of time. As will be seen, not only individuals but also organizations can be afflicted with various institutional types of chronopathy; among the most notorious organizational temporal malaises with evident negative ethical consequences are short-termism.[5]

8.2 AESTHETICS AND VALUE(S)

Pursuit of the common good, as well as respect for human rights, orient toward a state of human existence in which people feel secure, fulfilled, dignified, and free from suffering. Intuitively one grasps that human suffering is not something beautiful; on the other hand, human flourishing is something beautiful. One might say that in proportion to increased human suffering comes a decrease of the beautiful in human existence.

Having said this, it is necessary to consider an opposing view. Postmodern composer Karlheinz Stockhausen (whose own works music critic and philosopher Roger Scruton describes as "bulbous monstrosities which make maximum demands on the listener's attention and give next to nothing in return"[6]) seems to exalt human suffering and massive violation of the human rights of innocents – namely the terrorist attack on the World Trade Center's twin towers on 9/11 – as a form of art.

> Well, what happened there is, is of course – now you all have to adjust your brains – the greatest work of art that has ever existed. That spirits achieve in one act something we could never dream of in music, that people practice like mad for ten years, totally fanatically, for one concert. And then die. And that is the greatest work of art that exists for the whole cosmos. Just imagine what happened there. These are people who are so concentrated on this single performance – and then five thousand people are driven into resurrection. In one moment. I couldn't do that. Compared to that, we are nothing, as composers that is. (Hängg 2011)

To make such an assertion, Stockhausen surely must have a conception of art that is at war with the ideal of beauty. It is a postmodern deployment of art that is designed to shock and degrade human existence, not to celebrate it and elevate it. To situate, as Stockhausen does, such a horrendous infliction of human suffering and denial of human rights within the aesthetic sphere, to assert that the mass murder of innocent humans is the "greatest work of art that exists for the whole cosmos," is to simultaneously insult art, mock musical performance, and decouple them from their proper inheritance in the realm of the beautiful; it is to exalt malevolence, sanctify lawlessness and violence; it is to glorify cruelty, arrogance, and contempt for human dignity, freedom, and compassion. Victims of the WTC attack suffocated, were burned alive in intense heat, smoke and flames, falling to their death screaming in horror, their brains liquefying upon impact. They were all people like us: precious, irreplaceable loved ones belonging to families that still deeply miss them and grieve for them. Children, who are the most helpless and vulnerable in this world, were irreversibly rendered fatherless or motherless. Fathers and mothers lost their beloved sons and daughters forever.

To treat aesthetics as encompassing the hatred of that which is beautiful, to see human destruction and human rights crimes as forms of artistic expression, is to move aesthetics far away from its status as a branch of philosophy that deals with the nature and expression of beauty to the antithesis of that – it is to repudiate the core value that beauty carries for human existence.

Leaving Stockhausen's aberrations behind us now, and returning to the earlier path of argument, when human beings do not feel a sense of significance in life, when they do not enjoy a sense of dignity, when they do not feel a sense of security, then conditions for the creation of beauty, including apprehension of the sublime are compromised.

Yet even in the midst of great physical suffering, a sense of beauty can nurture the human spirit, helping one endure what would otherwise be insurmountable hardship. Viktor Frankl recounts how he and his fellow prisoners in Nazi concentration camps, even while stretched to the very limits of physical endurance – undernourished, sleep deprived, worked to the point of exhaustion, frostbitten – would at times find themselves enraptured by brief glimpses of beauty:

> One evening, when we were already resting on the floor of our hut, dead tired, soup bowls in hand, a fellow prisoner rushed in and asked us to run out to the assembly grounds and see the wonderful sunset. Standing outside we saw sinister clouds glowing in the west and the whole sky alive with clouds of ever-changing shapes and colors, from steel blue to blood red. The desolate grey mud huts provided a sharp contrast, while the puddles on the muddy ground reflected the glowing sky. Then, after minutes of moving silence, one prisoner said to another, "How beautiful the world *could* be." (Frankl 2004, p. 51)

In Frankl's estimation, such experiences, along with the staging of improvised cabarets, singing of songs, reciting of poems, and deliveries of satiric jokes, formed a part of some prisoner's ability to retain a sense of purpose, of meaning in life, which in turn increased their chances of physical survival.

The creation of music, art, philosophy, and literature, contribute to the aesthetic dimension of the greater good of humanity, but without fulfillment of physical needs like safety and health, participation in higher attainments becomes difficult. Looking past the materialist conception of *homo economicus* towards an understanding of man as a substantial unity of spirit and matter, one faces the deeper humanness of our existence, together with the richness of its emotional, intellectual, and spiritual aspirations. Whatever diminishes the human subject and forces him or her to live in a state of mere material subsistence, without fostering opportunities to think, learn, create, dream, and hope cannot reasonably be deemed beautiful.

According to this outlook, economic activities that increase suffering of human beings, either by depriving them of physical well-being or by hampering their communion with beauty, should be subject to heightened levels of scrutiny, and an added burden of explanation demanded for such practices. If there is evidence that economic activity diminishes the aesthetic of communal life, any purported claims that such a condition is warranted, should shoulder a heavy burden of justification.

There are, to be sure, special problems that arise if one attempts to place the domain of aesthetics (beauty) on the same plane as that of ethics (the good), and epistemology (truth). Aesthetic judgments, unlike ethical judgments and epistemic claims, after all, are grounded in taste. But is there any rational anchoring to matters of taste? If I claim that Debussy's music is superior to Snoop Dogg's rap, can I justify that assertion when someone else disagrees with it, if our comparative assessments simply express our respective subjective tastes?[7] This kind of relativist conception of aesthetics has prompted many to consider judgments about beauty to be purely subjective and therefore immune to criticism or rational debate. Yet in ancient thought beauty was regarded as an ultimate value, and one that is pursued for its own sake. Moreover, as an ultimate value, beauty, along with goodness and truth, was regarded as something the pursuit of which no further reason needs to be provided. If we inquire "why should I believe p?" the answer is "because p is true." If we ask "why should I pursue q?" a plausible reason is "because q is good." If we query "why should I value or admire r?" a reasonable reply is "because r is beautiful." But some thinkers would contend that whereas truth and goodness do not compete with each other, such is not the case for beauty (e.g., Scruton 2009).

For instance, Søren Kierkegaard – who regarded the aesthetic life in temporal terms, as linked to the present moment[8] – held that a sphere of existence in which beauty is pursued as the highest value is lower than a sphere of existence in which goodness and virtue are of supreme value (which in turn is lower to the religious sphere in which God is accorded ultimate value). By contrast, it is interesting to note that, according to received Thomistic scholarship, Aquinas considered truth, goodness and beauty to all carry the same status as "transcendentals": each is "being" (*ens*) rationally apprehended by means of a different modality (Gallagher 2006). Thus, for Aquinas, truth (*verum*) is being as known, goodness (*bonum*) is being as rightly desired, and (at least under the interpretation that counts beauty indirectly as among the transcendentals) beauty (*pulchrum*) is being as rightly admired.[9]

Nevertheless, for many philosophers the status of aesthetics as encompassing the province of ultimate values remains dubious in a way that ethics and epistemology are not.

8.3 HUMAN RIGHTS

It has been known from antiquity that there exists a law higher than written human decrees. In Sophocles' tragedy, Antigone points to a higher law that compels her to bury her rebel brother Polyneices, killed in a civil war, contrary to Creon's edict forbidding any burial of rebels as a sign of their disgrace. Concerning such unwritten laws, Antigone says "Not now, nor yesterday's, they always live, and no one knows their origin in time."[10]

The ancient conception of higher unwritten law was connected to aesthetic concerns. Insofar as the ancient Greek notion of music carried a wider meaning than it has for us, we find in it a conception of a higher law-like harmony. As an adjectival designation for the Muses – the goddesses reigning over arts and sciences – the notion of music pertained to human activities aimed at beauty and truth. Later on, this broadened conception can be seen in the thought of Boethius, who classified music into *instrumentalis, humana and mundana*, according to which harmony is found within the spheres of the human body, the human soul, and the physical world, respectively. Music is an ordering principle that keeps these three systems connected in a unified way (Grout 1960).

Stoic philosophy, originating in ancient Greece and expanding into the Roman Empire, contributed a concern for universal human dignity at the heart of the moral law. Subsequently the rich heritage of Roman jurisprudence emerged, especially as expounded by Marcus Tullius

Cicero, who wrote in the *Republic* that "there will not be different laws at Rome and at Athens, or different laws now and in the future, but one eternal and unchangeable law will be valid for all nations and all times" (Ebenstein and Ebenstein 2000, p. 133).

As well, the idea of an unseen higher law is at the foundation of the modern concept of rights. John Locke maintained that even in a state of nature there is a law recognized by all people which is implanted in human reason. Such a law of nature engenders natural rights discernible by all rational beings. The notion of natural rights is proclaimed in the United States Declaration of Independence:

> We hold these truths to be self-evident: that all men are created equal; that they are endowed, by their Creator, with certain unalienable rights; that among these are life, liberty, and the pursuit of happiness.

Such a conception designates rights that are taken to be independent of, and prior to rights established by particular political arrangements.

Even into the realm of international law, the notion of an unwritten eternal law has been vital. For instance, during the Nazi war crimes trials at Nuremberg jurisdictional limitations precluded prosecuting the crimes pursuant to the laws of the various participating nation-states. Accordingly, the indictments referenced "crimes against humanity."

Recourse to the idea of higher law has been central to many civil rights cases throughout United States history. Martin Luther King, Jr.'s famous "Letter from Birmingham Jail" (1963) decried the persistence of racial prejudice from extant law. As King writes, "A just law is a man-made code that squares with the moral law or the law of God." An unjust law is a code that is out of harmony with the moral law. To put it in the terms of Thomas Aquinas: "An unjust law is a human law that is not rooted in eternal law and natural law."[11]

For Aquinas, natural law is that part of the eternal law of the Creator that is presented to human reason. We are guided by a rational apprehension of the eternal law which is imprinted as precepts, rules of behavior, or broad principles of natural law. Because humans are autonomous beings they must choose to observe the law of nature through their own acts of free will. Natural law is a product of unaided reason. Human laws are positive laws that are, or should be, derived from natural law.

These days, to the extent that people think about an unwritten higher law, most of them situate the notion with human rights, which are seen as protecting basic liberties and justifying entitlements to basic needs. Ordinarily we associate deprivations of basic rights with the corresponding loss they bring to physical needs, although intangibles like freedom of conscience and freedom of expression are also considered within the scope of basic rights. Not surprisingly, we direct attention towards the various ways that public and private institutions, and other people violate human rights. A plausible rationale advanced by Martha Nussbaum (2000), Amartya Sen (2009), and others, for respecting such basic rights is that they support human capabilities. Ultimately we wish for humans to realize their capabilities for enjoyment of the good life. And living a good life, as Aristotle showed, is contemplation of intrinsically valuable things like truth, goodness, and beauty.

Quite a number of thinkers in the Western tradition, extending from Socrates and the Stoic philosophers to Schopenhauer and Adam Smith, espoused the notion that some form of deliberation constitutes the supreme good of life. Correspondingly, in Eastern thought, one sees this view endorsed in the Buddhist, Confucian, Zen and Taoist quest for a tranquil state of mind. Thus, Lao Tse's query runs:

> Do you have the patience to wait
> till your mud settles and the water is clear?[12]

Aristotle's ideas about contemplation bear a strong similarity to the Zen-like state creative artists experience from being so utterly focused that ordinary thought is suspended. When in this state, which is a kind of retreat into the refuge of the present moment, your troubles seem to disappear. The artist Botero said that he only started existing when working in his studio, which provided him with a refuge from the world's violence. He felt a superb fulfillment in finding harmony arising from a precise form coupled with precisely the correct color, a profound joy – which he likened to lovemaking – issuing from a magical, unexpected moment at which a sense of peace pervaded both the canvas and his heart.[13]

As you can see, what I am proposing is to shift our concern for human rights away from mainstream discourse towards a context that at first glance seems counter-intuitive. The context is framed by *aesthetics and temporality*, in order to initiate reflection about, on the one hand, threats to and, on the other hand, opportunities for promoting an "existential" awareness of certain kinds of human rights that are situated in an invisible, "higher" spectrum of economic life. Rather than considering human rights within a standard political frame of reference, I shall be treating them from an existential-aesthetic point of view.

Consequently, we are considering as potential "victims" of human rights deprivations not only the materially poor and the politically oppressed (Pogge 2007), but even the materially affluent and politically privileged segments of humanity. Of course, it goes without saying that by not assuming responsibility for future consequences of present actions, and for ignoring responsibility for past wrongs, one may be depriving others of various human rights. Yet among the non-obvious claims I am advancing is the proposition that when we are living an inauthentic life, trapped in time compression, or struggling against time as a perceived enemy, we are doing something that is in a sense much worse than what anyone else could do to us: we are depriving ourselves of our own basic human right to a serene habitation in the mind–body and on the good earth.

Consider temporally distressed characters, those who have wasted the gift of created time in their banality and self-absorption, such as the high-court judge portrayed by Tolstoy in *The Death of Ivan Illich*. In order to make this point in a more specific way that bears upon contemporary economic life in particular, I shall present the notion of *chronopathy*: a condition of temporal discordance that inhibits one's healthy in-dwelling within the dimension of time.

8.4 TIME

> At the centre of the debates about the metaphors for time,
> whether mathematical, physical, or philosophical,
> are questions about whether time is a threat or a gift.
>
> Stephen Happel (1993)

From the standpoint of physical science, time appears to move in one direction – the past lies behind, fixed and immutable. The future lies ahead and is not necessarily fixed. According to the Second Law of Thermodynamics, natural processes have a preferred direction of progress. Thus, heat flows from area of higher temperature to area of lower temperature. It is never the reverse, unless some kind of external work gets performed on the system in question. Thermodynamic processes reduce the state of order of initial systems, so entropy is an expression of disorder or randomness.

Ultimately, entropy is what determines the direction of the "arrow of time." Consider for instance how the gas combustion that makes a car run creates mechanical energy and heat. But no process in the universe will let the exhaust gases re-combine with the heat energy to reconstitute the original gasoline. The heat energy of the burning gasoline has reached a higher, irreversible state of randomization. The entropy of the system, and the universe, is irreversibly increased, as required by the Second Law of Thermodynamics.

Shifting one's focus from physics to economics, in an important way, *economic value* is analogous to *energy*: it becomes randomized as with the Second Law. Spending money is easier than earning and saving it. Once created, economic value requires infusion of energy from sources outside a system – competent strategy; contributions of capital or labor.

Indeed, without temporally ordered management, to organize and structure transactions, over time a business will fail, a victim of entropy.

8.5 THE RHYTHM OF BUSINESS

Doing business deeply engages economic, aesthetic, and moral phenomena which are themselves time-laden. Value creation – whether one is considering economic value, aesthetic value or moral values – is subject to a dynamic involving pulsations, with multi-tiered sequences passing through states of equilibrium, intensification, and resolution. Economic value rises and falls over time, normally understood within a market frame of reference (stocks, commodities, real estate, and labor).

There are metrical waves that constitute distinct rhythms within all aspects of business. They intertwine in intricate ways. Such rhythmic patterns appear in virtually all facets of business. One example is Elliott waves in trading (see Figure 8.1), which are based upon technical analysis used to represent financial market cycles and to forecast market trends. According to the model, market prices alternate between impulsive, or motive phases, and corrective phases on all time scales of trend.

Other examples of rhythmic patterns in business, to identify just two, are product sustenance life cycles (Figure 8.2) and technology "hype cycles" (Figure 8.3).

Within what frame of reference do aesthetic values rise and fall over time? And what about moral values? In contrast to economic value, it is difficult to identify commonly agreed-upon frames of reference. And yet, as regards aesthetic values, there are music, art, and film competitions which presuppose some authoritative judgments being rendered in that domain. And although taste is often seen as a matter of personal judgment, there are public impacts of private taste to be reckoned with; and communities of judgment (such as city councils and planning boards that establish standards for neighborhoods) presuppose at least some shared conceptions of aesthetic value (which are also connected to economic value).

Concerning moral values, it is commonplace to speak of their periodic rise and fall. For instance, a recent Gallup poll reported three-quarters of Americans saying that the country's moral values were declining, which

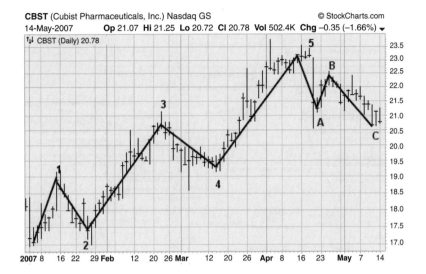

Figure 8.1   Elliott waves

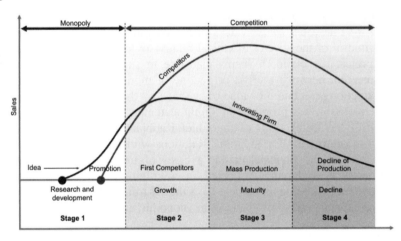

Figure 8.2   Product sustenance life cycle

they attributed to erosion of ethical standards, poor parenting, and dishonesty by government and business leaders. By contrast, only 14 percent of respondents thought that the country's moral values were on the rise. Increased diversity and the need for Americans to pull together in tough times were two of the reasons those respondents offered

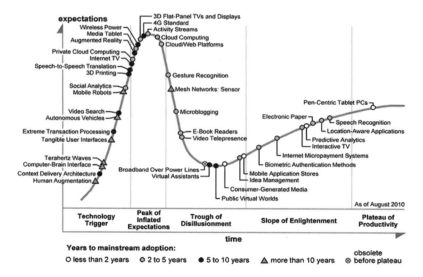

Figure 8.3   Technology hype cycle

(Alfonso 2012). However, the tricky part here is to specify, along with *which* values, just *whose* values one is deeming to be in a state of flux.

Mindful of the specter of ethical relativism looming in the background to protest the claim, it seems plausible to suppose that there is some connection between a crisis or decline of moral values and the massive destruction of economic value occasioned by the financial crisis. Such an interpretation was proposed in a joint statement of the Bilateral Commission of the Delegations of the Chief Rabbinate of Israel and the Holy See's Commission for Religious Relations with Jews, which identified at the root of the financial crisis "a crisis of moral values in which the importance of having, reflected in a culture of greed, eclipsed the importance of being and where the value of truth reflected in honesty and transparency was sorely lacking in economic activity."[14]

8.6 ST. AUGUSTINE

Augustine was among the earliest philosophers, perhaps the first, to take time seriously. He was surprisingly frank about the sense of mysteriousness and puzzlement that surrounds our conceptions of time: "What, then, is time? If no one asks me, I know; if I want to explain it to someone who does ask me, I do not know."[15]

Here is a brief summary of Augustine's inquiry about time, broken down into three parts:

1. How can these two kinds of time, the past and the future, be, when the past no longer is and the future as yet does not exist?
2. If the present were always present, and would not pass into the past, it would no longer be time, but eternity.
3. Therefore, if the present, so as to be time, must be so constituted that it passes into the past, how can we say that it is, since the cause of its being is the fact that it will cease to be?

In *De Musica*, Augustine gives a kind of mediation on the aesthetic thinking of Plotinus and Plato that was to exert a substantial impact on later medieval aesthetic approaches. For Augustine, we are all woven into a temporal tapestry. But music can help us move away from the world of sense toward the eternal, to gain access to a higher world seen with the eye of reason (O'Connell 1978). In his *Confessions*, Augustine offers an account of *distentio*: a dispersing we undergo in our experience of time which stimulates the mind's quest to reestablish its original unity.

Listen to what Augustine says about it:

> I am distracted amid times, whose order I do not know, and my thoughts, the inmost bowels of my soul, are torn asunder by tumult and change, until being purged and melted clear by the fire of your love, I may flow altogether into you.[16]

For Augustine, a person who is so distended can, with divine help, gain re-collection – delivery from the fragmenting temporal world into the unity from which one has fallen. Thus, in a recitation of a psalm or poem our mind is anticipating what is yet to come while simultaneously keeping in memory what has already passed. So far as we attain a degree of ordering or control over time we can approximate, though in a faint way, the character and perspective of eternity.

8.7 CHRONOPATHY

What I shall term *chronopathy* is a state of temporal dysfunction that afflicts not only individuals but also organizations. It can be manifested in individuals as busy-ness, or as taking refuge in the "now," or as a retreat into the future, in either case constituting a kind of temporal bad faith.

8.7.1   Busy-ness

The phenomenon of "busy-ness" has been discussed by a variety of commentators in the popular press. Here is some of what Tim Kreider (2012) has to say about what he calls the "busy trap":

> Living in the 21st century you've probably had to listen to people tell you how busy they are. It's the default response when you ask anyone how they're doing: "Busy!" "*So* busy." "*Crazy* busy." It is, pretty obviously, a boast disguised as a complaint. And the stock response is a kind of congratulation: "That's a good problem to have," or "Better than the opposite."

> Busyness serves as a kind of existential reassurance, a hedge against emptiness; obviously your life cannot possibly be silly or trivial or meaningless if you are so busy, completely booked, in demand every hour of the day ... . Idleness is not just a vacation, an indulgence or a vice; it is as indispensable to the brain as vitamin D is to the body, and deprived of it we suffer a mental affliction as disfiguring as rickets. The space and quiet that idleness provides is a necessary condition for standing back from life and seeing it whole, for making unexpected connections and waiting for the wild summer lightning strikes of inspiration ...

> It's not as if any of us wants to live like this; it's something we collectively force one another to do.

Similarly, Thomas DeLong (2011) locates busyness as a product of organizational culture in the following passage:

> The trap of busyness is so much a part of corporate culture that many times it clouds our vision of what's really going on. We expect to be busy; we don't know what to do when we're not. The trap of busyness causes us to move with such mindless speed that we're like the proverbial chicken running around with his head cut off. We plunge into our emails and meetings with a manic energy that forbids reflection, deeply honest conversations, and breaks from the routine.[17]

Readers wishing to glean something on the more practical side from this discussion are now invited to take part in the following self-assessment exercise, which is intended to stimulate reflection on your own engagement with time on a day-to-day basis:

1. When people ask "how are you?" you usually answer: "so busy", "crazy busy" or "busy but good."
2. You worry about how busy you'll be tomorrow.
3. You tend to get angry when others aren't as busy as you.
4. You stay awake thinking about everything that didn't get done.

5. You make a point of letting people know that you stay at work after hours.
6. You check emails over and over throughout the day and night.
7. You space out during conversations, thinking about other things you need to do.
8. You volunteer for things you don't really care about.
9. You often complain about how busy you are.
10. You make list after list to make sure you don't forget anything during the day.
11. You don't seem to have enough time to even clean your workspace or get organized.
12. You regularly eat in your car, or while standing, walking or working.
13. You use a phone when driving because "it's the only time you have to talk."
14. You never arrange for a day set aside each week mainly for rest and relaxation.

So, assuming you have taken the time to complete this quiz, how many "yes" responses do you have? What implications does that have for your life? (All responses will be kept in strict confidence.)

For organizations, the dysfunction is sometimes manifested as short-termism (driven by greed), or it may appear as "one-minute manager" syndrome. The disastrous results of short-termism are clearly seen in the financial crisis and need not be rehearsed here as they have been extensively discussed elsewhere by myself and others. As for the one-minute manager condition, which is insidious yet not often noticed, it arises as a delusion that complex matters can, under a simplistic master law of efficiency ("little time equals big results,") be quickly tackled with a rapid-fire leadership formula: goals, praisings, reprimands (repeat). What can be calamitous, however, is when issues requiring sustained reflection, whose deliberation are perceived to be inefficient or not amenable to crisp, definitive resolution are excluded from the communicative process and remain unspoken. So, over time, such "marginal" problems (which may be of great moral significance) take on the appearance of irrelevance and suffer devaluation by the too-zippy manager as well as the decapitated chickens scurrying about under his beck-and-call. Recall Ford's rush to get all those (exploding) Pintos to market.

8.8 IMPROVISATION AND TIME

Improvisation occurs in business just as much as it does in jazz music. In both domains, improvisation triggers concentrated interaction between *constraint* and *contingency*: particularization of the past for the present and the future.

Rather than seeking to evade or conquer time, improvisation enlists time in celebrating our human freedom.

8.8.1 Music as an Exemplar of Temporal Performance[18]

In teaching classes in business ethics and corporate social responsibility I will often introduce executive and graduate business students to live jazz improvisation ("jam sessions") and/or classical collaborative music ensemble performances in venues around New York City (or Brussels, depending on where I'm teaching that term), after which they pool their thoughts about what they have observed that is applicable to business management. Although by no means exhaustive, here are some examples of pedagogical insights for temporality in business management that may be gleaned from such performance régimes:

Reading scores and charts. In jazz parlance one speaks of the process of reading through the changes, or chord progressions along with one's co-improvisors. Similarly, managerial wisdom, when cultivated, can equip one to give an enlightened reading of the various "charts" that are connected with commercial life (business plans, bylaws, profit-loss statements) and to be adroit at "performing" them with insight, discernment, integrity and care. Many of the patterns confronted by business managers can be likened to those confronted by musicians.

Improving Patterns of Conversation and Communication. To lead wisely is to pay attention to, and become skilled in, the ways people create new understanding in the intricate back and forth of professional conversation. Communication is the sharing of created meaning; conversation is the creation of shared meaning. So to lead wisely is to pay attention to, and to become skilled in, the ways language shapes meaning and life. In the sense that music involves patterns of conversation, questions come up, because in conversation there are many questions that arise. Questions lead to answers, which lead to more questions. That is what makes the music continue in a coherent temporal flow: the questions and their answers.

Improving Patterns of Improvisation. Business management and leadership is often thought of in terms of conventional principles and rules: things we must do, and things we must not do in running an organization

– making it do what is was designed to do. But business management is also inevitably contextual and open-ended. Managers should be trained in how to apply principles and rules in a way that is sensitive to the situation. That doesn't mean established standards go out the window. It just means that even well-established rules need to be interpreted, and applied to the particularities of the case at hand. This requires sound judgment, and imagination. Business management is, in other words, often a matter of skillful improvisation.

The improvisational nature of management is particularly exposed when a company is faced with an organizational crisis. Yet it is by no means limited to such an extreme scenario. A crisis is, by definition, an unexpected set of circumstances; however, even day-to-day business activities in today's rapidly changing environment bring their own "crisis-like" challenges with which to contend. And it requires a set of skills closely aligned to those required for musical improvisation of the kind manifested by the virtuoso musician.

Looking further into the comparison, consider the following ways in which sustainable business management shares patterns with musical improvisation:

1. Management's stance towards the life of the enterprise must be *creative*. The best thing to do isn't in any pre-established script; it requires an ability to adapt to the peculiarities of every situation, and to exercise imagination.
2. Responsible management must be grounded in *structure*. Improvisation doesn't mean playing random notes. For a musician, improvisation normally means deviating from the melody while continuing to follow an underlying structure of some sort. Similarly, an organization is going to want to draw upon relevant moral principles, such as human rights norms, standards of environmental and social justice, as well as its own basic ethical structure, as provided by its Code of Ethics and its Mission, Vision, and Values statements, and so on.
3. Sustainability-minded management leans on *collaboration*. Improvising musicians take from each other both their cues and inspiration. They listen carefully to each other. No one of them dominates the others. The best improvisation happens among musicians who have played together before and who trust each other. Likewise, making sustainable business decisions often requires close collaboration between members of the firm (senior leadership, the company's technical and financial experts, the legal and compliance staff, and sales and marketing people), elements of civil society

(NGOs, NPOs, PVOs, activists, foundations), governmental agents, and many other stakeholders from communities that influence or are influenced by the enterprise.

4. At its best, business management is guided by *wisdom*. The expert musician knows how to play the expected notes, knows how to stick to the melody, but wisely chooses to deviate when deemed appropriate. Executives and managers who are leading a sustainable organization must likewise work from *phronesis*: knowledge of the nature of ethical obligation, insight into the company's own values, and sound judgment in balancing the interests of various stakeholders to create value.

5. To be a skilled manager requires *comfort* with the relevant concepts and vocabulary. A master improvisor reaches for unexpected notes and makes it look easy and natural. Likewise business leaders need a degree of comfort with the material at hand. For instance, to adequately cope with the many moral challenges that business confronts today requires that executives and managers be comfortable talking, thinking, and making decisions about ethics and moral responsibilities.

6. Leaders must have the courage to *confront uncertainty and to take risks*. Improvisation offers a model of contending with elements of risk and uncertainty analogous to those that attend many business decision-making arenas today.

Of course, the analogy between musical improvisation and business management is not perfect. But gaining awareness of the connections is a useful way of framing the task of applying knowledge and expertise to novel situations. Business leadership should be neither rigid nor random. Navigating through the sometimes perilous currents of business management requires a sound understanding of the underlying principles, and a comfort and willingness to adapt them responsibly to the needs of present situations.

8.9 ECONOMIC, AESTHETIC, AND MORAL VALUE(S)

Because they are linked to markets, and because markets are in flux over time, the objects to which we assign economic value undergo changes in valuation in a continuous temporal flow. What about the objects of aesthetic value, such as artwork and musical compositions? In addressing this question, it is important to recognize that there is some overlap between economic and aesthetic value. An original Picasso like his cubist oil painting *Le pigeon aux petits-pois*, which was stolen from the Musée d'art Moderne de la Ville de Paris in 2010 was at that time valued at approximately €23 million ($30 million). Leonardo da Vinci's *Mona Lisa* carried an assessed value of $100 million back in 1962. Adjusted for inflation for today it would be worth about $743 million, although some would alternatively refuse to assign any figure, deeming it to be priceless. While the economic value of a work of art is often enhanced by its widely recognized aesthetic value – its perceived beauty – these two spheres, the economic and the aesthetic, remain distinct. Something of great aesthetic value may carry little economic value and vice versa.

When it comes to reckoning moral value, we start to enter some rugged terrain. One thinks about the horror of equating the value of human life in a moral sense with some dollar amount in the actuarial sense. Recall the cost–benefit analysis memorandum that surfaced during the Ford Pinto trials. Part of the normative strength of human rights rests on the proposition that we cannot place price tags on people, as we do on appliances, without violating their inherent dignity and (priceless) moral worth. Certainly one of the important characteristics of the moral value of human rights is that it remains constant over time. It is not subject to "market swings." So in this sense human rights have a special *axiological atemporality*. On the other hand, our understandings of human rights may well undergo change over time.

Changes in moral values presumably affect how the moral value of human rights, as such, is comprehended. A society that does not lay much importance on values like freedom, equality, or dignity is not likely to extend recognition to or make effort to provide protections for human rights.

There are evidently significant connections between moral and economic value as can be seen, for instance, in the economic value of a well-reputed and trustworthy professional. If at least some of a lawyer's financial success has been the result of her honesty and integrity maintained in client relationships, then we see some potentially robust linkage: respecting a client's moral worth as a person may turn out to enhance the economic value of, on the one hand, that client as an asset (evidenced by a disposition of loyalty and preference for retaining the attorney in future legal matters) and, on the other hand, the economic value of the lawyer in the form of reputation capital. Innumerable other examples from other areas of business could be used to illustrate the same point.[19]

What should not be overlooked as well is the idea that there may yet be an element of beauty lurking within all of this. For there is something distinctly beautiful in business life when it attains that which is both profitable and noble, by doing well and also doing good. However, tastes surely differ on this point.

NOTES

1. The term "scientism" refers to a philosophical notion that refuses to accept the validity of any form of knowledge besides positive science. Scientism deems values to be mere byproducts of emotions and relegates the question of the meaning of life to the realm of the irrational or illusory.
2. "The unity of soul and body is so profound that one has to consider the soul to be the 'form,' of the body: i.e., it is because of its spiritual soul that the body made of matter becomes a living, human body; spirit and matter, in man, are not two natures united, but rather their union forms a single nature." *Catechism of the Catholic Church* 365.
3. St. Augustine, *Confessions* Ch. 11:26(33); Ch. 11:29(39).
4. Portmanteau of the Ancient Greek terms *chronos* (time) and *pathos* (disease).
5. To this one might add "one-minute managerial blatherskite," the arrogant attitude that all management problems can be crisply and most efficiently dealt with in exceedingly brief time spans.
6. Scruton, Roger, "The Post-Modern Ear", *Axess*, retrieved from axess.se/magasin/english.aspx?article=713 (accessed October 21, 2014).
7. A similar problem arises with regard to emotivist theories of ethics.
8. María Amilburu (1998) recites Kierkegaard as follows: "The best expression of the aesthetic existence comes down to saying that it lies in the moment," adding that, in consequence, "when pleasure is what someone wants, delay makes no sense."
9. Other scholars contend that Aquinas followed Aristotle in excluding beauty from the transcendentals (Aertsen 1996; de Bruyne 1947).
10. Sophocles, *Antigone*, lines 453–457.
11. According to Aquinas: "Human law is law inasmuch as it is in conformity with right reason and thus derives from the eternal law. But when law is contrary to reason, it is called an unjust law; but in this case it ceases to be a law and becomes instead an act of violence. ... Every law made by man can be called a law insofar as it derives from the natural law. But if it is somehow opposed to the natural law, then it is really not a law but rather a corruption of the law." Thomas Aquinas, *Summa Theologica*, I-II Q. 95, art. 2.
12. Tse, Lao, *Tao Te Ching*, Ch. 15.
13. Tasset, Jean-Marie, 'Fernando Botero: Life and Work Within the Century', retrieved from http://karaart.com/botero/tasset/life.html (accessed August 31, 2013).
14. Rome, March 27–29, 2012, 3.
15. *Confessions*, Bk. 11: Ch. 14 (17).
16. *Confessions*, Bk. 11: Ch. 29 (39).
17. Professor DeLong observes that some MBA graduates working on Wall Street admitted "[leaving] their suit coats on their chairs at the end of the work day to make it seem that they hadn't left for the night – that they were somewhere in the building doing work – when in fact they had gone home" (DeLong 2011).
18. This section has been adapted from my article '*Cura Personalis* and Business Education for Sustainability' (Jackson 2012b).
19. I have elsewhere provided an extended analysis of this kind of linkage between economic and moral value. See Kevin Jackson (2004), *Building Reputational Capital*, New York, NY, USA: Oxford University Press.

REFERENCES

Aertsen, Jan (1996), *Medieval Philosophy and the Transcendentals: The Case of Thomas Aquinas*, New York, NY, USA: Brill.

Alfonso III, Fernando (2012), 'Most Americans Say Moral Values in Decline', *Huffington Post* (October 8, 2012).

Amilburu, María (1998), 'Understanding Human Nature: Examples from Philosophy and the Arts', Twentieth World Congress of Philosophy, Boston, MA (August 1998), retrieved from http://www.bu.edu/wcp/papers/anth/AnthAmil.htm (quoting S. Kierkegaard, *L'equilibrie de l'esthetique et de l'ethique dans la formation de la personalité*, p. 207).

de Bruyne, Edgar (1947), *L'esthétique du Moyen Age*, Louvain: Éditions del'Institut supérieur de philosophie.

DeLong, Thomas J. (2011), 'The Busyness Trap', May 26, 2011, retrieved from http://blogs.hbr.org/cs/2011/05/the_busyness_trap.html (accessed October 21, 2014).

Ebenstein, William and Alan Ebenstein (2000), *Great Political Thinkers: From Plato to the Present*, Harcourt Brace College Publishers.

Frankl, Viktor E. (2004), *Man's Search for Meaning*, London, UK: Rider.

Gallagher, Daniel (2006), 'The Platonic–Aristotelian Hybridity of Aquinas's Aesthetic Theory', *Hortulus*, **2**(1).

Grout, Donald Jay (1960), *A History of Western Music*, New York, NY, USA: W.W. Norton, p. 7.

Hängg, Christian (2011), 'Stockhausen at Ground Zero', 15 *Fillip* (Fall 2011), retrieved from http://fillip.ca/content/stockhausen-at-ground-zero (accessed November 11, 2014).

Happel, Stephen (1993), 'Metaphors and Time Asymmetry: Cosmologies and Christian Meanings', in Robert Russell, Nancey Murphy and C.J. Isham (eds), *Quantum Cosmology and the Laws of Nature: Scientific Perspectives on Divine Action*, Rome: Vatican Observatory Publications.

Jackson, Kevin T. (2012a), *Virtuosity in Business*, Philadelphia, PA, USA: University of Pennsylvania.

Jackson, Kevin T. (2012b), '*Cura Personalis* and Business Education for Sustainability', *Business and Professional Ethics Journal*, **31**(2), pp. 265–288.

Kreider, Tim (2012), 'The "Busy" Trap', *New York Times*, June 30, 2012.

Luther King Jr., Martin (1963), 'Letter From a Birmingham Jail', April 16, 1963, retrieved from http://www.sas.upenn.edu/African_Studies/Articles_Gen/Letter_Birmingham.html (accessed August 31, 2013).

Nussbaum, Martha C. (2000), *Women and Human Development: The Capabilities Approach*, Cambridge, UK: Cambridge University Press.

O'Connell, Robert (1978), *Art and the Christian Intelligence in St. Augustine*, Oxford, UK: Blackwell, p. 69.

Plato, *The Republic*, in Benjamin Jowett, trans. (1888), p. 88.

Pogge, Thomas (ed.) (2007), *Freedom from Poverty As a Human Right: Who Owes What to the Very Poor?*, Oxford, UK: Oxford University Press.

Scruton, Roger (2009), *Beauty*, New York, NY, USA: Oxford University Press.

Sen, Amartya (2009), *The Idea of Justice*, Cambridge, MA, USA: The Belknap Press of Harvard University Press.

Tolle, Eckhart (2004), *The Power of Now*, Vancouver, Canada: Namaste Publishing.

9. Ecological economics: a new paradigm ahead

Ove Jakobsen

> When the last tree has been cut down, the last fish caught, the last river poisoned, only then will we realize that one cannot eat money.
>
> Native American saying.

9.1 INTRODUCTION

We are living in complex and turbulent times – "with amazing scientific discoveries, technological inventions, industrial and commercial expansion, population increase, social transformations, new systems of transportation and communication, vast educational and research establishments, ventures into space" (Berry 2007, p. 57) – in other words a brilliant time. But there is another more destructive aspect – "mountains are ripped apart for the underlying coal and ore deposits; rivers are polluted with human and industrial waste, the air is saturated with toxic substances, the rain is turned to acid, the soil is sterile with chemicals, the higher forms of life is endangered, the great mammals have been killed off almost to the point of extinction, the tropical forests are being ruined, and many coral reefs are endangered beyond repair" (Berry 2007, p. 57).

These are the negative side effects following the modern industrial society and are to a large extent the unintended consequences of the mechanistic worldview. Merton warned against "unanticipated consequences of purposive social action" (Merton 1936, p. 894), and he differentiated between the consequences in the following categories: (a) consequences to the actor, (b) consequences to other persons mediated through (1) the social structure, (2) the culture and (3) the civilization (Merton 1936, p. 895). According to Merton we could, to a large extent, interpret the destructive aspects of modernity as unintended consequences of a society which is far from being in harmony with the natural and social conditions.

Soon the continuing ecological losses may well begin to stress both the economic and social systems. As ecosystems become more degraded the greater is the risk that these systems will be pushed over the edge. According to Lindner; "We ... live in historically unprecedented times of risk, but also in historically unprecedented times of opportunity" (Lindner 2012, p. xxv).

9.2 FOCUS ON SYMPTOMS

If we try to solve these serious challenges by no more than a one-sided treatment of the most visible symptoms, a number of paradoxes could well be the consequence. For example initiatives to stimulate economic growth have been recommended to solve the financial crisis, while we know that continued growth in the economy will only serve to worsen the environmental problems. When the rich countries use billions of dollars to stimulate growth in production and consumption, the result widens the gap between rich and poor, in both the national and global perspectives. Growth in production and consumption in the rich countries often leads to reduced resource efficiency, the life cycle of products becomes shorter, the distance between production and consumption increases, and the amounts of waste grow dramatically. Our tendency to overexploit resources is currently reinforced not only by powerful technologies, but also by cultural norms, particularly those associated with the paradigm of economic growth which is, currently, globally dominant.

We don't talk to each other and this lack of interdisciplinary communication is a serious threat to the understanding of how the different symptoms hang together. Specialized fields of science have tended to focus on the different symptoms. Each specialty and each subject is increasingly isolated, partly as a result of its own specialized vocabulary of terms and expressions that are unintelligible to outsiders. Some would say this is a verbal electric fence set and designed to keep outsiders out but however we look at it the problem is the same: it is difficult to communicate across disciplinary boundaries. Into the vacuum comes abstract, specialized knowledge which sets aside general and practical insights. Alfred North Whitehead (1978), the English philosopher, warned nearly 100 years ago against what he called "the fallacy of misplaced concreteness." Whitehead believed that we tend to forget that theories and models are abstract representations of reality. Even more illusory is our insistence on equating between abstract knowledge and reality.

9.3 RADICAL CHANGES

When we look at the future through the lens of neo-classical economic theory, which focuses on nothing more than short-term profit maximization, the time horizon is too short and the perspective too narrow to contain the complex phenomena which include the relationships between ecological sustainability, social welfare and individual quality of life.

Evolution, both biological and cultural, has been characterized by slow development over long periods of time, followed by sudden revolutionary leaps of profound change. Scientific development is, according to the philosopher Thomas Kuhn (1962), characterized by revolutionary paradigm shifts. Kuhn argued that fundamental changes occurred only when the established explanations do not make the cut for solving society's challenges. Problems that could not be solved within the established paradigm were called anomalies. If the anomalies increase in number and severity science goes into a phase of crisis, which allows for a paradigm shift. This presupposes that an alternative paradigm, able to deal with the anomalies, is developed.

Multiple crises – financial, economic, food, energy – have caused governments and other bodies to look more critically at systematic and structural issues related to national and global economies. Since several crises converge to reach their maximum level of tension simultaneously we can conclude, in accordance with Max-Neef, that this is "a crisis for humanity" (Max-Neef 2010, p. 200). To solve the most urgent problems economic theory and practice has to go through radical changes. Both the financial crises, poverty crises and the climate crises remind us of the gravity of the problems. Most alternative measures of human well-being (alternative to the conventional measure of money flows as reflected in GDP) show that; "quality of life in the industrialized world peaked in the mid-1970s and has been going downhill ever since" (Dawson 2006, p. 12). In the same period GDP has continued to climb. According to Daly the consequences of this development are that, in addition to a loss of well-being, we also face a "possible ecological catastrophe" (Daly 2007, p. 14).

9.4 UNECONOMIC GROWTH

Daly (2007) believes most developed countries are now in a period of uneconomic growth, in which further growth in market economic activity is actually leading to a reduction in well-being instead of enhancing it. There is a period in which economic growth does contribute to improvement of well-being, but only up to the threshold point, beyond which, if there is more economic growth, well-being will begin to deteriorate. In a poor country that has not yet reached the threshold point, it is legitimate to point out that to overcome poverty economic growth is necessary. After the threshold the economy has reached a point in which the costs of growth outweigh the benefits.

Daly asks: "How can we fight poverty without growth?" He comes up with the following answer: "We might have to share!" (Daly 2007, p. 10). His answer is different from the message in the report from the World Commission on Environment and Development (WCED) which said that the best solution to the problems was to initiate "more rapid economic growth in both industrialized and developing countries" (Brundtland Report, WCED 1987, p. 89). To sum up, growth in the use of natural resources must give way to the "steady-state-economy", competition must be replaced by cooperation, generosity in sharing limited resources must be introduced to the economy to replace the principle of egocentric maximization of utility and profits. Development of quality of life must be more important than quantitative growth in GNP (Capra and Henderson 2009).

If we accept that the current environmental and social challenges cannot be solved by and within established economic theory and practice the way is clear for new and creative groundbreaking solutions. Since problem solving goes on at the meeting point between past and future, it is necessary to address the challenges with a thorough understanding of the social and economic developments up to the present day. In addition, it is essential to have realistic long-term visions for the future. To identify and address the major challenges, it is important that new ideas are rooted in individual and collective experience. It is neither desirable nor possible to force solutions that do not have a basis in human intuition, feelings and thoughts. Overwhelmed by, "the sheer quantity, complexity and brilliance of scientific knowledge, the interaction between our whole culture and the natural world, has become increasingly ignorant and insensitive" (Naydler 2009, p. 16). Here, then, is an aspect of the relationship between science and the contemporary ecological crisis which, despite being critical, is often overlooked.

9.5   REAL ECONOMY

Improved technology alone has found it difficult to reduce CO_2 emissions. Additional measures are required to address the climate crisis but these are difficult to implement without the radical switch from growth to de-growth economy. This same reasoning applies to the problems arising from the global financial and debt crisis. According to Benedicter (2011), it is impossible to restore the established system through legal and ethical adjustments alone. We need to develop new solutions based on a change from a competitive to a cooperative economy, based on an ongoing dialogue between all concerned stakeholders. A new balance between the real and financial economies is our goal.

According to Daly, banks in recent decades were "engines creating money out of nothing. ... They extended credit, bought stocks on the margin, and dealt in derivatives – a fancy name for betting with unregulated, multiplying insurance policies" (Stuckey 2009). Because of the dramatic explosion of assets produced, the illusion arose that wealth was increasing. But the wealth existed only on paper. Domination by the financial economy today is so big that; "the term anomaly may be appropriate – an infirmity phenomenon in society" (Berglund 2007, p. 140). Liquid assets within the financial economy are invested in stocks, bonds and currencies. What creates the anomaly is that the assets are only to a limited extent channeled back into the real economy. Following this line of reasoning the disproportionate relationship between the real economy and the financial economy explains some of the necessary conditions behind the financial crisis.

9.6 GREEN ECONOMY

To handle the challenges of our time, I have argued that there has to be a change both in economic theory and practice. How deep this change will need to be could be illustrated by drawing a demarcation line between "green economics" and "ecological economics". As a starting point we must accept that both perspectives are based upon a serious willingness to solve the environmental and social problems embedded in mainstream economics. Green economics by introducing changes based more or less on the same tool kit as used in mainstream economics and ecological economics by revising the ontological, epistemological and methodo-logical preconditions for economics.

As a tool in elaborating these questions I distinguish between different interpretations of economic growth along the variables "green economy" and "ecological economics" versus "short term" and "long term" action plans. To solve economic and environmental problems representatives for green economy accept that in a short term perspective increased growth has the highest priority. In a longer term perspective they argue that the growth should be as green as possible. For ecological economists growth is not part of the solution; indeed, on the contrary, growth is the core problem. In the short term it is necessary to move towards a de-growth economy. In the long term the focus has to turn towards qualitative development (Table 9.1).

Table 9.1   Different interpretations of growth

	Green economy	Ecological economic
Short term perspective	Economic growth	De-growth
Long term perspective	Green growth	Qualitative development

Arguments indicating that environmental responsibility is based on (green) growth are often found in the literature. To solve the problems we must have more resources to spend on the different enterprises. Greening the economical practice could be an efficient marketing tool to develop a good environmental reputation that is necessary to increase the company's competitive advantage and its profits. Economic internalization (Hopfenbeck 1992) could be one possible step in the process of greening the economy. When environmental and social costs connected to business activities are quantified and measured in the firm's accounting systems the problems connected to externalizing environmental damage are reduced. The idea is: by making the environment into a costly commodity business will be given an economic incentive to design environmentally friendly products, procedures and uses of resources. Following the same line of reasoning green taxes, laws and regulations are relevant tools.

Ecological economics accepts that because the traditional mechanical and linear way of thinking is limited, our problem solving often brings about unintended and undesirable effects. Financial and climate crises are examples of such unintended consequences. Holistic thinking, including adaptability, flexibility, learning, self-organization and cooperation are central in ecological economics. Ecological internalization implies that environmental and social responsibility are integral and integrated parts of business management. Creativity and divergent thinking are essential within ecological economics because it is more important to discover new questions than to find new answers to the old questions.

In accordance with this line of argument Max-Neef asserted; "it is no longer acceptable that Universities still teach economic theories of the nineteenth century in order to tackle twenty first century problems"

(Max-Neef 2010, p. 200). There seems to be a conflict between the physical impossible (continual growth) and the political impossible (limiting growth) (Daly 2007, p. 10). But the ecologic and economic crises we are facing in the beginning of the twenty-first century provide the most exciting opportunity for change. It is generally accepted that to break established habits we must see the benefits of the change *and* the cost of following the old track. Now, when we can clearly see the downside of the system we have been using, this is the moment to change our habits, our accounting, and our tired old assumptions about what the Earth can sustain. It's time to rein in our air money balloons and get our feet firmly planted on the real ground.

9.7 ECOLOGICAL ECONOMICS

Ecological economics is a field of economics that could bring the economic and ecological crisis down to Earth. Policies introduced in the next few years will make all the difference. Three questions of special importance arise and have to be addressed.

First, production and consumption must be sustainable in the long run. Economic growth, as both a "God" and an end in itself, is based upon the questionable assumption; "there are no limits to the planet's ability to sustain it" (Pearce 2001, p. 7). Instead sustainability implies recognition of the fact that natural and social capital are not infinitely substitutable by built and human capital, and that; "there are real biophysical limits to the expansion of the market economy" (Costanza 2008, p. 33). Hence, a sustainable economy must at some point stop growing, but it need not stop developing. In other words, there is no necessary connection between development and growth, and, conceivably, there could be development without growth (Georgescu-Roegen 1975).

Second, the distribution of resources and wealth must be fair. Fairness implies recognition that the distribution of wealth is an important determinant of social capital and quality of life (Costanza 2008, p. 33). We must move from an economy oriented toward the satisfaction of the wants of the rich part of the world, to an economy committed to satisfy the basic needs of all human beings. Instead of focusing on economic growth and increasing profits the global economy must include (possibly for the first time) moral considerations and equity.

Third, the allocation of resources must be efficient. Real economic efficiency implies the inclusion of all resources that affect sustainable human well-being in the system of allocation, not just goods and services being on the market. "Our current market allocation system excludes most non-marketed natural and social capital assets and services, which are huge contributors to human well-being" (Costanza 2008, p. 34).

Boulding introduced the metaphor "Spaceship economy" to illustrate the conclusion that the only way "man can survive is by recycling earth's resources after use instead of continuing to exhaust its mines and pollute its reservoirs" (Kerman 1974, p. 14). And we must remember that there are no passengers on the spaceship, only crew, in other words we are all co-responsible.

9.8 CONCLUDING REMARKS

According to Eisenstein the present convergence of crises, "in money, energy, education, health, water, soil, climate, politics, the environment, and more – is a birth crisis, expelling us from the old world into a new" (Eisenstein 2011, p. xx). Lindner (2012) describes how destructive competition must not be chosen at the expense of life-enhancing cooperation. Instead of firing the engine of capitalism and wealth creation by prioritizing selfishness, individualism and narcissism, the ability to say yes to love, kindness, generosity, sympathy and empathy alleviates the birth woes for a new world.

Boulding argued that "economics has rested too long in an essentially Newtonian paradigm of mechanical equilibrium and mechanical dynamics" (Boulding 1981, p. 17), a reasonable conclusion is that our current environmental and societal dilemmas are due, in part, to a much distorted perception of reality. According to Rees; "Modern economic society operates from an outdated mechanistic perception of the natural dynamics of the Earth" (Fabel and St. John 2007, p. 104).

Pearce goes a step further and argues that the failure to address metaphysical questions has led to many of the central errors of conventional economics. Therefore, economics needs an internal metaphysical critique. Instead of focusing on physics, quantitative measures and products economists should discuss metaphysics, qualitative values, and processes (Pearce 2001). In my opinion the critique from Pearce is both valid and relevant for understanding the negative symptoms following mainstream economy; in addition the critique is an argument for the need of ecological economics.

REFERENCES

Benedicter, R. (2011), *Social Banking and Social Finance: Answers to the Economic Crisis*, Dordrecht, Netherlands: Springer.

Berglund, S. (2007), 'The Function of Banks in the Economy', in S. Ingebrigtsen and O. Jakobsen (eds), *Circulation Economics – Theory and Practice*, Oxford, UK: Peter Lang.

Berry, T. (2007), 'The New Story – Comments on the Origin, Identification, and the Transformation of Values', in Arthur Fabel and Donald St. John (eds), *Teilhard in the 21st Century – The Emerging Spirit of Earth*, New York, NY, USA: Orbis Books.

Boulding, K. (1981), *Evolutionary Economics*, London, UK: Sage Publications.

Brundtland Report (1987), *Our Common Future*, WCED, Oxford, UK: Oxford University Press.

Capra, F. and H. Henderson (2009), 'Qualitative Growth', *Tomorrow's Company*, England/Wales, UK: The Institute of Chartered Accounts.

Costanza, R. (2008), 'Stewardship for a "Full" World', *Current History*, January.

Daly, H.E. (2007), *Ecological Economics and Sustainable Development*, Cheltenham, UK and Northampton, MA, USA: Edward Elgar Publishing.

Dawson, J. (2006), *Ecovillages – New Frontiers for Sustainability*, Dartington, UK: Green Books.

Eisenstein, C. (2011), *Sacred Economics – Money, Gift and Society in the Age of Transition*, Berkley, CA, USA: Evolver Editions.

Fabel, A. and D. St. John (2007), *Teilhard in the 21st Century – The Emerging Spirit of Earth*, New York, NY, USA: Orbis Books.

Georgescu-Roegen, N. (1975), 'Energy and Economic Myths', *Southern Economic Journal*, **41** (3).

Hopfenbeck, W. (1992), *The Green Management Revolution – Lessons in Environmental Excellence*, New York, NY: Prentice Hall.

Kerman, C.E. (1974), *Creative Tension: Life and Thought of Kenneth Boulding*, Ann Arbor, MI: University of Michigan Press.

Kuhn, T. (1962), *The Structure of Scientific Revolutions*, Chicago, IL, USA: The University of Chicago Press.

Lindner, E. (2012), *A Dignity Economy – Creating an Economy that Serves Human Dignity and Preserves Our Planet*, Lake Oswego, OR, USA: Dignity Press.

Max-Neef, M. (2010), 'The World on a Collision Course and the need for a New Economy', *Journal of the Human Environment*, **39** (3), pp. 200–210.

Merton, R.K. (1936), 'The Unanticipated Consequences of Purposive Social Action', *American Sociological Review*, **1** (6), pp. 894–904.

Naydler, J. (2009), *Goethe on Science – An Anthology of Goethe's Scientific Writings*, Edinburgh, Scotland: Floris Books.

Pearce, J. (2001), *Small is Still Beautiful*, London, UK: Harper Collins Publishers.

Stuckey, P. (2009), 'Air Money – or Bringing the Financial Crisis down to Earth', *This Lively Earth*, retrieved from http://thislivelyearth.com/2009/03/10/air-money (accessed March 10, 2009).

Whitehead, A.N. (1978), *Process and Reality*, Corrected edition by D. Ray Griffin and D. Sherburne (eds), New York, NY, USA: The Free Press.

PART III

From compliance and enforcement to
autonomy and responsibility

10. Personal responsibility for the greater good

Knut J. Ims and Lars Jacob Tynes Pedersen

10.1 INTRODUCTION

This chapter deals with the phenomenon of personal responsibility in organizational life. Specifically, we aim to shed light on the process by which individuals in organizations arrive at radical acts of personal responsibility despite inflicting considerable costs on themselves (and potentially on others). Thus, we investigate a particular variety of personally responsible behavior – acts that are characterized by autonomous, value-driven choice. The chapter relates personal responsibility to moral concerns for the broader implications of organizational action. As such, we address the relationship between personal responsibility and conceptions of the greater good. In doing so, we explore the nature of personal responsibility, and in particular, how the individual translates one's moral values into action.

The chapter builds on previous work by Ims and Pedersen (2013; Ims 2006), who discussed strategies of personally responsible behavior in organizations. Depending on the circumstances, Ims and Pedersen (2013) argue, different strategies can be considered as instances of personal responsibility. Voicing concerns to managers or colleagues when it may be personally costly to do so, exiting the organization, or staying in loyalty to the organization while attempting to change its practices from the inside, can all constitute responsible acts depending on the situation (cf. Hirschman 1970). In this chapter, we investigate the case of *exiting the organization as responsible action* by providing an in-depth analysis of a top manager's choice to resign from an organization for ethical reasons.

Our empirical setting is the case of Inge Wallage, who used the *exit strategy* in order to take personal responsibility. Wallage left her former position as vice president of communications in the Norwegian oil company Statoil, and instead chose to take on the role as communications director of Greenpeace. She later also left Greenpeace in order to join the non-profit IWA (International Water Association). We discuss Wallage's decision to take personal responsibility by leaving Statoil, as well as how her decision relates to her conceptions of a greater good. The empirical analysis builds both on several personal interviews with the case subject – both in person and via email – as well as with various sources of secondary data. In addition to the Wallage case, we also draw on some published accounts of people who spoke out about wrongdoings in their workplace. Thereby, we also shed light on some similarities and differences between exit and voice as strategies for personally responsible action (cf. Hirschman 1970).

We structure the remainder of the chapter as follows. First, we explore the concept of personal responsibility and its relation to role-mediated responsibility and common morality. Therein, we discuss the nature and scope of personal responsibility. Second, we investigate the case of leaving the organization as an example of acting personally responsibly. Thereby, we discuss how acting personally responsibly may relate to promoting or protecting the common good.

10.2 PERSONAL RESPONSIBILITY

What does personal responsibility entail? In an important sense, personal responsibility is about the individual's realization of his or her own beliefs and values in action (cf. Ims 2006). This can refer both to how the individual responds and acts to situations as they occur and to how the individual over a longer time acts in order to live in a manner he or she can justify. Moreover, personal responsibility is crucially about reflecting on the limits of role-mediated behavior. This means that in an organizational context, personal responsibility deals with (1) the individual's attempt to exercise professional roles in a manner that is consistent with values that are important for him or her, and (2) the individual's concern for the broader implications of his organizational acts, that is, how these acts promote or undermine the greater good. In order for responsible action in organizations to mean something more than simple obedience, it must be based on a certain *sense of responsibility*. That is, the individual actively reflects on, and takes seriously, the degree to which a given action transgresses a relevant norm or implies unacceptable consequences (Bovens 1998; Zsolnai 2008).

As proposed by Ims (2006), it is useful to distinguish between role-mediated responsibility, common morality and personal responsibility (see Figure 10.1). The individual's *role-mediated responsibility* refers to the responsibilities assumed by the individual when taking on a given role in the organization. These responsibilities are professional responsibilities, and they give allowances and limitations to the individual. For instance, a doctor *is allowed* to conduct medical examinations of patients and prescribe medications due to his or her role as a doctor, but the role also *limits* what are acceptable actions for the doctor, such as entering a romantic relationship with a patient. Hence, the role determines which types of behavior are acceptable and unacceptable and it places a set of responsibilities on the individual who takes on the role. Taking on the role thus implies accepting these responsibilities.

Second, the individual is bound by the *common morality* of her community or society. Communities have moral values and corresponding moral obligations that are relatively widely shared, and the individual is partially bound by these values and obligations. There is an interesting tension between common morality and professional responsibilities, as the ethical standards of professional groups may sometimes differ from those that are reflected in common morality. Common morality is constantly evolving through dialogue between members of the community and because of societal changes, and as professional roles change, they may also influence common morality.

Finally, the individual has a *personal responsibility* that is independent of the individual's roles and of her being part of a given community. This personal responsibility relates to the individual's role-mediated responsibilities, in the sense that the individual's willingness to take on and to perform according to the expectations to a professional role, depends on the degree to which the role is compatible with his or her personal morality. The question is which types of behavior the individual is willing to engage in as the performer of various roles.

The personal responsibility of the individual is also in tension with both common morality and role-mediated moralities. The individual's morality in part adheres to the community's moral tradition and sometimes implies making radical value choices that can conflict with that tradition (cf. Kekes 1991). In a similar way, the individual's personal values are in tension with the values that are reflected in his or her professional role. Any mismatch between these two sets of values necessitates a critical reflection on these value conflicts and a prioritization between them in choice and action. Thus, personal responsibility relates to one's own norm-horizon as well as to shared norm-horizons.

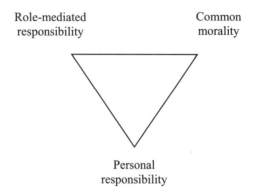

Source: Ims (2006).

Figure 10.1 The triangle of responsibility

From a psychological point of view, we consider a type of personally responsible action that can be considered as *self-determined behavior*. It is intrinsically driven because it relates to issues relevant to the individual's conscience or, more broadly, has implications for his or her life project (see Williams 1981). Williams writes that a ground project is one or several projects that are closely related to one's existence and which to a significant degree gives a meaning to one's life (Williams 1981, p. 12). The idea of a person's ground project provides "the motive force that propels him into the future, and gives him a reason for living" (p. 13).

We may assume that there may be a struggle between a person's internal world and the objective external world. Emphasizing the internal subjective world, we may localize responsibility in "Man the maker" (actor/agent). In the internal world, we perceive, interpret and judge what is going on in the objective world around us. Distinguishing between the internal world (life-world) and public world, we may see it as a bipolar concept, each pole named "Man the Maker" and "Man the Answerer", respectively (Niebuhr 1999; Harmon 1995; Ims 2006; see Table 10.1). Thus, we imagine a *dialectic between moral authorship and accountability*.

As human beings, we have an internal world within which ethical reflection can take place. The human freedom is the capacity to mentally withdraw and having freedom implies responsibility. One's ethic is social in meaning and in context, but personal in judgment and action. According to Kierkegaard, there are no genuine tests in morality, and our moral standards can only be chosen. The authority is that a person has

Table 10.1   A dialectic between moral authorship and accountability

Man the Maker	Man the Answerer
Internal world	External world
Subjective	Objective
Feelings	Rationalistic thinking
Can do	Must do
Self-reflection/authenticity	Self-deception/inauthenticity

chosen to utter his morality ("the subjectivity is the truth"). Rational arguments can do no more than to present us with alternatives. In any chain of reason, we finally reach a point where we have *to choose* to take a stand. Personal responsibility as construed in this chapter involves moving beyond narrow accountability and viewing one's actions in a horizon of a greater good.

10.3   THE CASE OF INGE WALLAGE: PERSONALLY RESPONSIBLE ACTION IN ORGANIZATIONAL LIFE[1]

In 2006, the Norwegian oil company StatoilHydro (hereafter referred to as Statoil, which is the company's current name) hired Inge Wallage. In the end of 2008, she was the company's Vice President of International Communications, at which point she made a radical and surprising decision. In her two years working with communications in Statoil, Wallage had spent a large part of her time justifying and defending Statoil's controversial oil sands venture in Canada and had grown increasingly uncomfortable with this task. Even though she had a powerful and prestigious position within a major oil company, Wallage decided to resign from her position in Statoil and instead start working for Greenpeace – a main antagonist to Statoil in the oil sands venture.

The reactions to Wallage's decision were varied. Statoil demanded that she should leave her post immediately. Former Statoil executives questioned her direct transfer to "the enemy", while business professors hailed Greenpeace's new recruit as a strategic coup (Andreassen 2009). Wallage explained her decision in an interview, wherein she stated that she wanted to be able to look back at her life and say that she had contributed to making the world a better place. Moreover, she asserted:

"We only have one planet, and we have to treat the globe with respect" (Kongsnes 2009, p. 6). She emphasized that she had entered her role in Statoil in order to contribute to a sustainable development in the company's operations, but that she had failed to do so. Finally, she explained her choice with reference to her responsibility towards her children, and said: "I hope that my children will grow up able to live on a planet that is still intact and that I have contributed to this through my work life" (Kongsnes 2009, p. 7).

According to Wallage, there were a couple of triggering events behind her remarkable change in employment. First, Wallage was contacted by a recruiter who was wondering if she was interested in being hired by Greenpeace International. It would mean that her salary would go down 60 percent compared with her salary in Statoil. This served as an opening for a new career, however, with a considerable decrease in wages. Second, Wallage recalls having the "feeling of being 'the odd one out' inside of Statoil" and this feeling "grew continuously". She felt that in Statoil they tried "to make [her] more and more Norwegian", even when she was hired for her international expertise and experience. Third, Wallage recalls, "[i]t was hard for me that my colleagues were treating Mother Earth as something that is not alive and other parts of the world as 'undeveloped' areas that were waiting for the 'Norwegian model', as if their societies did not have their own values that we should respect ... the lack of openness for different – non Norwegian – views was hard for me to swallow". Moreover, Wallage had grown tired of commuting. She was working in Norway during the week, with her family based in Amsterdam. "My children were turning into young teenagers and I needed to be home more. My son was quite outspoken about this. 'When will you come home and work in Amsterdam, mummy?'"

As this overview shows, the picture painted by Wallage is one of complex motivations, which included moral, cultural, practical and identity issues. Reflecting back on those events, Wallage emphasizes that the recruiter from Greenpeace arrived at the right time in her life. She had tried to get a job at Greenpeace in 2003, but was unsuccessful due to her lacking experience with NGOs and civil society organizations.

Was Wallage in doubt of whether her choice was the right one? Did she consider alternative options?

> "As soon as I was really with Greenpeace, I knew it was the right choice. I felt home very soon. I felt home in a way I had never experienced in my corporate years, not with any company I had been with. I could be myself, use my professional experience, but allowing for my gut to contribute too", Wallage said. She admits to have been "quite wary once I had taken the

decision to 'sign on the dotted line' of the Greenpeace employment contract, as I knew I was changing worlds ... I realized that it is pretty hard to move from the corporate world to the NGO world. ... I knew this was my chance and I better grab it. ... I could always go back to the corporate world."

Wallage further admits that even if Greenpeace would not have worked out for her, she would have wanted to leave Statoil. And resigning was not something she considered as radical. She had resigned "quite a few times before, moving from one company to the next".

An important question with regard to Wallage's strategy is why she did not deliberate on other action alternatives within Statoil as a responsible choice. Wallage's perception is that she "might have considered staying if I could really have been part of contributing to the new business area of green energy/renewable. The problem with all traditional energy companies, not just for Statoil, is that exploration and production is their main business".

Wallage had tried and rejected other action alternatives that were compatible with her fundamental objective of contributing to a sustainable future. Her ethical action was grounded in a deep sense of personal responsibility towards stakeholders like her children, nature and future generations, and more generally for contributing to a sustainable future. The change of jobs would enable her to engage in work that was consistent with the values to which she felt a profound obligation.

Wallage further elaborated on what personal responsibility means for her. According to Wallage:

[E]veryone in this world has a responsibility to live and act in a way that does not harm others. That is the bare minimum. To me it means that I need to have done as much as I can to make this world a better place. I don't understand how people can look into the mirror and live with themselves knowing that what they do is not really good.

Moreover, she added: "[t]he impact – environmental, but also social – to some of the (oil) exploitation that is happening through/around the business of exploration and production of oil and gas is incredible. ... We (the world) are out of balance completely. The world cannot handle this anymore, the rising temperatures should tell it all. ... Because there is not enough resources, we need to share and come up with new solutions."

Wallage wonders why people in the world of business apparently do not feel the urgency like it is felt in civil society – that the world needs to be "changed in order to be environmentally and socially fair". Wallage concludes that she feels "an ever-increasing sense of responsibility to work hard to find different ways to get people on the journey for a sustainable world. ... I feel a responsibility to the future generations, to reference the Native American proverb 'we don't inherit the Earth for our ancestors, we borrow it from our children'."

When asked about her decision to leave Greenpeace after a few years and start working for IWA, Wallage offered the following explanation:

> [T]here were a variety of factors that played a role in my decision, one that I did not take lightly as I had so enjoyed my time and contribution to Greenpeace and its vision/mission. However, it became clear that after 4.5 years my time as a change agent had come to an end. ... In addition, Greenpeace was going through changes, a reorganization and decentralization with more power to the national and regional offices and with its "centre/ headquarters" (which is where I worked) becoming much smaller. Even though I agreed with the overall approach, I did not agree with the diminishing role of the global communications function at the central HQ or at the most senior level. This was not in line with what I express overall (at communications conferences and such). And though I would have been happy to stay at Greenpeace longer, I wanted the choice to stay to be a positive one.

Wallage also clearly expressed that there was an attraction to the work IWA offered:

> The fact that I joined the IWA was for a variety of reasons: first of all, I wanted to continue my quest to contribute to a better world. Secondly, I found working for water extremely meaningful. ... And lastly, the Executive Director had clearly indicated that I would not only join as the Communications and Engagement Director, but as a management team member who would work on the overall IWA strategy and implementation.

So were there relevant similarities or differences between the choice of leaving Statoil and the choice of leaving Greenpeace? Wallage elaborates:

> The similarity of leaving Greenpeace was that I was into something new. However, it is much easier to think of the difference of leaving Statoil and joining Greenpeace. Leaving Statoil and joining Greenpeace was a personal "Great Transition" for me in joining the quest to actively contribute to a sustainable world. However much Statoil and its employees like to think they do so too, not in the way one does when working in civil society. Furthermore, Statoil is engaged in activities that cannot be part of a sustainable world. I could no longer be part of that; I had to change/leave. Hence, joining Greenpeace meant actively working to change the world for the better and try to end wrong practices. The choice of leaving Greenpeace and joining the IWA was, therefore, a continuation of the quest to contribute to a better world.

10.4 DISCUSSION: PERSONAL RESPONSIBILITY AND THE GREATER GOOD

In this section, we discuss Wallage's account of her choices in light of the notion of a personal sense of responsibility. One way to understand Wallage's choices is through the lens of Taylor's (1989) concept of strong evaluations. Taylor explored the background of our moral and spiritual intuitions. He coined the term strong evaluations, which refers to evaluations that are closely connected to a person's identity. One might say that they are related to the question "what kind of person do I want to be?" Strong evaluations are the second order assessments of our first order desires and preferences. That is, our strong evaluations reflect our moral horizon and the manner in which we assess our desires and preferences from a moral point of view; thus changing our behavior in ways that are more in line with our desired identity. The contrast to strong evaluations are so-called weak evaluations, which refer to following our immediate desires and preferences. By doing so, argues Taylor, we may easily end up not fulfilling our life. Strong evaluations are thus central to the realization of moral values that we hold to be important.

What is Wallage's moral framework or moral horizon? She points to the values of respecting mother earth and future generations and thereby ensuring a sustainable future. Taylor (1989) describes three axes relating to our strong evaluations: respect, fulfilment and dignity. Taylor argues that there are differences even within given cultures with regard to how respect, fulfilment and dignity are understood and acted upon. We believe that all the three axes are relevant in the case of Wallage. With regard to the first axis, respect for ecology and nature is at stake in how Wallage sees her practice and her choices. However, the second axis – fulfilment – is perhaps the most relevant in her case. A number of questions may be asked with regard to what constitutes a fulfilled (as opposed to a meaningless) life. When Wallage decided to leave her prestigious position in Statoil and get a position in Greenpeace, she knew that this would mean a considerable cost for her personally. Some doors would be closed for her in the future – not only in Statoil, but perhaps even in big corporations in general. How can a director in a big oil corporation who chooses to move directly to the big enemy be trusted'?

In Taylor's (1989) sense, persons have an orientation towards the good, and this is central to our identities. Persons define themselves by reference to where they stand with respect to their orientation to this good. The identity of the individual serves as a frame of reference that provides a horizon of meaning. This moral space defines what is good or bad, what is worth doing and what is not (Taylor 1989, pp. 25–32). Asking questions within this framework about what is good helps us understand who we are. The articulation of this framework is never complete, and can rather be seen as continuous work-in-progress. According to Taylor (1989, p. 42), one of the most basic aspirations of human beings is the need to be connected to what we see as good and what is of fundamental value. What kind of life is worth living and what would be a meaningful life?

In a Taylorian sense, we may ask: What are Wallage's strong evaluations? Did she search for a life of unity or purpose? What kind of life does she consider as worth living? When Wallage points to the fundamental value of ecological sustainability, it is clear that she is not reducing her moral motivation to strive for only one good: pleasure and happiness in a shallow sense (Taylor 1989, p. 332). This shallow kind of happiness makes all human desires equally worthy of consideration and thus eliminates "strong evaluations". Wallage's actions are not reducible to pleasure-seeking. To the contrary, she makes choices that may hinder future career opportunities and that lead to direct and significant personal and social costs as she criticizes and exits her former employer. In doing so, she is able to act in accordance with her standards for what constitutes a justifiable work life.

Reflexivity is central to our moral understanding and the danger is to think of ourselves as the center of the world (Taylor 1989, pp. 138–139). We can only see ourselves properly if we see ourselves in relation to some standard. However, in the modern world it is problematic to determine what constitutes this standard and this horizon. Nietzsche coined the term "God is dead" to wipe away the whole horizon. In this context, Augustine is the moral philosopher *par excellence*, who opens up the inward space and engages in radical reflexivity. Augustine accentuates the conflict between one's knowledge about the good, the immediate desires and the will. The will is not simply dependent on knowledge. This is the space of "moral choice", and a main problem is the phenomenon of weakness of the will – "akrasia".

The problem is how to create a meaningful life in harmony with one's desires? In Wallage's case, it may be more meaningful to apply Aristotle's concept of happiness as "eudaimonia". The main content in the Aristotelian concept of eudaimonia is that it is based on activity and the judgment of a whole life. It is a teleological concept viewing human life as consisting in the pursuit of ends. While individual actions and projects may be judged as being virtuous or not, a single good action is not enough to evaluate a man's goodness. A complete life requires virtuous activities, and in such a view, pleasure cannot be the sole purpose of man.

Pleasure that accompanies virtuous activities may be seen as "added perfection – like the bloom of youth to hose in their prime" (Aristotle 1935/51, p. 259).

Wallage is able to remain independent of the opinions of her colleagues and openly protest against the exploitation of oil sands in Canada. What is at stake? Wallage was concerned about being an instrument for activities that she saw as destructive. She was concerned that the requirements of her role were incompatible with her personal sense of responsibility as well as the moral standards of significant others – primary among them her children. According to Vetlesen (2004), we can fear being transformed into mere means when we make efforts to adapt to the ever-increasing demand for growth and change. Sennett (1998) writes about the "corrosion of character" and also points to how the modern workplace and society may easily make us into "flexible instruments". This may lead to the dissolution of the vitality of the self, and make us into commodities. "The attitude to the self in such a situation is one of ruthless exploitation" (Vetlesen 2004, pp. 138–139).

Wallage seems to have a clear ground project in Bernard Williams' (1981) sense. She repeatedly emphasizes the importance to take responsibility for Mother Earth. This appears to be closely related to her existence, and gives her a reason for living. The choice of Greenpeace as an employer for Wallage is not accidental. She had actively attempted to join Greenpeace earlier and her wish to join had been strong for years. However, Wallage admits that even without the possibility of a position in Greenpeace, she would have left Statoil. Her life project could not be reconciled with Statoil's conventional exploration and production of fossil energy, and her choice allowed her to reconcile her own standards with those of a new employer. The decisive moment in the long process of leaving Statoil for Greenpeace was perhaps Wallage's walk in a park in Amsterdam. She tells: "It was as a sudden revelation. I cannot stay with Statoil any longer. I have to do something else with my life". This was a moment of awakening for Wallage.

An interesting comparison can be made to Emma O'Reilly's (2014) story, which is about organizational voice – an alternative approach to responsible action (Hirschman 1970; see also Ims and Pedersen 2013). O'Reilly revealed the inside story of being the person closest to Lance Armstrong in his early cycling career. In the meantime, Emma learned about several young cyclists who died due to doping, "senseless, tragic deaths of talented riders". She had experienced the doping culture from the inside and in 2001 she chose to speak out to a journalist.

O'Reilly claimed that her aim was to clean up the sport. However to confront the world's most winning cyclist Lance Armstrong for systematically doping, Emma had to pay her price. She was attacked for her allegations by Armstrong's lawyers, and she revealed that blowing the whistle had made her feel disloyal to her former colleagues and in particular to Armstrong himself. She thus felt that she deserved everything she got, including harassment and being sued for her disloyalty. According to O'Reilly (2014, p. 194), "[t]his time, along with the numbness came a new, overpowering emotion that ate away deep inside. Guilt." As in the case of Wallage, both prior to and after the choice, there were strong emotions accompanying her reflections of the situation and what was at stake.

What was O'Reilly's moral horizon? She was "brought up to tell the truth, that lying was a sin", and said that "[f]or years I had felt guilty ... I even doubted the values I'd been brought up to believe in: a sense of honesty at all costs" (O'Reilly 2014, pp. 276–277). However, our interpretation of Emma's whistleblowing is that it is not the truth as such, but rather the people involved, that ultimately are at stake. Primarily, Emma seems to consider the fate of the young riders who die because of doping. In fact, Emma stands in a web of human relationships that she has to manage and protect.

Wallage also told about feelings of guilt. In her case, it is not so clear from where this feeling of guilt came. In this context, we can perhaps interpret Wallage's guilt as a deep inner voice that spoke to her – stemming from deep moral sources that place a demand on us when we do not live up to our own standards. In Wallage's case, there was a considerable discrepancy between her ideals and the feeling of being complicit in destructive oil sands extraction in Canada. According to Taylor (1989), we all have a demand laid upon us from our deep inner sources. We may think of this as a kind of moral intuition. We feel the demand like a burden when we violate moral standards. A similar phenomenon is coined "the ethical demand" by the Danish philosopher Knud Løgstrup (1956/91). It emerges from the spontaneous life utterances of human beings – like trust, openness, and compassion.

Earlier in the chapter, we introduced a dialectic concept of responsibility, which included the tension between self-reflection and authenticity on the one hand versus self-deception and inauthenticity on the other hand (Harmon 1995; Niebuhr 1999). There are different degrees of self-deception. Myopic vision or tunnel vision is one example, while an emphasis on means at the expense of ends may be another. Moreover, role-mediated responsibilities may lead individuals into self-deception, as most acts and even transgressions may be justified with reference to the role-holder's accountability to superiors in the organization. Bandura et al. (2002) discussed how corporate transgressions often take place when otherwise pro-social managers adopt socially injurious corporate practices. This is possible by construing situations and decisions in a manner that downplays their agency in the situation and thereby also their responsibility for eventual adverse outcomes.

We may view Wallage's exit from Statoil as her unwillingness to accept the notion that production of oil sands for energy usage morally justifies the detrimental environmental effects. She expresses how no longer holding her former position feels like breaking free from a practice she could not support. Again, an interesting parallel from the Lance Armstrong story can shed light on such a feeling of emancipation. Tyler Hamilton, who was Lance Armstrong's "trusted lieutenant" with the US Postal Service team, and a member of his inner circle, has also admitted the truth about substance abuse (Hamilton and Coyle 2012). Hamilton won an Olympic gold medal, but was later found guilty of doping and exiled from the sport. He wrote:

> The world works in strange ways. I know that old saying that when God closes a door He opens a window. I think that saying is really talking about the resilience of truth. I've come to learn that truth is a living thing. It has a force inside it, an inner springiness. The truth can't be denied or locked away, because when that happens, the pressure builds. When a door gets closed, the truth seeks a window, and blows the glass clean out. (Hamilton and Coyle 2012, p. 271)

An interesting question is whether the aftermath of such personally responsible action that Wallage, O'Reilly and Hamilton carried out, leads them to act personally responsibly also in other instances. In the quote above, Hamilton refers to the cathartic and energizing feeling of breaking out of his prior behavioral patterns. Perhaps are there even long-lasting behavioral changes when individuals are able to live lives that are more authentic and that are in alignment with moral values that are important to them?[2]

10.5 CONCLUDING REMARKS

In this chapter, we have explored personal responsibility and the greater good as a dual perspective, primarily by shedding light on Inge Wallage's journey from a public role-mediated defender of oil sands in Statoil to becoming an adversary to the same practice as an executive in Greenpeace.

Wallage's attitudes and acts appear to be defining characteristics of her as a person. These responses refer to much more than one single act. They may rather be seen as long and more or less continuous processes across time. Emotional and cognitive impulses led her to transcend her own narrow self-interest in response to different stakeholders through authentic and active dialogues; dialogues outside of her respective working environment – with her partners and close friends.

The actions of Wallage cannot be reduced to a performance of social, professional or organizational roles. To the contrary, she went beyond her roles as a good team player or communication director. She transcended those roles in order to realize what she saw as essential values tied to a greater good. For Inge Wallage, this related to her life project and to ecological sustainability and future generations. Similarly, in the case of Emma O'Reilly, the value of truth and the concern for young cyclists at risk led her to sacrifice her loyalty to her employer and her colleagues. The values at stake were so pressing for Wallage and O'Reilly that they had to be acted upon – even at the foreseen high personal and social cost, which became a sort of self-inflicted pain.

Both Wallage and O'Reilly had developed reflexivity about the ethical norms of their societies and a capability to display empathy or compassion with others with whom they shared a common environment (cf. Zsolnai 2008, p. 166). This type of actions could be interpreted as reflecting a type of personal development that might be called secure-autonomous persons with a strong sense of self. Emotions are a central feature of a person's character and together with personal values they constitute persons as extended selves who identify with a larger community. The challenge is to go "beyond self" when the self is defined in a narrow way. Arne Næss (1999) writes about the extended self, clearly influenced by Gandhi's view of the oneness of sentient beings. According to this view, we are all part of a web of life and, consequently, what we do to others we do to ourselves. Wallage clearly expressed dismay about her complicity in the destruction of the environment and how she could not defend standing idly by while the future planet of her children was placed at risk.

The famous organization scholar James March has said that undermining the self-interest doctrine may be the most important project of the twenty-first century (Zsolnai 2014). In business, economics, politics and everyday life, the doctrine of self-interest is pervasive. It is even demonstrated that in business, people who act altruistically do not have the courage to talk about their true motivation, but camouflage it by using the vocabulary of self-interest (Ferraro et al. 2005). Singer (2010) similarly argues for the need to challenge the norm of self-interest in order to obtain a better life. More altruistic behavior will lead to more flourishing and higher quality of life for both the altruist and the beneficiary, argues Singer. The major problem is that the norm of self-interest is an ideological belief, "resistant to refutation by the behavior we encounter in everyday life" (Singer 2010, p. 77). We tell stories about our acts of compassion and put a self-interested face on them. The norm of self-interest is self-enforcing and socially pernicious. According to Singer, the necessary change is to develop a culture of giving, which requires more openness, putting a face on the needy, and a better understanding of the greatly underplayed pleasure in altruistic behavior (Singer 2010).

To use Henrik Ibsen's famous concept, Wallage had to face the "compact majority" in the leadership group in Statoil, when she resigned and told them that she would take on a new position in Greenpeace. For Wallage, her new position in Greenpeace – and later also in IWA – again enabled her to flourish in her work. Her competency could be used for a greater good and her sense of personal responsibility and the work that was required of her in her new roles were aligned. Personal responsibility assumes that each individual may make a difference. The story of Wallage – much like the story of O'Reilly – illustrates that personal responsibility ultimately is connected to freedom and dignity, and the ability to live one's life autonomously and in pursuit of the realization and protection of important values.

NOTES

1. This section is based on qualitative interviews with Inge Wallage, both in person and via email. Also, parts of the case description are based on Ims and Pedersen (2013).
2. In order to strengthen the validity of our interpretations, we used communicative validation (e.g., Ims 1987, pp 183–187). This implies examining whether or not the analyzed individual can recognize the manner in which he or she is depicted and interpreted, or if it is far-fetched or "off the mark". This kind of communicative validation also has an important ethical aspect, since it necessitates that the interviewee is given the opportunity to comment, correct or deepen the answers given during the interview process. For this reason, we sent a complete draft of this chapter to Inge Wallage, who has given feedback on our use and interpretation of the data analyzed in this chapter. She had no objections to our interpretations.

REFERENCES

Andreassen, K. (2009), '– Oppsiktsvekkende kritikk [Eyeopening criticism]', *Stavanger Aftenblad*, June 9.

Aristotle (1935/51), translated by P. Wheelwright (the translation contains selections from seven of the most important books of Aristotle, amongst other from *The Nicomachean Ethics* which is the central source in this chapter), New York, NY, USA: The Odyssey Press.

Bandura, A., G.-V. Caprara and L. Zsolnai (2002), 'Corporate Transgressions', in L. Zsolnai (ed.), *Ethics in the Economy – Handbook of Business Ethics*, Oxford, UK: Peter Lang, pp. 151–164.

Bovens, M. (1998), *The Quest for Responsibility: Accountability and Citizenship in Complex Organisations*, Cambridge, UK: Cambridge University Press.

Ferraro, F., J. Pfeffer and R.I. Sutton (2005), 'Economics Language and Assumptions: How Theories can Become Self-Fulfilling', *Academy of Management Review*, **30** (1), pp 8–24.

Hamilton, T. and D. Coyle (2012), *The Secret Race. Inside the Hidden World of the Tour De France: Doping, Cover-ups, and Winning at all Costs*, London, UK: Bantam Press.

Harmon, M.M. (1995), *Responsibility as Paradox: A Critique of Rational Discourse on Government*, London, UK: Sage Publications.

Hirschman, A.O. (1970), *Exit, Voice, and Loyalty: Responses to Decline in Firms, Organizations, and States*, Cambridge, MA, USA: Harvard University Press.

Ims, K.J. (1987), *Leder i dialog. En studie av informasjonssøk med metoder for personlig utvikling* (Manager in Dialogue: A study of Information Search with Methods for Personal Development). Bergen: Universitetsforlaget.

Ims, K.J. (2006), 'Take it Personally', in L. Zsolnai and K.J. Ims (eds), *Business within Limits: Deep Ecology and Buddhist Economics*, Bern: Peter Lang, pp. 219–268.

Ims, K.J. and L.J.T. Pedersen (2013), 'Ethical Action and Personal Responsibility', in L. Zsolnai (ed.), *Handbook of Business Ethics: Ethics in the New Economy*, Oxford, UK: Peter Lang, pp. 127–150.

Kekes, J. (1991), *Moral Tradition and Individuality*, Princeton, NJ, USA: Princeton University Press.

Kongsnes, E. (2009), 'StatoilHydro-sjef ville ikke forsvare oljesand-prosjekt [StatoilHydro executive would not defend oil sand project]', *Stavanger Aftenblad*, June 8, pp. 6–7.

Løgstrup, K.E. (1956/1991), *Den etiske fordring* (The Ethical Demand), København: Gyldendal.

Næss, A (1999), *Økologi, samfunn og livsstil, utkast til en økosofi*, Oslo: Bokklubbens kulturbibliotek.

Niebuhr, H.R. (1999), *The Responsible Self. An Essay in Christian Moral Philosophy* (originally published in 1963), Kentucky, USA: Westminster John Knox Press.

O'Reilly, E. (2014), *'The Race to Truth'. Blowing the Whistle on Lance Armstrong and Cycling's Doping Culture*, London, UK: Bantam Press.

Sennett, R.R. (1998), *The Corrosion of Character: Work in the 'New' Capitalism*, New York, NY, USA: W.W. Norton & Co.

Singer, P. (2010), *The Life You Can Save. How to Do Your Part to End World Poverty*, New York, NY, USA: Random House Trade Paperbacks.

Taylor, C. (1989), *Sources of the Self. The Making of the Modern Identity*, Cambridge, UK: Cambridge University Press.

Vetlesen, A.J. (2004), *A Philosophy of Pain*, London, UK: Reaction Books.

Williams, B. (1981), *Moral Luck: Philosophical Papers 1973–1980*, Cambridge, UK: Cambridge University Press.

Zsolnai, L. (2008), *Responsible Decision Making*, New Brunswick, NJ, USA: Transaction Publishers.

Zsolnai L. (2014), 'Economics, Ethics and Spirituality', in *Beyond Self: Ethical and Spiritual Dimensions of Economics*, Oxford, UK: Peter Lang.

11. Developing a framework for critiquing multi-stakeholder codes of conduct

S. Prakash Sethi and Donald H. Schepers

11.1 INTRODUCTION

Recent years have seen the development of a number of non-state regulatory regimes (e.g., the UN Global Compact, the Extractive Industry Transparency Initiative, the Forest Stewardship Council, etc.). A number of articles have commented on a variety of these regimes. Ann Zammit (Utting and Zammit 2006, 2009; Zammit 2003) has written extensive critiques on the Global Compact, as have also Georg Kell (Kell 2003, 2005; Kell and Levin 2003), Andreas Rasche (2009; Rasche and Kell 2010) and John Ruggie (2001, 2002, 2008, 2010) in its defense. Sethi and colleagues have examined the Extractive Industries Transparency Initiative (2006). The Forest Stewardship Council has received a great deal of attention (Gulbrandsen 2008; Pattberg 2005a; Schepers 2010). Schepers (2011) has examined the governance issues in the Equator Principles.

One potential framework that has been used to examine such non-state (and hence non-democratic) regimes has been that of input and output legitimacy (Bäckstrand 2006, 2008; Scharpf 2001), where input legitimacy measures elements such as stakeholder representation and voice, and output legitimacy measures various elements of impact, including such items as monitoring. This is consistent with the work of Ostrom (1990) which examines non-state regulatory regimes from the aspects of input, stakeholder involvement, governance, and outcome measures.

This chapter proposes an alternative framework for examining the quality of such non-state regulatory regimes. It evaluates such regimes on the basis of various measures that are included in the code itself weighed against cohesiveness among the members of the coalition governing the code. Specifically, we link code effectiveness to (a) the specificity and materiality of the voluntary code is provisions, strength of governance, and implementation structures; and (b) the cohesiveness among sponsoring group members. We developed our framework from an earlier analysis of a large number of voluntary codes of conduct sponsored by individual companies, industry groups, and multi-stakeholder-based organizational entities. The last category, of multi-stakeholder codes is primarily international in scope, and cover either specific issues (e.g., sustainability, project finance, anti-corruption, etc.), or broader concerns of public policy (e.g., human rights, poverty reduction, etc.).

Based on this framework, we identify eight pre-conditions that could be used to identify the strengths, weaknesses, and potential pitfalls that present different types of codes from universal, industry-wide, and individual company-sponsored codes of conduct.

In the present chapter, our focus is limited to industry-wide codes of conduct. In our view, industry-wide codes represent perhaps the most area for improving corporate performance and social accountability. It should be noted here that we do not define corporate social responsibility (CSR) to be limited to corporate philanthropy or good corporate social responsibility corporate citizenship. Instead, we define corporate social responsibility pertaining to negative externalities or costs that are imposed by the companies on society, through the companies which under the logic of competitive markets, should be borne by the companies. These costs include, among others, environmental degradation, harmful consequence for public health and safety, and unsafe labor practices, to name a few.

We believe this framework contributes to the literature by offering a methodology for critiquing non-state codes of conduct using attributes of both the stakeholder groups that constitute the membership of the code governance structure, as well as attributes of the code itself, linking such analysis to code effectiveness. We suggest that this framework provides academics and practitioners alike with a stronger set of tools whereby extant codes can be moved to greater effectiveness and future codes can be more suitably constructed.

The four industry-wide codes included for analysis are: International Council of Mining and Minerals: Sustainable Development Framework (ICMM); Kimberley Process Certification Scheme (KPCS): A Voluntary Multi-group Initiative to Control Trade in Conflict Diamonds; the Equator Principles: Supporting Sustainable Development in infrastructure project through lending by investment banking institutions; and, the Forest Stewardship Council: an industry NGO Coalition to support sustainability forestry practices.

Although, these codes represent specific industries, they also differ significantly from each other in terms of membership, governance structure, scope of activities and measures of transparency. Hence they provide an excellent prism with which to examine the saliency of these codes in achieving their goals.

11.2 ANALYTICAL FRAMEWORK FOR EVALUATING VOLUNTARY CODES OF CONDUCT

Over the last two decades, there has been a plethora of voluntary initiatives by companies, industry groups, and regional and global bodies that call for creating voluntary standards in those aspects of corporate conduct that are inadequately addressed in prevailing legal and regulatory mandates. For example, in a recent study of over 514 corporate social responsibility–sustainability (CSR-S) reports published by large corporations from around the world, it was found that 452 (88 percent) had created their company-based codes of conduct. Additionally 137 (39 percent) indicated participating in one or more industry-wide codes; while another 144 (32 percent) acknowledged participating in at least one universal code of conduct (SICCA 2010). The resulting codes have addressed issues that are important to broad segments of society and aimed at changing corporate conduct to more adequately address those issues. Most of these issues are collectively stated as environment, social and governance (ESG) issues.

A voluntary code of conduct is in the nature of "private law" whereby an institution makes a public commitment to certain standards of conduct. The "private law" character of voluntary codes of conduct gives the SOs a large measure of discretion as the nature of commitment, issues to be covered, and the measures by which its adherence to self-created standards would be measured. However, it should be emphasized that the private law character of voluntary codes does not reduce the obligations of the SOs, whether they are individual companies, industry sectors, or other types of groups. Rather, it increases their burden to ensure that skeptical critics and the public-at-large believe in the responses and performance claims of the SOs (Sethi 2011). The success of the system depends on the ability of the SOs to create and sustain a high level of transparency and credibility that is commensurate with the nature of the particular code and its built-in societal expectations promoted by the code's sponsors (Kell and Ruggie 1999; Kolk and van Tulder 2005; Laufer 2006; Rodrik 1997; Ruggie 2001; Sethi 2003a, 2003b, 2011).

Another important point to note is that the nature of voluntariness, and by implication the flexibility afforded to the companies, depends on the premise that the SOs and their critics share a common interest in improving the underlying conditions of impacted groups and regions and that it is in the interest of all parties to resolve these issues within realistic constraints of available financial resources and competitive conditions (Sethi 2003a, 2003b, 2011).

11.3 VOLUNTARY CODES DEALING WITH CORPORATE SOCIAL RESPONSIBILITY – SUSTAINABILITY ISSUES

Voluntary codes that address CSR-S issues (these are also generally referred to as environment-sustainability, societal and governance issues, or ESG) present a unique set of challenges for both the sponsors and those who would be impacted by their actions. In direct contrast to the more traditional codes of conduct by business organizations, CSR-related codes of conduct call for the individual company and industry-based SOs to voluntarily undertake additional costs toward reducing negative externalities emanating from their operations, which may adversely impact their overall profitability and competitive position in the market-place (Ostrom 1990). It should also be noted that the ability and willingness of various companies to absorb these costs would most likely differ and thereby impact their ability and willingness to adhere to their voluntary principles or standards (Schepers 2010, 2011; Sethi et al. 2011a, 2011b).

Nevertheless, these voluntary codes of conduct serve an important business and social purpose. From the business perspective, these voluntary codes provide individual companies, industry groups, and other forms of private sector collectives with mechanisms to develop solutions that are focused, take cognizance of the SOs' special needs and public concerns, and are economically efficient. They engender public trust through "reputation effect" (Kapstein 2001; Sethi 2003). This is a proactive stance and perhaps the best of all possible worlds. It provides scope for experimentation and building consensus, and facilitates the enactment of public law. From the public's perspective, voluntary codes avoid the need for further governmental regulation with the prospect of onerous regulatory conditions. They also allow the moderate elements among the affected groups to seek reasonable solutions to the issues involved (Sethi 2003a, 2003b).

Although a substantive body of literature and research has been generated over the last 20+ years, this research has largely focused on different types of voluntary codes and their relative strengths and weaknesses, i.e., individual company codes, group-based industry codes, and universal or multi-sector codes. Second, voluntary codes have been classified in terms of their sponsorship or patronage, i.e., nongovernmental organization (NGO) sponsored codes, government–industry sponsored, multi-sector aid and development organization codes, or codes developed under the auspices of government bodies, e.g., the European Union.

The effectiveness and viability of a voluntary code of conduct would depend, to a large extent, on two sets of factors:

1. The structural characteristics of the particular types of codes and their consequential strengths and weaknesses that are embedded in the code and that would require external mechanisms to enhance their effectiveness and integrity assurance.
2. The internal factors, i.e., incentives and disincentives available to individual companies or industry groups that would induce or discourage the extent of their compliance with a particular code.

In this chapter, we begin by creating a schematic framework (Figure 11.1) to demonstrate the interrelated nature of SOs and their ability to create and implement different types of voluntary codes of conduct.

Although, this framework can be equally effective in evaluating all types of codes, we have confirmed our analysis to only industry-wide codes given space constraints. The codes included for our analysis are:

1. International Council of Mining and Minerals: Sustainable Development Framework (ICMM).
2. Kimberley Process Certification Scheme (KPCS): A Voluntary Multi-Group Initiative to Control Trade in Conflict Diamonds.
3. The Equator Principles: A Voluntary code for oversight of large-scale loans for Infrastructure Projects and their sustainability.
4. The Forest Stewardship Council: an industry-based private-public initiative to ensure bio-diversity and sustainability in forest harvesting.

These codes are measurable of the immense diversity that is symptomatic of differing challenges presented by industry characteristics, leadership orientation and the gap that exists between comparable actions and societal expectations.

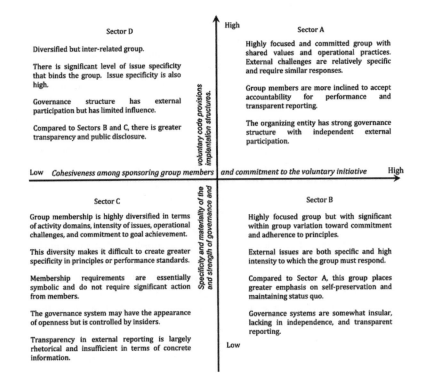

Sector D

Diversified but inter-related group.

There is significant level of issue specificity that binds the group. Issue specificity is also high.

Governance structure has external participation but has limited influence.

Compared to Sectors B and C, there is greater transparency and public disclosure.

High   Sector A

Highly focused and committed group with shared values and operational practices. External challenges are relatively specific and require similar responses.

Group members are more inclined to accept accountability for performance and transparent reporting.

The organizing entity has strong governance structure with independent external participation.

Low   *Cohesiveness among sponsoring group members*   *and commitment to the voluntary initiative*   High

voluntary code provisions implantation structures.

Specificity and materiality of the and strength of governance and

Sector C

Group membership is highly diversified in terms of activity domains, intensity of issues, operational challenges, and commitment to goal achievement.

This diversity makes it difficult to create greater specificity in principles or performance standards.

Membership requirements are essentially symbolic and do not require significant action from members.

The governance system may have the appearance of openness but is controlled by insiders.

Transparency in external reporting is largely rhetorical and insufficient in terms of concrete information.

Sector B

Highly focused group but with significant within group variation toward commitment and adherence to principles.

External issues are both specific and high intensity to which the group must respond.

Compared to Sector A, this group places greater emphasis on self-preservation and maintaining status quo.

Governance systems are somewhat insular, lacking in independence, and transparent reporting.

Low

Figure 11.1   *Confluence of member characteristics and motivations, and the scope of principles and implementation structures in creating effective voluntary codes of conduct*

This framework has been developed through our analysis of a large number of voluntary codes of conduct promulgated by individual companies, industry groups, and multi-sector and global organizations. These include, among others, codes sponsored by individual companies and focused on the company's own operations; industry-based codes that are focused on (a) major industry members, or (b) members of the entire supply chain in an industry; and universal codes. The last category covers codes by international or multi-purpose organizations that focus on specific issues, e.g., pollution control, or address broader concerns of public policy, e.g., human rights, poverty reduction, minimizing income equalities, to name a few (Sethi and Schepers 2013).

This analysis suggests that the relative effectiveness in goal achievement from the perspective of the code sponsors and their credibility with their external community depends on the confluence of two sets of factors. These are (a) the cohesiveness of the SO in shared interest in formulating and implementing the voluntary standards; and (b) the scope and specificity of enumerated standards, the integrity of governance and accountability structures that would ensure effective implementation, monitoring, and public disclosure of the code sponsors' activities.

It is important to note here that the purpose of this exercise is not to create distinctions between strong and weak codes, but to suggest structural attributes of various types of voluntary codes and the type of approach necessary to ensure the viability and credibility of these codes both for the SOs and also their external constituencies.

The first dimension is defined by the number of participating entities; cohesiveness of their purpose; their view of the socio-political environment; and their willingness to share the costs and benefits of implementing a particular code of conduct. It suggests that the level of cohesiveness invariably suffers with every increase in the number of participants and the divergence in their views as to the scope of voluntary principles, method of implementation and monitoring, and discipline activities.

The second dimension consists of the nature and scope of the principles, or specific undertakings that are incorporated in the voluntary principles or code of conduct. As membership becomes more heterogeneous (either in business or region of operation), application specificity decreases, and principles become more aspirational than compliance-oriented.

The two issues of adverse selection and free riders can be explained using these dimensions. The primary driver of adverse selection is the number of participating entities (Andreoni and McGuire 1993; Conlon and Pecorino 2004; Inderst 2005; Lenox and Nash 2003; Wilson 1980). As the number of participants increases, it makes it difficult to maintain both the group cohesiveness and code specificity since a code must accommodate the members' increasingly divergent interests. This within group variability makes it tempting for an increasing number of free riders to become code members. The number of free riders (those unwilling to share costs, but gladly reap benefits) also increases with a decline in the group's cohesiveness and consequent loss of efficient governance. In other words, a more generalized code whose sponsoring group lacks cohesiveness of purpose and shared interest proves very attractive to free riders. At the same time, it discourages best performing companies from doing more than what is minimally required so as not to share the benefits of their efforts with free riders. This situation also appeals to the companies with the worst track record who would be quite interested in joining the group at the first opportunity to enhance their otherwise poor reputation by publicizing their group membership, i.e., adverse selection. Unfortunately, adverse selection – when pronounced – could be quite detrimental to the survival and success of the group, since it would discourage high performing companies from joining the code group for fear of sullying their reputation.

In general, Sector A provides the best framework for creating a voluntary code of conduct that is both efficient and effective for the sponsoring companies or industry groups while at the same time engendering public trust and credibility from society's viewpoint. As an SO, a single company is in the best position to create a voluntary code that addresses the company's conduct in response to external socio-political challenges. The company has a large measure of control as to how it meets its commitments under the code and takes steps to ensure that performance measures are credible to its various stakeholders. To date this approach has been largely used by companies that are facing a crisis of public confidence in their business model and operation and must respond in a forceful manner regardless of the activities of other companies in that industry. The two recent examples of this approach are those of Mattel, Inc., with its Global Manufacturing Principles (GMP), and Freeport-McMoran Copper & Gold, Inc. and its operations in Papua, Indonesia (Sethi et al. 2011a, 2011b). In the case of industry groups, the best examples of this genre are Forest Stewardship Council and its sustainable forestry program (Whelan and Dwinnells 2011), and Chemical Industry's Responsible Care Program (King and Lenox 2000).

Sector B represents cohesive but embattled groups who must exhibit high commitment to codes of conduct but face structural and market-based constraints in implementing those codes. When faced with in-group variability these groups resort to weak code compliance accompanied by insular governance and information control. This approach allows member companies to appear to fulfill the standards, while at the same time not costing the business much in the way of operational discomfort. Some of the industry-wide codes falling in the sector would include: International Council of Mining and Minerals (ICMM), US Defense Industry Initiative, and Healthcare Group Purchasing Industry Initiative.

Sector C represents the type of voluntary codes and participating groups that have both low level of cohesiveness among members of the group, and also low specificity in the code elements and performance requirements. An SO, involving one or more industry groups and geographical/political regions, faces a more challenging environment in the creation and implementation of a voluntary code of conduct. The code elements and principles by necessity must be universal in character to appeal to a large number of diverse companies and industries. The sustainability of such a code, therefore, makes it inevitable that (a) principles are defined in very broad terms, i.e., they are mostly aspirational, and (b) the enabling requirements for meeting these rules are necessarily minimal.

On the face of it, these codes seem to have little practical usefulness in achieving their proffered purpose. Therefore, to make them work, they must have a sense of moral or ethical coherence that would induce subscribing group members to demonstrate adherence to those principles at some level of credibility. For this to happen, it is necessary that the SO (a) has a high level of social credibility for its moral stance, (b) uses that moral stance or halo effect to cajole member organizations to demonstrate good faith effort in some form, and (c) uses its proverbial soap box to discourage companies from exploiting the code's credibility and reputation through adverse selection and free riders (Cragg 2005).

These voluntary codes generally embrace large groups from diverse industries, regions, and regulatory environments and enumerate principles more germane to common issues faced by entire communities. There is considerable variance of opinion and outlook both within and between groups. Hence, common purpose is at best described in abstract terms leaving considerable room for differing interpretations and thus skepticism as to the sincerity and commitment of its sponsors. Examples include the Global Compact, as well as Voluntary Principles for Security and Human Rights, jointly sponsored by the governments of United States and United Kingdom.

Sector D represents voluntary codes where the SOs are more diversified (but interrelated) than in Sectors A and B, but less diversified than Sector C. The common binding agent is issue specificity that necessitates group members to work together. Issue specificity is also strong from the perspective of the external community and thus adds extra pressure for the members to respond collectively. Strong external scrutiny necessitates a governance structure with greater independence and requires more transparency and accountability. In real terms, however, the independence of the governance structure is more apparent than real. The internal conflicts between diversified but interrelated groups mandate greater corporate control and less scrutiny over their actions. Nevertheless, strong external pressures lead to more concrete and timely disclosure than is found in Sectors B and C. Some of the examples of these codes are: Kimberley Process Certification System (KPCS) which deals with the issues of conflict and blood diamonds; The Equator Principles which monitor project finance lending by financial institutions for projects where environmental, human rights, land expropriation are important issues; and the Extractive Industry Transparency Initiative (EITI) which deals with mining–government relations.

The aforementioned discussion should not be construed to mean that with the exception of single company codes, generally found in Sector A, all other types of codes are structurally flawed and, therefore, provide limited credibility to their sponsors and engender little public trust to give them long-term traction. Instead, we suggest that all types of codes are indeed relevant in their specific context, and serve important business purpose as well as issues of public concern.

Instead, the analytical framework points to certain policy options and operational practices that companies and industry groups as well as code sponsors would need to adapt to mitigate the structural shortcomings of their code apparatus and thereby improve the cost effectiveness of the SOs operational policies and programs, minimize negative externalities, and also maximize public good that forms the core basis and *raison d'être* of these voluntary codes of conduct.

Our extensive analysis of a very large number of all types of voluntary codes of conduct and relevant literature together with multi-year field experience in creating, implementing, and monitoring voluntary codes have led us to synthesize eight conditions that can be applied to ensure a higher level of effectiveness and public credibility of different types of voluntary codes (Sethi 2011). It should be noted here that these pre-conditions are not absolute but relative, i.e., the extent of their application would depend on the location of a particular code in our analytical framework, its structural shortcoming, and the extent to which these shortcomings must be corrected through meeting a certain level of compliance with the eight pre-conditions described below. These are:

1. The code must be substantive in addressing broad areas of public concern pertaining to industry's conduct.
2. Code principles or standards must be specific in addressing issues embodied in those principles.
3. Code performance standards must be realistic in the context of industry's financial strength and competitive environment. The industry should not make exaggerated promises or claim implausible achievements.
4. Member companies must create an effective internal implementation system to ensure effective code compliance.
5. Code compliance must be an integral part of a management performance evaluation and reward system.
6. The industry must create an independent governance structure that is not controlled by the executives of the member companies.

7. There must be an independent external monitoring and compliance verification system to engender public trust and credibility in the industry's claims of performance.
8. There should be maximum transparency and verifiable disclosure of industry's performance to the public. Standards of performance disclosure should be the sole province of the code's governing board (Sethi 2011).

11.4 CODE 1: INTERNATIONAL COUNCIL ON MINING AND METALS SUSTAINABLE DEVELOPMENT FRAMEWORK (ICMM)

There has been growing recognition on the part of the mining companies that the status quo has become untenable. Mining companies around the world are being confronted with protests and demonstrations that often turn violent and lead to loss of human life, damage to property, and disruption in production operations. At the same time, they are being subjected to lawsuits in their home countries with potential damage awards in the billions of dollars.

In response, a group of mining companies organized under the aegis of the International Council on Mining and Metals (ICMM), created a set of guiding principles called the Sustainable Development (SD) Framework.

The initiative, however, instantly became a subject of intense criticism by some of the largest and influential nongovernmental organizations in the area of environmental protection and sustainable development. These groups accused the industry of creating an organization that is completely controlled by the industry.

11.4.1 The MMSD Project

In the late 1990s, rising public concern over environmental and social harm attributed to the extractive industry induced some of the leading companies in the industry to take steps to assure the public that their operations were conducted in a socially responsible manner and were compatible with sustainable development. One outcome of this movement was a new Global Mining Initiative (GMI), and through it the creation of the Mining, Minerals, and Sustainable Development (MMSD) project.

From its very inception, the GMI effort was spearheaded by three of the world's largest mining companies: Rio Tinto, Western Mining Corporation, and Phelps Dodge Corporation2. The companies' CEOs, Robert

Wilson, Hugh Morgan, and Douglas Yearley, played leadership roles in creating the project. The start-up funds for the MMSD project were provided by 27 companies, with each contributing at least $150,000, for a total of approximately $4 million. However, by the time its initial report was completed, the project had exceeded $7 million.

Launched in April 2000, MMSD was conceived as a wide-ranging research and consultation project. Therefore, it was felt that a study should be conducted in an objective and independent manner to ensure its credibility to the industry's external stakeholders. The MMSD project took two years to set up multi-stakeholder dialogue and conduct thorough research. It included four regional partnerships, each with its own governance structure; about 20 national projects; 23 global workshops; and 175 working papers. According to the project documents, it involved more than 5,000 participants from various stakeholder groups from all over the world. During this period, 21 project bulletins were issued and sent to 5,000 stakeholders to report on the progress and to seek feedback on the draft report.

Critics of the industry, however, remained skeptical. They argued that the process was stage managed to stretch it over a long period of time to avoid the necessity of substantive action by way of changing mining practices. The industry was accused of selecting NGOs that were friendly to its perspective and who may otherwise be relatively uninformed about the topic. This situation led to a boycott of the MMSD project by many NGOs who were considered knowledgeable and experienced about issues pertaining to the extractive industry and sustainable development. The MMSD project was also criticized for inadequacy in participation on the indigenous peoples and other impacted groups.

11.4.2   Creation of Sustainable Development Framework: The Core Principles

ICMM was formally established in October 2001 by the extractive industry leadership through the expansion of duties of another mining industry association – International Council on Metals and the Environment (ICME). Subsequently, at a 2002 conference in Toronto, the responsibilities to implement the recommendations of the MMSD report were given to the newly formed council. Between October 2001 and May 2003, ICMM initiated a wide variety of programs and activities that focused on setting standards for the industry's performance, creating international policy and collaborative networks, and catalyzing change for sector-wide action.

Finally, in May 2003, more than three years after the creation of the MMSD project, ICMM announced in the form of the Sustainable Development (SD) Framework, which would henceforth guide the actions of the extractive industry. The SD Framework outlined ten core principles against which the ICMM's members would measure their sustainable development performance (Table 11.1).

Table 11.1　ICMM SD Framework – explanatory statements

Corporate Governance Principle 1: Implement and maintain ethical business practices and sound systems of corporate governance.	Develop and implement company statements of ethical business principles, and practices that management is committed to enforcing.
	Implement policies and practices that seek to prevent bribery and corruption.
	Comply with or exceed the requirements of host-country laws and regulations.
	Work with governments, industry and other stakeholders to achieve appropriate and effective public policy, laws, regulations and procedures that facilitate the mining, minerals and metals sector's contribution to sustainable development within national sustainable development strategies.
Corporate Decision-making Principle 2: Integrate sustainable development considerations within the corporate decision-making process.	Integrate sustainable development principles into company policies and practices.
	Plan, design, operate and close operations in a manner that enhances sustainable development.
	Implement good practice and innovate to improve social, environmental and economic performance while enhancing shareholder value.
	Encourage customers, business partners and suppliers of goods and services to adopt principles and practices that are comparable to our own.
	Provide sustainable development training to ensure adequate competency at all levels among our own employees and those of contractors.
	Support public policies and practices that foster open and competitive markets.

Human Rights Principle 3: Uphold fundamental human rights and respect cultures, customs and values in dealings with employees and others who are affected by our activities.	Ensure fair remuneration and work conditions for all employees and do not use forced, compulsory or child labor.
	Provide for the constructive engagement of employees on matters of mutual concern.
	Implement policies and practices designed to eliminate harassment and unfair discrimination in all aspects of our activities.
	Ensure that all relevant staff, including security personnel, is provided with appropriate cultural and human rights training and guidance.
	Minimize involuntary resettlement, and compensate fairly for adverse effects on the community where they cannot be avoided.
	Respect the culture and heritage of local communities, including indigenous peoples.
Risk Management Principle 4: Implement risk management strategies based on valid data and sound science.	Consult with interested and affected parties in the identification, assessment and management of all significant social, health, safety, environmental and economic impacts associated with our activities.
	Ensure regular review and updating of risk management systems.
	Inform potentially affected parties of significant risks from mining, minerals and metals operations and of the measures that will be taken to manage the potential risks effectively.
	Develop, maintain and test effective emergency response procedures in collaboration with potentially affected parties.
Health and Safety Principle 5: Seek continual improvement of our health and safety performance.	Implement a management system focused on continual improvement of all aspects of operations that could have a significant impact on the health and safety of our own employees, those of contractors and the communities where we operate.
	Take all practical and reasonable measures to eliminate workplace fatalities, injuries and diseases among our own employees and those of contractors.
	Provide all employees with health and safety training, and require employees of contractors to have undergone such training.
	Implement regular health surveillance and risk-based monitoring of employees.
	Rehabilitate and reintegrate employees into operations following illness or injury, where feasible.

Environment Principle 6: Seek continual improvement of our environmental performance.	Assess the positive and negative, the direct and indirect, and the cumulative environmental impacts of new projects – from exploration through closure.
	Implement an environmental management system focused on continual improvement to review, prevent, mitigate or ameliorate adverse environmental impacts.
	Rehabilitate land disturbed or occupied by operations in accordance with appropriate post-mining land uses.
	Provide for safe storage and disposal of residual wastes and process residues.
	Design and plan all operations so that adequate resources are available to meet the closure requirements of all operations.
Biodiversity Principle 7: Contribute to conservation of biodiversity and integrated approaches to land use planning.	Respect legally designated protected areas.
	Disseminate scientific data on and promote practices and experiences in biodiversity assessment and management.
	Support the development and implementation of scientifically sound, inclusive and transparent procedures for integrated approaches to land use planning, biodiversity, conservation and mining.
Material Stewardship Principle 8: Facilitate and encourage responsible product design, use, re-use, recycling and disposal of our products.	Advance understanding of the properties of metals and minerals and their life cycle effects on human health and the environment.
	Conduct or support research and innovation that promotes the use of products and technologies that are safe and efficient in their use of energy, natural resources and other materials.
	Develop and promote the concept of integrated materials management throughout the metals and minerals value chain.
	Provide regulators and other stakeholders with scientifically sound data and analysis regarding our products and operations as a basis for regulatory decisions.
	Support the development of scientifically sound policies, regulations, product standards and material choice decisions that encourage the safe use of mineral and metal products.

Community Development Principle 9: Contribute to the social, economic and institutional development of the communities in which we operate.	Engage at the earliest practical stage with likely affected parties to discuss and respond to issues and conflicts concerning the management of social impacts.
	Ensure that appropriate systems are in place for ongoing interaction with affected parties, making sure that minorities and other marginalized groups have equitable and culturally appropriate means of engagement.
	Contribute to community development from project development through closure in collaboration with host communities and their representatives.
	Encourage partnerships with governments and nongovernmental organizations to ensure that programs (such as community health, education, local business development) are well designed and effectively delivered.
	Enhance social and economic development by seeking opportunities to address poverty.
Independent Verification Principle 10: Implement effective and transparent engagement, communication and independently verified reporting arrangements with our stakeholders.	Report on our economic, social and environmental performance and contribution to sustainable development.
	Provide information that is timely, accurate and relevant.
	Engage with and respond to stakeholders through open consultation processes.

11.4.3 ICMM's Governance and Structure

ICMM is governed by its members, which currently include 19 major companies and 30 commodity and regional trade and industry associations. Its governance structure from the outset was completely insular and had no formal representation from outside the industry. Association members were also represented by the Associations Coordination group.

11.4.4 ICMM's Programs and Activities

Over the period of 2003–2009, ICMM primarily focused its efforts and resources in two areas: Developing a series of position papers that would clarify its principles; and, preparing toolkits and participating in evaluation studies to assist industry members in implementing ICMM principles and to enhance sustainable business practices in their operations.

From all accounts, it was a prodigious effort, if progress can be defined in terms of sheer volume of paperwork. More than 700 documents were produced and included in ICMM's online library over that period. ICMM also engaged in a broad range of activities that would suggest progress in implementing the substance of its ten core principles.

11.4.5 Environmental Stewardship

Among its principles, the ICMM SD Framework calls for sustainable development and environmental stewardship of global mining operations. Under the umbrella of the Environmental Stewardship program, ICMM has been working on a number of projects to help mining companies in diversity standards and procedures for improved operational management. These include, among others, integrated mine closures, biodiversity, resource endowment initiatives, community development toolkit, mineral taxation, social economic development, materials stewardship, and health and safety.

11.4.6 Analysis and Evaluation

Notwithstanding the massive scale of activities undertaken by ICMM, it is not clear what, if anything, these activities have achieved in the more effective implementation of ICMM principles. For the most part the toolkits imply that the mining industry is in a nascent stage of development and thus needs a coordinated effort to develop implementation tools that are both cost efficient and operationally effective. The problems confronting the industry are well known and the industry includes some of the world's largest companies. What is necessary, therefore, are not new tools, but determination to take effective action.

Based on our analytical framework, we find a number of industry-designed actions that make ICMM potentially less effective. For example, among the eight pre-conditions listed, we suggest that code principles must be specific, and the performance measured must be realistic in magnitude and time frame. There must be an effective internal implementation system, management performance evaluation, independent governance structure, and an independent external monitoring and compliance verification system. Finally, there must be maximum transparency and disclosure to the public.

In this section we undertake a systematic analysis of the ICMM's principles, policies, programs, and implementation procedures. In particular, we examine (a) the specific elements of the program content; (b) the operational framework; (c) the governance structure; and (d) accountability assurances that are intended to enhance or deter the industry in meeting its promises to society.

11.4.7 ICMM's Principles: Gap between Promises and Performance

A careful reading of the ten principles in the SD Framework suggests that they are primarily inspirational in character, with heavy emphasis on "intent" and call for "commitment" on the part of member companies. A major flaw of these principles lies in their lack of specificity. For example, the first principle states its goal to "implement and maintain ethical business practices and sound system of corporate governance." However, there is no discussion of what constitutes "ethical business practices," or a "sound system of corporate governance."

To take another example, consider principle six, which calls for "continual improvement of our environmental performance." Unfortunately, such a statement does not call for a company to include its current level of environmental performance and what would constitute acceptable level of improvement.

Principle ten calls for effective and transparent engagement with stakeholders, including "independently verified reporting arrangements." However, ICMM does not provide any information regarding how company performance would be independently verified and how results would be reported to the public. ICMM also does not suggest any approaches to what the industry would do in the event that a member company's verification procedures are lacking in independence. Nor does it indicate what the industry might do in the event that a member company declines to make its findings public with regard to its compliance with the ICMM framework.

ICMM's governance structure is completely insular and controlled entirely by the member companies. It has no independent output from those who are most likely to be impacted by the industry's strategic orientation and operational policies. Its very inception and governance council has been made up of the CEOs of all ICMM member companies, two elected representatives from the member associations, and ICMM's president. It meets twice a year to set the strategic direction for ICMM and decide on policy. The council is composed of 17 members, who are senior executives of ICMM's member companies.

In this sense, ICMM's current governance structure is closer to that of industry-based trade associations, which are formed to protect industry members' interests in their traditional business activities. It fails to meet the criteria of independence. It even falls below the standards adopted by other industry groups in natural resources, manufacturing, and internationally oriented industry–trade associations, which seek to involve nonindustrial stakeholders at the governance and consultative levels.

It seems strange for an industry to opt for such a governance structure where (a) it is under severe public criticism; (b) lacks public trust and confidence in industry's assertions of responsible behavior; and (c) the industry needs to demonstrate a good-faith effort and transparency in its conduct. A review of ICMM's plans indicate that even if all of the proposals currently under review are implemented, they are unlikely to improve the quality of code implementation in terms of delivering results that are meaningful; have direct relation to societal expectations; and accurately and objectively measure individual company performance.

11.4.8 Corporate Accountability and Performance Verification

ICMM's current guidelines indicate that independent monitoring and public reporting are to be voluntary and at the discretion of individual companies. Principle ten calls for implementation of effective and transparent engagement, communication, and independently verified reporting arrangements with all relevant stakeholders.

GRI reporting procedures, however, have their primary focus on self-reporting, where organizations are provided with a large measure of flexibility in choosing and interpreting various standards of performance and carry no requirements for level of compliance and carry no requirements for independent external verification.

11.5 CODE 2: KIMBERLEY PROCESS CERTIFICATION SCHEME (KPCS): A VOLUNTARY MULTI-GROUP INITIATIVE TO CONTROL TRADE IN CONFLICT DIAMONDS

The Kimberley Process Certification Scheme (KPCS) was created in 2003 to control the illegal mining and trade of diamonds, variously called "conflict diamonds" or "blood diamonds," from war-torn countries in Africa. Money earned from the sale of these diamonds has been used to finance ethnic and territorial fights by local warlords and tribal chiefs, culminating in systematic mass killings, gross human rights violations, atrocities against women and children, genocide and ethnic cleansing, forced migration, and sectarian violence against civilians. More often than not, these atrocities have been concentrated among the poorest countries in Africa.

The KPCS is a collective effort combining the resources and cooperation of global governing bodies, national governments, the business community, and civil society organizations. In this sense, the initiative belongs to a genre of "global governance systems" that attempts to bring together private-sector players, national governments, and operatives from nongovernmental organizations (representing the public interest or speaking for disenfranchised groups). The philosophical approach is that of consensus building wherein all participants would voluntarily agree to regulate their conduct to achieve a commonly agreed end goal. Sanctions, where necessary and justified, are imposed with extreme reluctance, if ever. Instead, transparency and peer pressure are applied to encourage the recalcitrant members to become participants in good standing.

Unfortunately, the scorecard with regard to global governance systems has not been encouraging even where the primary parties are national governments operating under the aegis of well-established global organizations, such as the United Nations and its Security Council, or the European Union. This segment is drawn primarily from Sethi and Emelianova (2011). The challenges of multiparty coordination are far more complex, because national governments, business groups, and NGOs often have conflicting agendas and utilize differing means to achieve desired outcomes. These sharp disagreements are inevitable where gains from becoming a free rider can be substantial and where any sanctions for noncompliance are likely to be perfunctory.

11.5.1 Antecedents to the Creation of the KPCS

The diamond industry has never been without severe conflicts and human rights abuses or environmental degradation regardless of whether they were committed by Western colonizers, leaders of the diamond mining industry, and, more recently, corrupt governments and self-styled freedom fighters. Most conflict diamonds are produced in the economically underdeveloped African countries that also suffer from ineffective and corrupt government bodies and a general lack of judicial systems and oversight. These countries are often subject of political instability and long histories of human rights abuses. The second half of the twentieth century was marked by a series of violent political conflicts, civil wars, and rebel movements in Central and Western Africa, including

Sierra Leone, Angola, Liberia, and other African countries. Reports produced by the United Nations and many reputable nongovernmental organizations indicate that diamond exploration in Western and Central Africa was largely conducted under the direct or indirect oversight of national governments or rebel groups. The proceedings of this rough-diamond trading were used to fuel violent conflicts that resulted in the destruction of villages and towns, and death and injury to millions of civilians.

11.5.2 Impetus for the Establishment of the KPCS

In July 1998, Global Witness, with support from Partnership Africa Canada and other NGOs, spearheaded a campaign to expose the nexus between diamond smuggling and the civil war. Whether they liked it or not, transnational corporations engaged in these operations found themselves accused of cooperating, or at the very least, benefiting from the environmental degradation and human rights abuses emanating from these operations.

The campaign and intense public scrutiny prompted the United Nations Security Council to impose sanctions on the Angola government, prohibiting the direct or indirect export of rough Angolan diamonds. In May 2000, driven by the common goal to regulate illicit diamond trade, the South African diamond-producing states, representatives of the diamond industry, and the NGOs came together in Kimberley, South Africa, to formulate an action plan to end the conflict-diamond trade and debilitate the diamond-funded violence in the war-torn regions of southern Africa.

In December 2000, the United Nations General Assembly endorsed the creation of a global certification scheme to legitimize the trade of rough diamonds. It became apparent to industry leaders that the diamond industry faced a major challenge to its business if diamonds were perceived not as symbols of long-lasting love, luxury, and wealth, but as symbols of corporate greed and exploitation, and drenched in the blood of innocent victims. The campaign against blood diamonds, complete with portrayals of the limbs of children cut off by rebels in Sierra Leone, effectively countered the soft focus of the diamond ring as an object representing love and commitment. The drive for the industry's change from resistance to cooperation was spurred by De Beers, the industry leader that stood to lose the most from declining diamond sales. In the same year, the World Federation of Diamond Bourses and the International Diamond Manufacturers Association jointly created the World Diamond Council (WDC) with the mandate to develop a tracking system for trade in rough diamonds and to prevent their illicit use.

After two years of discussions, in November 2002, the UN, state governments, the diamond industry, and nongovernmental organizations launched the Kimberley Process Certification Scheme. This was an international certification scheme for rough diamonds. It was essentially a national certification scheme with internationally agreed minimum standards.

11.5.3   Implementing the KPCS

The Kimberley Process Certification Scheme implementing document describes the goals of the project, its governance-system deliberative bodies, organization and decision-making structures, responsibilities for monitoring performance, and public disclosure. The system displays exhibits all the hallmarks of a highly bureaucratic and structured system that is intended to coordinate and manage the activities of various stakeholders' nations, business groups, and nongovernmental organizations. It sets out not only procedures, but also detailed instructions for implementing them. Consensus building and deliberate negotiations are of paramount importance, and the leadership is rotated to indicate a sense of equality and egalitarianism.

The KPCS presents a paradox in terms of goal and means, performance, and accountability. The organization's entire focus is devoted to managing conflicts among the participating groups to prevent the trade in illicit diamonds. The assumption being that regulated and certifiable trade is beneficial for all parties, who are expected to respond positively to incentives of generating higher revenues and disincentives against violations that may result in consumer boycotts and unwelcome attention from national regulatory bodies, NGOs, and the news media.

A healthy sense of skepticism is in order, however. Illicit diamonds, by their very nature, move through informal and secretive channels, where Oppenheimer at best can claim an educated guess. Estimates by other observers have ranged between 10 and 25 percent of all diamonds mined, and an even higher percentage of diamonds mined in countries where national governments appear to be willing partners in such trade, or that may be unwilling or unable to control it. These greater estimates raise the problems of controlling illicit diamond trade to a significantly higher order of magnitude, with accompanying challenges of controlling their mining and trade.

11.5.4   Governance Structure of the KPCS

The Kimberley Process Certification Scheme is overseen by an annually appointed Chair representing a state government. The Chair is responsible for supervising the KPCS, the functioning of the working groups and committees, and general administration. There are six working groups that manage the KPCS, each of which is headed by a Chair and has its own organizational structure and members. The first chair assignment went to South Africa in 2003. The KPCS has an elaborate organizational structure with various bureaus and sections to manage various aspects of its operations, supply chain monitoring, certification-process auditing, communication, and public disclosure. These include the Kimberley Process Working Group on Monitoring (WGM), the Kimberley Process Working Group on Statistics (WGS), the Working Group of Diamond Experts (WGDE), the Working Group on Artisanal and Alluvial Production (WGAAP), the Participation Committee (PC), the Rules and Procedures Committee (RP), and the Selection Committee (SC).

11.5.5 Participation in the KPCS

Participation in the KPCS is open on a nondiscriminatory basis to all applicants engaged in the diamond business and who are willing to comply with the requirements of the scheme. Participants are also required to provide details on the laws, regulations, rules, procedures, and other practices they will follow in executing the Kimberley Process. As per requirements, KP participants are allowed to import or export rough diamonds only from other KP members.

The diamond industry's trade body – the World Diamond Council – and civil society groups Global Witness and Partnership Africa Canada are engaged in the creation and the implementation of the Kimberley Process. Further discussions with regard to the involvement of civil society organizations and the diamond industry in the annual reporting process at a national level, reflecting the KP's tripartite (industry, governments, and NGOs) structure are in process.

11.5.6 Implementation of the KPCS

The Kimberley Certificate issued by countries should meet the minimum requirements as prescribed by the KPCS. The certificate should carry the title "Kimberley Process Certificate" and a statement declaring that the diamond handling has followed the provisions listed in the KPCS. Other prerequisites are that the certificate should include the country of origin, unique numbering with the Alpha 2 country code, tamper- and forgery-resistant packing, date of issuance, date of expiration, issuing authority, identification of exporter and importer, number of parcels in the shipment, carat weight of the shipment, and the value of the shipment.

The certificate may also comply with the several optional features and procedures included. The scheme mandates that the shipment of rough diamonds can only be exported or imported to and from a co-participant country in the Kimberley Process, and should be accompanied by a government-validated, forge-proof, and uniquely numbered Kimberley Process certificate describing the shipment's contents.

It should be noted that KPCS compliance varies with the level of participation in the certification process. Consequently, different participants in the diamond-trade channel follow different measures.

11.5.7 Self-regulation as the Foundation of the KPCS

The entire edifice of the KPCS is designed to facilitate self-regulation on the part of all participants. However, for self-regulation to work it must create systems and procedures that maximize positive incentives for the participants; that is, collective and cooperative action would be beneficial to the self-interest of all participants while at the same time enhancing society's benefits. While self-regulation affords maximum opportunity for the participant to establish common principles or standards of conduct, it can also be used by the participants to vary their level of compliance on the basis of self-interest and thereby undermine the integrity of the entire process.

11.5.8 Accomplishments of the KPCS

The KPCS has been in operation since 2003. It is, therefore, pertinent to ask as to how well the system has accomplished its objective of eliminating illegal or conflict diamonds from the legitimate supply chain. This is, however, not an easy question since no one has any control over the groups that mine and trade in illicit diamonds. The assumption that success of the KPCS in improving legal trade in diamonds would result in (a) reducing production and trade in illicit diamonds, and (b) limiting, if not eliminating the ability of warring groups to find ways to mine and sell diamonds to buy weapons, is simply unsustainable as a matter of logic, and ignores the reality of the situation as it exists and is apparent to everyone. Therefore, if the ultimate purpose initiative is to reduce violent conflict and human rights abuses, the KPCS must take into consideration the motives and means available to the fighting groups and the price they are willing to pay – engaging in atrocities to maintain their hold on the production and marketing of illicit diamonds.

Our analysis, however, leads us to conclude that KPCS's claims of success are quite porous and subject to differing interpretation by the priorities of asserting institutions. The KPCS's official document states that the KP has done more than just stem the flow of conflict diamonds; it has also helped stabilize fragile countries and supported their development. As the KP has made life harder for criminals, it has brought large volumes of diamonds onto the legal market that would not otherwise have made it there.

(a)   A more skeptical, but equally plausible, perspective would suggest that: An increase in the flow of certified diamonds may result, at least in part, from the phenomenon of "certification capture"; that is, the certification process has been contaminated and thereby allows illicit diamonds to pass through certified channels. The system is akin to money laundering, where money from illegal activities is sanitized by passing it through legitimate channels.

(b)   The success of the certification process may simply result in increasing the risk of trading in illegal diamonds and thereby reducing their price for the producers of those diamonds. Thus, rather than discouraging the production of conflict diamonds and thereby reducing violent conflicts, the system may have the perverse effect of increasing violence and human rights abuses since the warring parties would need to produce more diamonds to generate a similar amount of money to support their military activity.

11.5.9   Misuse of Documentation

The entire edifice of the KPCS depends on proper documentation and the integrity of various agents in the supply chain.

Any loopholes in the paper trail, therefore, jeopardize the overall effort. Unfortunately, as critics note, these loopholes occur in various stages of the diamond trade. What is most disturbing is that the KPCS lacks effective mechanisms and controls over the certification process, leaving implementation and compliance reporting for certification entirely to local governments and industry participants. These problems have been identified by various NGOs with deep involvement with the KPCS, and also by various UN, US, and other governmental bodies in the course of exercising their oversight responsibilities.

11.5.10   Supply Chain Regulation and System of Warranties

Crossing borders and changing hands from diggers and middlemen to exporters, diamond trading corporations, diamond cutters, laboratories, and reserves, a diamond finally reaches consumers in the retail jewelry market. However, this also seems to be the point where the stream of guarantees dries out. Not only is the claim of conflict-free weakened by multiple transactions and changes of ownership, in many cases it is not even existent. In March 2004, Global Witness conducted a survey of 33 US retail stores to verify their compliance with the promises to combat conflict-diamond trade. The survey showed that only 17 percent of the surveyed stores were able to respond in writing about their policies on conflict-free diamonds and warranty system implementation. At the same time, 88 percent of sales people, when asked about store policies, were not aware of the conflict-free warranty requirements.

11.5.11 Kimberley Process Oversight and Compliance Enforcement

Weak or nonexistent control of the governments over the diamond production, corrupt systems, and absence of a regulatory and legal framework for supply chain compliance already creates a shaky platform for self-regulation. Added to that is a lack of coordination and oversight on the part of the KPCS. Current interpretation of the KPCS lacks any specifics on the mechanisms and norms of assessment, evaluation, and reporting of countries' self-governance. Some member countries of the KP agreement, such as Russia, which is the second-largest diamond producer in the world, even showed reluctance to disclose diamond trade statistics.

Many member countries of the KPCS were repeatedly pointed out by NGOs and media reports to be in violation of the agreement, smuggling diamonds, and abusing human rights. However, KPCS reaction to such allegations is very slow and consequently largely ineffective.

11.5.12 The KPCS: An Assessment

The aforementioned discussion and analysis leads us to conclude that notwithstanding the seriousness of the problem and the enormity of the challenge, we should expect at best modest results and restrained expectations. We should not build exaggerated hopes of creating a new world order that is both self-sustaining and self-regulating, and that given time and goodwill among participants would lead us to a nirvana here and now rather than in life hereinafter.

Admirers and supporters of the KPCS present it as an "innovative attempt to end conflict by cutting off the ability of combatants to finance war via diamonds." In terms of process, the KPCS is presented as an outstanding example of an inclusive approach involving nation-states, the private sector, NGOs, and international and multilateral organizations. Unfortunately, when stripped of the usual hype and hyperbole, the KPCS is not an innovative model. Instead it is an overly bureaucratic framework with cumbersome and ever-growing rules and regulations, which are often found to be violated by various parties to such an extent that it makes the entire system suspect. The very institutions that are supposed to certify performance and assure integrity are found to be its worst offenders. Despite the lip service, the diamond industry, from major corporations to retailers, seems to have done very little by way of promoting the sale of certified diamonds or educating consumers to demand such verification.

11.6 THE EQUATOR PRINCIPLES: A PROMISE PERFORMANCE GAP

Infrastructure financing is a major part of large-term investments around the world. Given their very nature infrastructure projects raise serious questions of environmental degradation, and in many cases, abuse of human rights of the indigenous people and other groups who are disenfranchised from their lands. Infrastructure lending also involves multilateral lending on the part of the World Bank and other international bodies such as international financial corporation, and many regional development banks (Schepers 2011).

11.6.1 Antecedents to the Creation of the Equator Principles

Project finance is a risk diversification strategy used in developing major projects with massive up-front costs and long-term payouts, such as telecommunications, extraction, pharmaceutical, or power generation projects. In such investments, one underwriting bank syndicates the loan (60–80 percent of the project cost) to other banks, spreading the risk. For the project firm, the risk is limited to the firm's equity stake (20–40 percent of the project cost) in the project alone. The only recourse banks have, should the project sour, is the project itself.

The third partner in such ventures is the government whose country hosts such projects. Profit sharing agreements (PSAs) delineate how the profits will be shared between all the partners. PSAs usually include as a first step that all infrastructure costs will be paid before profits are shared. The government bears risk only under conditions where the PSA is threatened by increases in infrastructure cost, as happened in the Sakhalin II development (Swann 2005), and that risk is essentially limited to a decrease and/or delay in anticipated revenues. The direct antecedents to the EP are the principles and guidelines of the World Bank and the International Finance Corporation (IFC). Firms applying for funding are required to conduct both a Social Impact Assessment and an Environmental Impact Assessment.

The largest concern for project finance deals is that they often occur in remote, ecologically sensitive areas, and impact indigenous peoples. The Sakhalin II project, for example, has damaged ecologically sensitive salmon spawning grounds used by natives (Kuprewicz 2006), and endangered the local grey whale species (*International Oil Daily* 2004). The history of such problems stretches back to the World Bank's efforts at project finance. The difficulties that occurred gave rise to what were the Safeguards, now Performance Standards (PS). Two World Bank projects in particular have been cited for their role in bringing the environmental and social issues to the fore in banking decisions: (1) the Polonoroeste road project in Brazil; and (2) the Narmada dam project in India (Wade 1997). Both projects precipitated resettlement problems, though neither included such issues in the assessment of the project. In Polonoroeste, the road construction swelled the population in the target area from 620,000 in 1982 to 1.6 million in 1988. In the Narmada project, the dam (in which the Bank eventually declined to participate due to resettlement problems) would have displaced 40,000 households due to the dam and portions of another 68,000 households from the attendant canals.

The profit incentive in project finance serves to exacerbate the externality problem, particularly in developing economies. Such economies and their governments experience high volatility, providing investors with a "get in and get out" mentality that gives little concern to either environmental or social problems created as a result of the venture (Sauermann 1986). The governments of the countries where such projects occur have little incentive to stem the externality problem. They are often weak, ineffective, and unable or unwilling to monitor the projects and their effects.

The project finance sector of international banking has been under fire since the mid-1960s, when the World Bank and International Finance Corporation were severely criticized for loans made in the hope of enlarging the scope of bank activities (Bello 1994; Budhoo 1994; Chossudovsky 1997). These loans created severe negative externalities involving environmental, social, and human rights abuses in developing economies, in turn creating antagonism against the World Bank and IFC.

For multinational banks, the story was similar. Project finance loans were made in developing nations to firms in the pharmaceutical, energy generation, and extraction industries, to name but a few. These industries exploited the local areas in which they operated, creating multiple negative externalities that were left for the peoples in those areas to contend with (Houlder 1999; Kynge 2000; *The Australian* 2000; Moss 2001).

In April 2000, the Rainforest Action Network (RAN) confronted Citigroup. This attack led to the creation of the Equator Principles (EP), a system of process- and content-based principles governing environmental, social, and human rights issues. Instituted in 2002, the EP have been both praised and reviled by different constituencies. Banks have used them to varying degrees to enhance their reputation and avert social disapproval, particularly in developed economy markets (Wright and Rwabizambuga 2006).

11.6.2 The Equator Principles as Private Governance

In its revision (initially released on August 16, 2004), the IFC sought the twin goals of flexibility and integration. Flexibility, it argued, is required for the multiple scenarios confronted in project financing (International Finance Corporation 2006). The PS, the IFC contends, are more integrated, giving more emphasis and scope to client management of social issues in conjunction with environmental issues. The IFC highlights a better approach to community engagement, requiring "free, prior and informed consultation" and "broad community support" (International Finance Corporation 2006, p. 2) for each project. Further, the IFC notes that labor and community health standards have been strengthened, and the IFC will ascertain that the client has the capacity to implement the Action Plan and social/environmental management system required.

NGOs have been quick to point out the various issues left untended or weakened in the revisions. The Environmental Defense Fund alleged that the PS revisions weaken the social and environmental standards, not strengthen them as IFC argued (Lawrence 2005). These criticisms are pertinent in that the revision of the EP followed the revision of the PS, and the criticisms of the PS pertain equally to the revised EP. These criticisms again underline the suspicion that in the tension between investor rights and responsibilities, investor rights will win the day (Muchlinski 1999; Newell 2001).

11.6.3 Structure and Operation of the Equator Principles

The EP was promulgated in 2003, with ten banks as original adoptees. In the six years since, that number has grown to 68, with a revision of the EP in July 2006. In the first half of 2006, Equator Principles Financial

Institutions (EPFI) underwrote only 34 percent of project finance debt in emerging economies. The EP mandates that all loans an EPFI participates in must be EP-compliant. That leverage pushed the EP-compliant debt offerings in the first half of 2006 to 93 percent (Ellis and Caceres 2006).

11.6.4 Governance Mechanism and Lack of Transparency

The governance mechanism at the EP is a restricted system. There is a management system headed by an EPFI Chair, assisted by a Steering Committee and IFC Engagement committee. In addition, there are seven working groups (Adoption, Best Practices, Climate Change, Governance, Outreach, Scope Review and Stakeholders). Within the Stakeholders committee are three subcommittees: NGOs, SRI (socially responsible investors), and Clients. The members of the governance structure include EPFIs only. The NGO subcommittee provides a "forum for discussion", per the EP website (see http://equator-principles.com), but there is no other avenue for stakeholders such as NGOs or other affected parties such as indigenous peoples to have input into the governance structure.

The EP is a set of principles that exist by common agreement among adopting banks. It should also be clear that these banks do not sign anything; rather, the term "adopt" appears to have been carefully chosen to highlight the voluntary nature of the EP. Some banks appear to be highly (and even beyond) compliant with the EP (Lawrence 2005). Such compliance can only be determined by disclosure, however, and the majority of the banks appear to be low in disclosure of either EP performance or process data (BankTrack 2006, 2007). As such, they lack one of the most important elements of compliance, i.e., the EP does not have the ability to seek dismissal of any EPFI for conduct.

This minimal governance mechanism is a fundamental flaw, indicative of a very weak "sword" (Prakash and Potoski 2007), and little moral legitimacy from appropriate structure (Suchman 1995). Adding to the loss of moral legitimacy, another impact of this lack of governance is on the issue of adverse selection. EPFIs have little disincentive to join the collective, and face few sanctions should they not comply with the strictures of the EP. This lack of governance is made more deeply troubling by the lack of transparency (yet another "weak sword"; Prakash and Potoski 2007) and evidence of little in the way of moral legitimacy (Suchman 1995). Secondly, transparency involves openness regarding the monitoring and publication of outcomes of the activity of those governed by the agreement. On the first count, the EP does attain a certain level of transparency, as NGOs are invited to comment on the draft proposal of the revisions, and found their comments were well received.

11.6.5 Effectiveness of the Equator Principles

Lacking effective central governance and firm transparency, the EP amounts to a self-regulatory environment wholly contained within each adopting bank. Public confidence and, hence, moral legitimacy in a self-regulatory environment depends on effective and reliable monitoring and disclosure (Prakash and Potoski 2007; Sethi 2003). With each bank withholding information on its performance standards and procedures, and little in the way of monitoring or external governance, visible investments become the indicator of rigor of application of the EP. Very few banks disclose projects they have declined to invest in, perhaps due to fear of chasing away future prospects. On the investment side, EP adoptees have invested in questionable projects. Eight EPFIs invested in the Sakhalin II oil and gas project which threatened the feeding and spawning grounds of the only grey whale population in the world, as well as the fishing grounds of the indigenous peoples (*International Oil Daily* 2004; Kuprewicz 2006). Barclays, another EP-adoptee, is invested the Trans Thai-Malaysia Gas pipeline. Little poverty reduction is predicted, and much damage to the local ecosystem and reduction of living standards for local communities appears quite probable (Globalpolicy.org 2005).

Given that the EP is an internal self-regulatory mechanism, the integration of the EP mechanisms within each bank therefore become critical in ensuring the EP maintains moral legitimacy. There are two critical issues for within-bank governance: (1) what internal management systems are established in response to the adoption of the principles; and (2) what capacity (i.e., personnel) does the bank then put in place to administer the principles? With respect to the first issue, BankTrack's (2005) "Unproven Principles" report indicates that a number of banks have simply adopted the EP, and do not have or do not disclose what mechanisms are in place to review proposals.

11.6.6 The Content of the Equator Principles

The current EP contains ten principles in addition to the Preamble (Equator Principles 2006). The Preamble begins with a statement that as financiers, these banks play a role in the promotion of environmental stewardship and social development. The scope of the EP has been expanded. Initially, the EP applied only to projects in excess of US$50m, now US$10m. In addition, the revised EP applies to advisory as well as financing activities. This is commendable, as these revisions follow the lead of the more forward-thinking EPFIs.

A major issue is absence of metrics in the revised EP. In order for a code to be considered legitimate, there must be clear and measurable metrics associated with the code (Sethi 2003). The appeal to a framework devoid of metrics renders monitoring meaningless, and eliminates moral legitimacy. Without objective verifiable metrics to measure performance, performance and the subsequent local outcomes become interpretation. For example, the requirements of "free, prior and informed consultation" and "broad community support" mentioned in the fifth principle offer no specific guidance as to what might constitute such consultation or support.

11.6.7 Conclusion

From our analysis, we conclude that the Equator Principles fail to meet all of the eight pre-conditions enumerated earlier in varying degrees. The principles lack specificity, have insular and opaque governance structure, and lack transparency. Above all, they do not provide viable measures for performance assessment and do not have any means of compliance assurance.

11.7 CODE 3: FOREST STEWARDSHIP COUNCIL

The Forest Stewardship Council (FSC) is a global private governance system overseeing the sustainability and biodiversity of the world forestry system through certification of forests and forestry processes and products, and is perceived as the strongest of the various certification schemes available (Domask 2003; Gulbrandsen 2004).

For over 30 years, various forms of self-regulatory behaviors have emerged in the governance of multinational corporations (MNCs). Such self-regulation has emerged in large part due to the absence of government regulation (Cashore and Vertinsky 2000; Sethi, 2011, 2003; Sethi and Schepers, 2013). This has been labeled a shift from government to governance (Peters and Pierre 1998). Three main factors have attributed to this shift, government rollback (Cashore and Vertinsky 2000), ineptitude on the part of governments (Peters and Pierre 1998), and deterritorialization due to globalization (Matten and Crane 2005). Government rollback and deterritorialization have certain elements in common. Both are premised on the notion that governments are much less effective agents of regulation in a globalized marketplace. Governments that might regulate specific behaviors domestically find that same task much more difficult in the international market.

This forces nations to compete for firm location on the basis of regulation. Government ineptitude (Peters and Pierre 1998), either in regulation or enforcement, has similar outcomes. Governments may construct conflicting regulations at national, state, and local levels, or more often, governments provide little in the way of either monitoring or enforcement. The outcome of this process is the creation of a self-regulatory space where government regulation has been the norm.

11.7.1 The Forest Stewardship Council

The FSC is a global governance system that oversees a system of certifiers as well as regional and national networks in the forestry products industry. This system of certifiers issues two types of verification. First, these certifiers certify that logging operations are done in accordance with its Principles & Criteria, as well as any regional accommodations approved by the FSC, within specific forest boundaries. Second, these certifiers also issue chain-of-custody certificates that accompany any forestry product from certified forests through the supply chain, and mandate such things as amount of non-FSC-certified materials allowed. Such chain-of-custody certificates allow those in the supply chain to be assured they are purchasing materials produced according to FSC guidelines. The FSC, therefore, has three levels of standards: standards that apply to accreditation of certifiers, standards that apply to forestry operations, and standards that apply to operations along the supply chain.

The initial guidelines for the FSC were drafted in 1993 by a group of 126 participants, consisting of various NGOs, retailers, unions, and indigenous peoples (Pattberg 2005b). The space for the private governance system was created by a deadlock among governments on a regulatory regime that would have applied in place of FSC. There have been (and still are) other forms of "soft law" (Gulbrandsen 2004; Sethi 2011; Laufer 2006) that could fill this governance space, but lack in some manner or other.

To maintain its legitimacy as a global governance organization, the FSC does not allow governments to join, and the FSC accepts no contributions from commercial enterprises. Certifiers pay fees for accreditation, and commercial enterprises pay fees for certification, portions of which go to the FSC and the certifier. In addition, there are donations from foundations and other sources.

The FSC mission is to promote "environmentally appropriate, socially beneficial, and economically viable" forest management (http://www. fsc.org/ en/about/about_fsc/mission). FSC Principles & Criteria deal with: compliance with laws, international treaties and agreements where applicable; land tenure and usage rights; indigenous people's rights; benefits from the forest, including such elements as watersheds and fisheries; environmental impact; management plan; monitoring and assessment; maintenance of high conservation value forests; and plantations.

There have been four drivers that have pushed firms to certify their forests or forest products through FSC or some other governance scheme. Primary among these has been buyer groups and NGOs (Domask 2003; Espach 2006). In the buyers group are retailers such as Home Depot in the US, and B&Q in the EU. Increasing such demand are requirements such as those imposed by the Green Building Certification Institute and its Leadership in Energy and Environmental Design (LEED) program, as well as the WTO endorsement mentioned earlier. Pulp and paper companies are also demanding chain-of-custody certificates before buying forestry products for their industry. Environmental NGOs, such as WWF and Greenpeace, have been instrumental in pushing certification, particularly certification through the FSC.

The capital markets are providing two additional drivers. Investment banks are beginning to require forestry firms to comply with FSC or some other scheme. HSBC in particular has required specifically FSC certification as a condition for capital. Socially responsible investors have also begun examining forestry and chain-of-custody certification as a pre-condition for investment.

In sum, FSC governance extends in two manners. First, it extends to the forest management system itself, examining the sustainability and monitoring the management plan of each forest. Second, it extends to the product line emanating from the certified forests through the chain-of-custody system. This system allows retailers and other users to maintain their own credibility regarding the use of certified forest products. FSC has attempted to maintain its own credibility through its governance and certification system. Finally, FSC is a market-based system, using consumer and investor demand, coupled with NGO pressure, to persuade firms to obtain certification (Espach 2006; Gulbrandsen 2004).

11.7.2 Challenges to the Legitimacy of the FSC

There are five main challenges to the legitimacy of the FSC as a certification scheme: the existence of alternative schemes; the lack of throughput and market access; the plantation issue; the cost of certification, particularly with small farmers and those located in developing countries; and illegal logging.

11.7.3   Alternative Certification Schemes

At least 50 alternative certification schemes are in current usage (Domask 2003), ensuring a more than adequate supply of certification schemes should any one prove unsustainable. Of these, the ones that appear in the literature (aside from the FSC) most frequently are the Canadian Standards Association (CSA), the Programme for Endorsement of Forest Certification Systems (PEFC), ISO 14001, and the Sustainable Forest Initiative (SFI). Of the various initiatives, only FSC, PEFC, and ISO 14001 are global in nature. The remainder are national, with SFI covering both the US and Canada. The major global competitors to the FSC are PEFC and ISO 14001, and hence I will concentrate on those standards.

ISO 14001 has inherent flaws as a certifier of forests and forest products. The ISO system accredits management practices, and therefore concentrates on process, not product. It certifies the process of instituting an effective environmental management system, but it does not certify the content of the management system. The moral legitimacy of such a scheme is therefore limited, as it does not examine the outputs from the system. Hence, companies that use such a standard might also use other standards to supplement ISO 14001. Both Weyerhaeuser and International Paper do exactly that, using the SFI principles to govern soil, water quality and forestry practices, while using the ISO 14001 standard to certify their environmental management system (http://www.weyer haeuser.com/environment/, http://www.internationalpaper.com/Our%20 Company/Environment/EnvironmentalStewardship.html). The one very real threat to the FSC from the ISO standard arises from the WTO's recognition of ISO 14000 series as legitimate public standards. This may have the effect of making ISO 14001 a ceiling, as other more stringent standards may be in violation of WTO (Clapp 1998). The ISO standard, therefore, while giving instant recognition, offers limited legitimacy to those subscribing to it, and very limited legitimacy to those subscribing to it without also subscribing to some other environmental standard practices.

11.7.4   Conclusion

FSC is, in many ways, one of the best codes of conduct covering a particular industry. In term of our pre-conditions, it has efficiently handled the issue of governance, consensus building with various stakeholders, and creating a market-system of incentives that would provide their own pressures for the member companies to adhere to certification criteria. The shortcomings of the system are to be found in the relatively high cost of the system which (1) discourages small errors, and (2) free riders that seek entry into the system because of the low threshold of percentage of timber (10 percent) in an entire load that would qualify for the FSC certificates.

REFERENCES

Andreoni, J. and M.C. McGuire (1993), 'Identifying the Free Riders', *Journal of Public Economics*, **51** (3), p. 447.

Australian, The (2000), 'The Australian Lenders back West African Pipe Dream', *The Australian*, June 8, p. 27.

Bäckstrand, K. (2006), 'Multi-stakeholder Partnerships for Sustainable Development: Rethinking Legitimacy, Accountability and Effectiveness', European Environment: *The Journal of European Environmental Policy* (Wiley), **16** (5), pp. 290–306.

Bäckstrand, K. (2008), 'Accountability of Networked Climate Governance: The Rise of Transnational Climate Partnerships', *Global Environmental Politics*, **8** (3), pp. 74–102.

BankTrack (2005), 'Unproven Principles: The Equator Principles at Year Two', retrieved from www. banktrack.org/doc/File/Our%20Publications/BankTrack%20Publications/050606%20Principles,the%20Equator%20Principles%20at%20year%20two.pdf (accessed July 7, 2006).

BankTrack (2006), 'Shaping the Future of Sustainable Finance: Moving from Promises to Performance', retrieved from www.banktrack.org/doc/File/Our%20Publications/BankTrack%20/Publications/0_060126%20Sustainable%20Finance%20full%20report.pdf (accessed June 26, 2006).

BankTrack (2007), 'Mind the Gap: Benchmarking Credit Policies of International Banks', retrieved from www.banktrack.org/download/mind_the_gap/0_071221_mind_the_gap_final.pdf (accessed June 15, 2009).

Bello, W. (1994), 'Global Economic Counterrevolution: How Northern Economic Warfare Devastates the South', in K. Danaher (ed.), *50 Years Is Enough: The Case against the World Bank and the International Monetary Fund*, Boston, MA, USA: South End Press, pp. 14–19.

Budhoo, D. (1994), 'IMF/World Bank Wreak Havoc on Third World', in K. Danaher (ed.), *50 Years Is Enough: The Case against the World Bank and the International Monetary Fund*, Boston, MA, USA: South End Press, pp. 20–23.

Cashore, B. and I. Vertinsky (2000), 'Policy Networks and Firm Behaviors: Governance Systems and Firm Responses to External Demands for Sustainable Forest Management', *Policy Sciences*, **33**, pp. 1–30.

Chossudovsky, M. (1997), *The Globalization of Poverty: Impacts of IMF and World Bank Reforms*, London, UK: Zed Books.

Clapp, J. (1998), 'The Privatization of Global Environmental Governance: ISO 14000 and the Developing World', *Global Governance*, **4**, pp. 295–316.

Conlon, J. R. and P. Pecorino (2004), 'Policy Reform and the Free-rider Problem', *Public Choice*, **120** (1/2), pp. 123–142.

Cragg, W. (2005), *Ethics Codes, Corporations and the Challenge of Globalization*, Cheltenham, UK and Northampton, MA, USA: Edward Elgar Publishing.

Domask, J. (2003), 'From Boycotts to Global Partnership: NGOs, the Private Sector, and the Struggle to Protect the World's Forests', in J.P. Doh and H. Teegen (eds), *Globalization and NGOs: Transforming Business, Government, and Society*, Westport, CT, USA: Praeger Publishers, pp. 157–186.

Ellis, S. and V. Caceres (2006), 'Equator Principles Financing: the International Fallout', *Infrastructure Journal*, September/October, pp. 73–76.

Equator Principles (2006), retrieved from www.equator-principles.com/principles.shtml (accessed May 4, 2006).

Espach, R. (2006), 'When is Sustainable Forestry Sustainable? The Forestry Stewardship Council in Argentina and Brazil', *Global Environmental Politics*, **6**, pp. 55–84.

Globalpolicy.org (2005), 'A Big Deal? Corporate Social Responsibility and the Finance Sector in Europe', retrieved from www.globalpolicy.org/socecon/tncs/2004/0904bigdeal.pdf (accessed June 6, 2006).

Gulbrandsen, L.H. (2004), 'Overlapping Public and Private Governance: Can Forest Certification Fill the Gaps in the Global Forest Regime?', *Global Environmental Politics*, **4**, pp. 75–98.

Gulbrandsen, L.H. (2008), 'Accountability Arrangements in Non-State Standards Organizations: Instrumental Design and Imitation', *Organization*, **15** (4), pp. 563–583.

Houlder, V. (1999), 'Green Guns Turn on the Financiers: Environment Campaigning: Environmentalists have Become Increasingly Aware of the Pivotal Role of Finance in the World Economy', *Financial Times*, February 9, p. 15.

Inderst, R. (2005), 'Matching Markets with Adverse Selection', *Journal of Economic Theory*, **121** (2), pp. 145–166.

International Finance Corporation (2006), 'Policy on social and environmental sustainability', retrieved from http://www.ifc.org/ifcext/sustainability.nsf/Content/EnvSocStandards (accessed June 29, 2006).

International Oil Daily (2004), 'Greens Warn Banks off Sakhalin: Summer Production Season Starts', *International Oil Daily*, May 31, retrieved from http://web.lexis-nexis. com.remote.baruch.cuny. edu/universe/document?_m¼85ecdab77f22e510fdc564d12535a59f&_docnum¼230&wchp¼dGLbVzz-zSkVA&_md5¼1298a6528b5c851aaf7d930cccf3ac61 (accessed June 6, 2006).

Kapstein, E. B. (2001), 'The Corporate Ethics Crusade', *Foreign Affairs*, **80** (5), pp. 105–119.

Kell, G. (2003), 'The Global Compact: Origins, Operations, Progress, Challenges', *Journal of Corporate Citizenship*, **11**(Autumn), pp. 35–49.

Kell, G. (2005), 'The Global Compact: Selected Experiences and Reflections', *Journal of Business Ethics*, **59** (1), pp. 69–79.

Kell, G. and D. Levin (2003), 'The Global Compact Network: An Historic Experiment in Learning and Action', *Business and Society Review*, **108** (2), pp. 151–181.

Kell, G. and J.G. Ruggie (1999), 'Global Markets and Social Legitimacy: The Case of the "Global Compact"', *Transnational Corporations*, **8** (3), pp. 101–120.

King, A.A. and M.J. Lenox (2000), 'Industry Self-Regulation without Sanctions: The Chemical Industry's Responsible Care Program', *Academy of Management Journal*, **43** (4), pp. 698–716.

Kolk, A. and R. van Tulder (2005), 'Setting new Global Rules? TNCs and Codes of Conduct', *Transnational Corporations*, **14** (3), pp. 1–27.

Kuprewicz, R.B. (2006), 'Operations on Sakhalin II Transmission Pipelines', retrieved from www. pacificenvironment.org/downloads/Accufacts%20Final% 20Sakhalin%20Report%202-24-06.pdf (accessed July 6, 2007).

Kynge, J. (2000), 'Doubt over Three Gorges Power Demand', *Financial Times*, March 10, p. 10.

Laufer, W. (2006), *Corporate Bodies and Guilty Minds: The Failure of Corporate Criminal Liability*, Chicago, IL, USA: The University of Chicago Press.

Lawrence, S. (2005), 'Marching Backwards into the Future', *Environmental Finance*, November, retrieved from www.environmenaldefensefund.org/ documents/5058_EnvFinance%20IFC%20Nov05text. pdf (accessed July 26, 2006).

Lenox, M.J. and J. Nash (2003), 'Industry Self-Regulation and Adverse Selection: A Comparison Across Four Trade Association Programs', *Business Strategy & the Environment* (Wiley), **12** (6), pp. 343–356.

Matten, D. and A. Crane (2005), 'Corporate Citizenship: Toward an Extended Theoretical Conceptualization', *Academy of Management Review*, **30**, pp. 166–179.

Moss, N. (2001), 'Ecuador Gives go-ahead to Dollars 1.1bn Oil Pipeline', *Financial Times*, June 8, p. 9.

Muchlinski, P. (1999), 'A Brief History of Business Regulation', in S. Picciotto and R. Mayne (eds), *Regulating International Business: Beyond Liberalization*, Basingstoke, UK: Macmillan, pp. 47–59.

Newell, P. (2001), 'Managing Multinationals: The Governance of Investment for the Environment', *Journal of International Development*, **13**, pp. 907–919.

Ostrom, E. (1990), *Governing the Commons: The Evolution of Institutions for Collective Action*, New York, NY, USA: Cambridge University Press.

Pattberg, P. (2005a), 'The Institutionalization of Private Governance: How Business and Nonprofit Organizations Agree on Transnational Rules', *Governance: An International Journal of Policy, Administration, and Institutions*, **18**, pp. 589–610.

Pattberg, P. (2005b), 'What Role for Private Rule-making in Global Environmental Governance? Analysing the Forest Stewardship Council (FSC)', *International Environmental Agreements*, **5**, pp. 175–189.

Peters, B.G. and J. Pierre (1998), 'Governance Without Government? Rethinking Public Administration', *Journal of Public Administration Research and Theory*, **8** (2), pp. 223–243.

Prakash, A. and M. Potoskl (2007), 'Collective Action Through Voluntary Environmental Programs: A Club Theory Perspective', *The Policy Studies Journal*, **35**, pp. 773–792.

Rasche, A. (2009), '"A Necessary Supplement": What the United Nations Global Compact Is and Is Not', *Business & Society*, **48** (4), pp. 511–537.

Rasche, A. and G. Kell (2010), *The United Nations Global Compact: Achievements, Trends, and Challenges*, Cambridge, UK: Cambridge University Press.

Rodrik, D. (1997), *Has Globalization Gone too Far?*, Washington, DC, USA: Institute for International Economics.

Ruggie, J.G. (2001), 'Global_governance.net: The Global Compact as Learning Network', *Global Governance*, **7** (4), pp. 371–378.

Ruggie, J.G. (2002), 'The Theory and Practice of Learning Networks: Corporate Social Responsibility and the Global Compact', *Journal of Corporate Citizenship*, **5** (Spring), pp. 27–36.

Ruggie, J.G. (2008), *Promotion and Protection of all Human Rights, Civil, Political, Economic, Social and Cultural Rights, Including the Right to Development*, New York, NY, USA: United Nations.

Ruggie, J.G. (2010), *Business and Human Rights: Further Steps Toward the Operationalization of the "Protect, Respect and Remedy" Framework*, New York, NY, USA: United Nations.

Sauermann, D. (1986), 'The Regulation of Multinational Corporations and Third World Countries', *South African Yearbook of International Law*, **11**, pp. 55–77.

Scharpf, F.W. (2001), 'Notes Toward a Theory of Multilevel Governing in Europe', *Scandinavian Political Studies*, **24** (1), pp. 1–26.

Schepers, D. (2010), 'Challenges to Legitimacy at the Forest Stewardship Council', *Journal of Business Ethics*, **92** (2), pp. 279–290.

Schepers, D.H. (2011), 'The Equator Principles: A Promise in Progress?', *Corporate Governance*, **11** (1), pp. 90–106.

Sethi, S.P. (2003a), 'Globalization and the Good Corporation: A Need for Proactive Co-existence', *Journal of Business Ethics*, **43** (1/2), pp. 21–31.

Sethi, S.P. (2003b), *Setting Global Standards: Guidelines for Creating Codes of Conduct in Multinational Corporations*, Hoboken, NJ, USA: Wiley.

Sethi, S.P. (2005), 'The Effectiveness of Industry-based Codes in Serving Public Interest: the Case of International Council on Mining and Metals', published in a special issue of *Transnational Corporations* (United Nations Conference on Trade and Development, Geneva, Switzerland), **14** (3), pp. 55–99.

Sethi, S.P. (2011), *Globalization and Self-Regulation: The Crucial Role that Corporate Codes of Conduct Play in Global Business*, New York, NY, USA: Palgrave Macmillan.

Sethi, S.P. and O. Emelianova (2006), 'A Failed Strategy of Using Voluntary Codes by the Global Mining Industry', *Corporate Governance*, **6**, pp. 226–238.

Sethi, S.P. and O. Emelianova (2011), 'International Council of Mining and Minerals Sustainable Development Framework', in S. Prakash Sethi (ed.), *Globalization and Self-Regulation: the Crucial Role that Corporate Codes of Conduct Play in Global Business*, New York, NY, USA: Palgrave Macmillan, pp. 161–188.

Sethi, S.P. and D.H. Schepers (2013), 'United Nations Global Compact: The Promise – Performance Gap', *Journal of Business Ethics*, February.

Sethi, S., D. Lowry, E. Veral, H. Shapiro and O. Emelianova (2011a), 'Freeport–McMoRan Copper & Gold, Inc.: An Innovative Voluntary Code of Conduct to Protect Human Rights, Create Employment Opportunities, and Economic Development of the Indigenous People', *Journal of Business Ethics*, **103** (1), pp. 1–30.

Sethi, S.P., E. Veral, H. Shapiro and O. Emelianova (2011b), 'Mattel, Inc.: Global Manufacturing Principles (GMP) – A Life-cycle Analysis of a Company-based Code of Conduct in the Toy Industry', *Journal of Business Ethics*, **99**, pp. 483–517.

SICCA (2010), 'Making Sense of CSR Reports 2010', www.sicca-ca.org.

Suchman, M.C. (1995), 'Managing Legitimacy: Strategic and Institutional Approaches', *Academy of Management Review*, **20**, pp. 571–610.

Swann, R. (2005), 'Shell Shocked again on Sakhalin-II Costs: Big Russian Oil, LNG Project now Pegged at $20-bil; Delayed a Year to 2008', *Platts Oilgram News*, **83** (135), p. 1.

Utting, P. and A. Zammit (2006), *Beyond Pragmatism: Appraising UN-Business Partnerships* (No. UNRISD/PPMBR1/06/1), Geneva: United Nations Research Institute for Social Development.

Utting, P. and A. Zammit (2009), 'United Nations–Business Partnerships: Good Intentions and Contradictory Agendas', *Journal of Business Ethics*, **89**, pp. 39–56.

Wade, R. (1997), 'Greening the Bank: The Struggle over the Environment, 1970–1995', *The World Bank: Its First Half Century*, Vol. 2, Chapter 13, Washington, DC, USA: The Brookings Institution.

Whelan, T. and E. Dwinnells (2011), 'The Role of Certification in Protecting the World's Forests', in S.P. Sethi (ed.), *Globalization and Self-regulation: The Crucial Role that Corporate Codes of Conduct Play in Global Business,* New York, NY, USA: Palgrave Macmillan, pp. 191–210.

Wilson, C. (1980), 'The Nature of Equilibrium in Markets with Adverse Selection', *Bell Journal of Economics*, **11** (1), pp. 108–130.

Wright, C. and A. Rwabizambuga (2006), 'Institutional Pressures, Corporate Reputation, and Voluntary Codes of Conduct: An Examination of the Equator Principles', *Business and Society Review*, **111**, pp. 89–117.

Zammit, A. (2003), 'Development at Risk: Re-Thinking UN–Business Partnerships', Geneva: South Centre and UNRISD.

12. Socratic dialogue – designed in the Nelson–Heckmann tradition: a tool for reducing the theory–practice divide in business ethics

Johannes Brinkmann

12.1 INTRODUCTION

The present chapter is about *Socratic dialogue* as a specific small group conversation process design suggested by the German philosophers Leonard Nelson and Gustav Heckmann (inspired by Plato's classical dialogues with Socrates as the ever-questioning main person, or communication "midwife"). This specific design is presented first, more or less as a short guided tour through some recommended literature. Then, three dialogue examples are presented and discussed. The chapter suggests that the business ethics community with its discourse ethics and stakeholder-dialogue tradition should consider and try out this design for how to walk the talk, offering the dialogue participants a learning by doing experience of what an ideal moral conversation could look like.[1]

12.2 SOCRATIC DIALOGUE

Socratic dialogue (subsequently: SD) refers to a specific small group discussion process, following the design suggested by the German philosophers Leonard Nelson and Gustav Heckmann (inspired by Plato's classical dialogues with Socrates as the ever-questioning main person, or communication "midwife"). On one of more and more Socratic dialogue "facilitator" websites, this design is presented as follows:

> Socratic Dialogue is practiced in small groups with the help of a facilitator, so that self-confidence in one's own thinking is enhanced and the search for truth in answer to a particular question is undertaken in common. No prior

philosophical training is needed, provided participants are motivated to try the method, are willing to contribute their honest thoughts and to listen to those of others. The questions, drawn mainly from ethics, politics, epistemology, mathematics and psychology, are of a general and fundamental nature. The endeavour of the group is to reach consensus, not as an aim in itself, but as a means to deepen the investigation. (http://www.sfcp.org.uk/ [accessed May 28, 2014])[2]

In addition to the classical texts by Leonard Nelson (1922/1949) and Gustav Heckmann (e.g., 1981) there are a number of short and useful introductions to the SD methodology (such as Kessels 1996; Krohn 1998 or Birnbacher 2010). In this chapter a few fragments from these sources can be presented, as a guide to further reading and a frame of reference for the dialogue examples.

12.2.1 "Indispensable Features"

A first useful reference is Dieter Krohn's distinction of *four "indispensable features" of SD* in the Nelson–Heckmann tradition, "meant to promote autonomy in thinking: philosophical insights [which] may be gained only by those who engage in the process of knowing in their own mind. External influences should only stimulate such independent thinking" (Krohn 1998, pp. 131–132; for an English translation, see for example http://www.sfcp.org.uk/socratic-dialogue-2/ [accessed May 28, 2014]; italics added by present author).

1. *Starting with the concrete and remaining in contact with concrete experience*: Insight is gained only when in all phases of a Socratic Dialogue the link between any statement made and personal experience is explicit. This means that a Socratic Dialogue is a process which concerns the whole person.
2. *Full understanding between participants*: This involves much more than verbal agreement. Everyone has to be clear about the meaning of what has just been said by testing it against her or his own concrete experience. The limitations of individual personal experience which stand in the way of full understanding should be made conscious and thereby transcended.
3. *Adherence to a subsidiary question until it is answered*: in order to achieve this, the group is required to bring great commitment to their work and to gain self-confidence in the power of reason. This means on the one hand, not giving up when the work is difficult,

but on the other, to be calm enough to accept, for a time, a different course in the dialogue in order then to return to the subsidiary question.

4.   *Striving for consensus*: This requires an honest examination of the thoughts of others and being honest in one's own statements. When such honesty and openness towards one's own and other partici- pants' feelings and thinking are present, then the striving for consensus will emerge, not necessarily the consensus itself.

12.2.2   Rules

Another useful way of understanding and presenting SD is by its *rules*, for the facilitator, the participants and for the procedure (Birnbacher 2010, pp. 223–230; Table 12.1 and transl. from German by present author):[3]

Table 12.1   Roles and rules

Facilitator role (rights and duties)[4]	Participant role (rights and duties)	Rules of procedure
1. Restrained and cautious 2. Neutral and protecting the slow thinkers 3. Further mutual understanding 4. Stay with the question 5. Aim at a consensus	1. Talk understandably 2. Try to understand one another 3. Stick to one's own experience 4. Voice uneasiness	1. Topic develops within the group 2. Dialogue departs from own experience 3. All important mentioned thoughts are written down 4. Substantial and meta dialogue are kept apart

12.2.3   Dialogue Process Design

At least if there are newcomer participants, a Socratic Dialogue typically starts with an *introduction* by the facilitator, in his/her own words, about the dialogue process, about the distinction between substantial dialogue versus meta and strategic dialogue,[5] and the rules of the game and not least about the facilitator role (cf. Heckmann in Birnbacher and Krohn 2002, pp. 73–91). The theme or *topic of the dialogue*, often in a question sentence, can be given in the invitation or as part of the introduction. Theoretically, one can also start with first agreeing on a topic as a first dialogue stage. Once the topic is given and clear, the next step consists in inviting *participant stories*, that is the participants are asked to share self-experienced stories which in their opinion best illustrate the dialogue topic (if one wants to or needs to save time, one can also ask the participants to identify, write down and bring suitable, relevant stories to the dialogue). These stories, or at least short forms of them, are then written down on posters, for example using a flip-over device. Out of these stories, *one story has to be chosen* by consensus, as the best illustration of the theme and by assumed productivity for the following dialogue.[6] (Sometimes, one can reduce the number of stories in two steps. First, they could be discussed in small breakout groups of 2–3 participants who have to select "theirs", and then *the* story would be selected from the pre-selected set.)

In the next step which one can call *preliminary story examination*, the story and its author are asked questions for a better and deeper and more common understanding of his or her story. From its start to its end, the whole dialogue process is *documented* on a growing number of num-bered, hand-written poster sheets, which in turn are posted on the walls, present and accessible to the dialogue participants.

The rest of the dialogue can be summarized under the headline of *regressive abstraction*, or with a quotation from Jos Kessels (1996, p. 61):

> [T]o generate … insight through the analysis of a single, realistic example. This method is called regressive abstraction. It implies that, starting from a concrete example, the questioner asks "backward", investigating the pre-suppositions that the example is based upon (regression). By making these explicit … we discover the foundations on which these judgments are based. This makes it possible to examine them, sharpen or justify them, and hold them to scrutiny. Thus we may develop general insights (abstraction).[7]

Now and then this methodology is visualized as an hour glass (see Figure 12.1 on the next page, taken from Kessels et al. 2009, p. 40).

12.3 PUBLISHED DESCRIPTIONS OF DIALOGUES[8]

A truly empathetic description of a SD related to a business ethical topic is *Stan Van Hooft's protocol* of a three day dialogue in Melbourne (Van Hooft 1999), about the topic "What can philosophy offer enterprise?" On eight pages (out of 11) the author tells the story as a story, without too many abstractions and evaluations inserted (the introductory two pages present the methodology and a one page author's reflection section conclude the paper). The selected example story refers to the storyteller's experience of marriage counseling as avoiding ethical questions related to

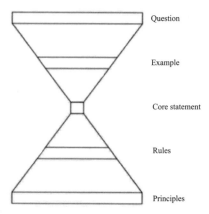

Question

Example

Core statement

Rules

Principles

Source: Kessels et al. 2009.

Figure 12.1   The hour glass model

power, responsibility and right–wrong issues, and that philosophy was
underexploited in such value-free, relativist approaches (Van Hooft 1999,
p. 115), in a next step elaborated a bit further using seven specifications
(p. 116). The group then develops formulations about "what philosophy
is", referring to the example, in nine points (pp. 116–120). Then, on day
three, the group feels "ready to approach the dialogue's central question",
and brainstorming results in six tentative answers (pp. 120–122). Then, in
a final "attempt", six suggestions came up for formulating "an answer to
the dialogue question", for example (e): "establishing a continuing
'space' within the enterprise, and 'owned' by it, for this discourse"
(p. 123). And, as the author observes, a "non-consensual outcome was
appropriate to the varied nature of philosophy itself" (ibid.).

Similarly thorough and empathetic is *Ute Siebert's description* of a
six-day(!) dialogue, facilitated by herself, about "How free is a human
being when making a decision?", found in the appendix of her published
PhD thesis (Siebert 2001, in German, pp. 285–296, now and then
referring to 11 posters, text on pp. 297–299). The selected story is about
a participant's decision to give up her plan to become a school teacher, as
a consequence of becoming increasingly uncertain, i.e. questioning her
motives and identity during her trainee stage after college (see e.g.,
p. 297).

A much shorter (half-day) dialogue is summarized by *Rene Saran*,
taking place at Hampstead school, with 10 Students from Years 8 and 9
and the Headteacher, Tamsyn Imison, trying to address and answer the
question "Is bullying a fact of life?" (the description is accessible online,

see http://www.sfcp.org.uk/an-example-socratic-dialogue/ [accessed May 28, 2014]). The SD description is nicely organized with a left column where a SD structure in general terms is elaborated a bit further in prose (this structure is then illustrated by quotations from the specific SD, in a right column):

- examining the question
- suggesting examples from personal experience
- selecting an example to focus on
- questions
- response from example giver
- generalizing from the example
- evaluation

After some adequate preparation, the following story was selected "as an example to focus on":

> Some students got hold of a photo of me. They photocopied it. They wrote nasty comments on some of the copies (slag, bitch). Some were stuck up in the corridor of the English block. A boy told me: "These are being handed round school." I and my sister threw a lot of them away. The action made me feel small, I had done nothing to the bullies. This time the bullying was the last straw and I had to tell the teachers again, this time saying something had to be done because I could not handle it anymore. Meanwhile I have learnt to cope, but I don't like the way the bullies get at my friends in order to get at me. The bullies are always in a group, which is threatening. (ibid.)

12.4 THREE SELF-EXPERIENCED EXAMPLES

Reading more or less empathetic descriptions of dialogues is clearly the second best alternative, compared with experiencing a dialogue oneself as a participant, at least once, but rather twice or even more often. Not quite consistent with that, perhaps, three dialogues (which the author participated in) are summarized in text table format (see Tables 12.2 and 12.3). The first two dialogues took place in the context of gatherings in Springe and Würzburg respectively, arranged by the German *Gesellschaft für sokratisches Philosophieren* (http://www.philosophisch-politische-akademie.de/gsp.html [accessed May 28, 2014]). The third dialogue took place in my private home south of Oslo, in Norway. All three dialogues were conducted in English.

In addition to these simplified descriptive summaries one can briefly address how one could try to understand and to evaluate such dialogues, both on their own terms and by external criteria, in hindsight.

First, the most important understanding and evaluation is supposed to be addressed and agreed on by the dialogue participants themselves as assumed owners of the dialogue process, as a *meta-dialogue* about the respective substantive dialogue in progress. One could say that there is an idealistic assumption of shared responsibility for voicing (and not voicing) any concerns about the dialogue process. Such meta-dialogues took place in all three dialogues, but were (wondering in hindsight) perhaps now and then underexploited, since voicing uneasiness can feel uneasy in itself, especially if the dialogue might have reached a point of no (easy) return (the author's own meta-dialogue II notes suggest that some principal objections related to the group dynamics and the acceptability of the chosen story were not mentioned during the dialogue, only off-record to the facilitator).

The responsibility for understanding and evaluating the dialogue process continuously is not only shared among the participants (in the meta-dialogue), but also between the meta-dialogue (or the participants) and the *facilitator*, who by definition has responsibility for facilitating the substantive dialogue. In the three sample dialogues the same person facilitated dialogues I and III, and played the role perhaps somewhat more self-confidently (or actively), than the dialogue II facilitator did (who could for example, theoretically, have stopped the choice of the story).

Most likely, one sees some avoidable traps and unexploited opportunities better *in hindsight* than when one is still in the dialogue, and as an experienced facilitator more likely than for example as a newcomer participant. Such reflections in hindsight (and for learning for the future) can be either an additional or even a better understanding and evaluation on the dialogue's own terms, of the assumed unique key success factor type (or the contrary), or more or less inspired by criteria such as the ones presented earlier in this chapter: "Krohn's four indispensable features", facilitator and participant role performance, following or deviating from the proper rules of procedure, advantages and disadvantages of the chosen story, speed and quality of the story examination and elaboration, and not least speed, quality and conclusion of the regressive abstraction process. Rather for illustrating the last mentioned thoughts about wise evaluations in hindsight than for claiming wise evaluations in hindsight of the referred-to dialogues, another text table can be used (see Table 12.4).

Table 12.2 Three self-experienced examples

	August 2011	February 2012	July 2012
Dialogue Question/ Topic	What is a just decision? (I)	What does it mean to work on oneself? (II)	Taking risks responsibly (III)
Experience: shared stories (short forms)	• Just grading, general (stakeholder) and specific considerations • Poor country student doesn't pay college fee • Student grade decision • Working in father's firm • Failing a dissertation • Handling plagiarism	• Stress reduction course • Morning exercises • Weight loss • Mindfulness • Becoming better at taking and implementing decisions • Bracelet • Forgiveness	• Going off with a stranger • Mexican guys • Trust my intuition • Becoming a farmer without experience • Giving up everything to go to university • Travel logistics stress • Rescue line
Experience: selected story	It was a just decision to give NN a second chance in respect of an assessed essay for his degree. His first attempt had been totally plagiarized and was a fail. The tutor X concerned spoke to me, I was K's personal tutor. I asked X if she would agree to my having a talk with NN about the plagiarism and what had motivated NN in doing this, i.e. what had been the reason as NN was perfectly able to write his own essay. X agreed. In the conversation NN never denied that he had copied, but could see no wrong in this. NN and I then discussed the academic conventions for authors citing precise references when quoting other people's work. I said, at the extreme his action could be seen as stealing other people's intellectual property. This would be dishonest. In the end he saw the point.	(Confidential nuclear family story, about how to handle it wisely): Working on myself is walking through significant life situations towards unconditional love.	NN went from living a very secure life with a secure home and a supportive community to living without this security in order to study. NN was aware that NN was giving up a great deal and wasn't certain what the outcome would be but it was worth the risk. When NN weighed up making this move against keeping this security it felt like the better thing to do. As NN felt driven towards achieving greater financial independence and to be a better role model for NN's son, then aged 7. It felt like a risk to give up the security NN had, but NN believed that to be the more responsible thing to do to pursue the aim going to university.

	August 2011	February 2012	July 2012
Dialogue Question/ Topic	What is a just decision? (I)	What does it mean to work on oneself? (II)	Taking risks responsibly (III)
Questions examining the selected story and author's responses	Why was it a just decision to give NN a second chance by writing a new essay on another subject? **Reasons:** a) First generation student in the late 1970s b) At first did not understand why plagiarism was wrong c) Teasing out why authors cite references d) I knew that NN was honest e) Knew that NN had some personal problems f) NN did not deserve to have his final grade prejudiced by a failed essay	Focusing on what is the meaning of walking/working and of unconditional love (examples) a) How does it work on a daily basis? b) Does the presented problem really express unconditional love? c) How does the story owner change in the process? d) Which further steps seem necessary? e) How much support from others is needed/wished/ refused when it comes to working on oneself?	**What is the risk for NN?** NN: Moving to a flat that we couldn't have for long was a big risk because we could end up homeless. There was also a risk to my son's well-being if we didn't move. … I saw my personal risk in failure if I did not get my degree and secure a good job. I felt that achieving the above was an important part of being a responsible parent. 1: Risk and responsibility in this case are tightly interconnected because of NN's role as a single mother. NN: I was aware that reports had shown life outcomes of lone parents' families were … more negative and therefore I saw it as part of my responsibility … to improve life chances. I felt that it was my responsibility to make that choice. 2: NN thought that she didn't want to be labeled as a bad parent. 3: Everyone has to take responsibility for [one's] own choices. 2: How did you weigh up? NN: Part of the decision was wanting to be in charge of my own future and not wanting to rely on luck, other people or faith.

| Abstractions developed | Examining reasons
 • Follow rules and procedures versus focus on the unique aspects of the case
 • Personal tutor's advocacy | What are the criteria/indicators of working on oneself in the example?
 a) The aim is attainable and profitable <br> b) That the story owner changes to change <br> c) That the story owner decided to change <br> d) Reaching inner peace <br> e) Distinguish between working on oneself and the result <br> f) Discipline <br> g) Noticing milestones on this path is helpful | The important aspects NN weighed up at that time included
 • Doing nothing
 • Relying on others
 • Wanting to achieve a good life for me and my son
 • Wanting to be a responsible … person
 • Not being responsible for an undesirable future
 • Doing all I could for realizing an alternative, desirable future
 • Lose a good community I was part of
 • To lose a secure home, permanently
 • Being a good role-model for [the] son
 • Improving [NN's] economy

 Group's/ group members' definitions:
 • 1/2: Taking a risk responsibly means minimizing the likelihood of something bad happening
 • 4: Is the possibility of a huge loss included in (implied by) risk taking?
 • NN: Taking risk involves making a choice (group consents: C)
 • NN: Risk is taking a chance on the outcome of our action being either positive or negative. Taking risk responsibly is understanding and weighing up these possibilities in order to make an informed choice |

	August 2011	February 2012	July 2012
Dialogue Question/ Topic	What is a just decision? (I)	What does it mean to work on oneself? (II)	Taking risks responsibly (III)
As long as we got	The participants' answers to their reading of the story ("reasons for calling a decision just"; selection): ● The action implied in the decision resolves the existing problem; the decision takes into account both individuals involved and present practice and regulations; the decision does not unduly harm other people ● Uses proper process for maximizing good consequences, minimizing harm/criticism The participants' view of the essence of the topic ● A judgment that entails action, which takes into account particular circumstances and can be justified in accordance with recognized norms ● Is a responsible decision that takes into account its consequences after having considered the situation and the people in it ● Is a decision which has to be based on particulars of the case and a decision maker's concept of justice ● Balances wisely relevant criteria, esp. case particulars against impartiality and reference to past/present/future aspects, ideally reached by dialogue rather than individually	There are three elements in working on oneself: a) Understanding, reflection, awareness, mindfulness b) Skills to live, how-to techniques c) Control, adapt, master, responding Conclusions: 1) To work on oneself means to consciously learn new patterns of adaptive behavior 2) Working on oneself is obtaining skills in order to attain an intended outcome 3) Choosing to do the *right* thing with deep empathy towards oneself and others. In the process, it is possible to let go of patterns or find new ones. It is a learning process that happens on a daily basis. It is going towards a goal and there are tools available to support this work	Acting responsibly (individual silent brainstorming), (*: mentioned by all but one): ● Weighing, balancing pros and cons ● Risk conscious ● Take action ● Competence ● Ability ● Decision-making ● Be prepared to be brave ● Be prepared to sacrifice ● Reflecting* ● Value others* ● Thinking about all possible outcomes* Taking risk involves making a choice, and to do so responsibly, means to collect as much available information as possible. Then evaluate it based on the consequences of (for?) all those affected by [the] decision and its outcomes: C.

250

Table 12.3   Three dialogues compared by criteria

Criteria	Dialogue I	Dialogue II	Dialogue III
Dialogue on its own terms	Homogeneity of participants' professional backgrounds makes consensus-building almost too easy	Psychological dialogues can be more risky than ethical ones?	Private home context and ambience matters
Krohn's features		Barriers to full understanding among participants	
Facilitator role	Experience and self-confidence matter	Too cautious?	Experience and self-confidence matter
Participant roles		Voice uneasiness can sometimes be difficult	Host role and responsibility for choice of topic could interfere
Procedure	Fully exploited meta-dialogue is perhaps unrealistic	Fully exploited meta-dialogue is perhaps unrealistic	Fully exploited meta-dialogue is perhaps unrealistic
Topic	Easy to relate to for most participants	Touchy and therefore confidential	
Story	Productive	Story is a good illustration of the topic, but group co-ownership more or less impossible	Productive
Story examination and elaboration	Ok	Subjective experience doesn't easily become inter-subjective	Ok
Regressive abstraction	Short but ok	Inspiring and interesting, strongest part of the dialogue	Good at developing relevant aspects
Conclusion	Interesting range of (compatible) participant views	Explicit, perhaps under-communicating that abstractions can conceal disagreement	A rather long list of 9–11 common denominators

12.5 THE USE OF SOCRATIC DIALOGUE FOR BUSINESS ETHICS TEACHING AND RESEARCH

During many years of *business ethics teaching*, I have used SD several times as an element in my introductory business ethics courses,[9] inspired by the founder Nelson's statements such as this one: "The Socratic method ... is the art of teaching not philosophy but philosophizing, the art not of teaching about philosophers but of making philosophers of the students" (Nelson 1949, p. 1). Not the least, SD was presented to the students as an operationalization of discourse ethics, with stakeholders rather than professional philosophers as the sources and owners of "their" ethics, understood as a well-founded consensus about potentially controversial issues.[10]

Another field of application could be *business ethics research*, in particular action research. In such a context, it makes sense to try out SD as an arrangement which would combine mainly three aspects: (1) the well-known advantages of focus groups when it comes to small group brainstorming, (2) discourse ethical and moral conversation ideals, and (3) rewarding the individuals and their organization for their participation with a positive experience of individual and organizational learning (cf. Kessels 1996).

Still another self-experienced example can help as an illustration. In the context of a pilot study with the working title "Listening to the ones not blowing the whistle"[11] it was decided to focus on the following theme: "wise reactions to disputable practices" (as a working translation of the Norwegian legal language term, *kritikkverdige forhold*, critique-worthy circumstances). Because of the research function, an independent facilitator was used, with significant experience with this technique, so that the researchers could concentrate on observation of the process. The dialogue lasted for approximately four hours, as a trade-off between the ideal 8–12 hours and the need of recruiting the participants in their paid working hours (cf. Herestad 2002). Because of the pilot function of this Socratic short-dialogue the participants were invited to share any reflections after the dialogue by email, and in addition a short qualitative follow-up questionnaire was emailed to the participants some four weeks after the session, asking them for their thoughts and reflections after the dialogue, both about moral muteness and about the assumed strengths and weaknesses of Socratic dialogue as a potential best practice model for moral conversations, generally structured by a rough interview guide.

12.6 SOCRATIC DIALOGUE AS A CATALYST[12] FOR REDUCING THE THEORY–PRACTICE DIVIDE IN BUSINESS ETHICS?

Business ethics is an example of applied ethics, theory and reflection *about* a field of practice, such as business (or medicine etc.). An easy approach could be to equal applied ethics with this and only this, being "about" a field or a study object (which it is applied to). More ambitiously, could be, for example, to demand *that* such ethics (or rather: a specified piece of it) is both applicable and really applied, more or less successfully. In a next step one could then ask *if* business ethics is applicable or applied (or relevant, if one prefers). If this is *not* the case, one could ask whose fault and responsibility the lacking use of academic business ethics is, if business ethics (as theory for a practice) is a *Bringschuld* or a *Holschuld*. Or in short, one could understand practical relevance of business ethics as theory as a productive question (and as an unproductive assumption), referring to the subheading for this chapter as such a constructive–critical (or productive) question, instead of postulating that we as theorists by and large can be content with trying to reach rather than actually reaching our practitioner target groups. Or with still less words: Business ethics as theory, or as a discipline, is not (or should not be) about itself, only.

Three references can serve as illustrations. First, one could refer to *Richard Rorty's* advice to the business ethics community (Rorty 2006), for example in teaching contexts. Especially within teaching one can try to concentrate Rorty's reasoning, about our co-responsibility as business ethicists for improving the world, into a number of pieces or theses (cf. Brinkmann 2009, p. 22). In the context of the present chapter the following pieces fit nicely: "Business ethicists might do better to think of themselves as social engineers working on site-specific projects. The two most useful tools for such work ... are narratives, whether historical or fictional, and what Laura Nash calls 'context-specific guidelines'" (Rorty 2006, p. 377), "Whether a narrative is historical or fictional does not matter as much as whether it enables the reader to put herself in the shoes both of those making difficult business decisions and of those affected by such decisions" (p. 378). As described above, SD asks for and focuses on the participants' self-experienced narratives as raw material for developing and agreeing on context-specific guidelines. Also, one learns typically to put oneself in the shoes of the story-owner and the other participants as story-co-owners as the process unfolds (while it depends on the topic and situation to what extent external stakeholders are addressed during the dialogue).

A second reference could be two thought-provoking papers which address the theory–practice divide can be mentioned briefly, written by *Georges Enderle*. According to him, "thinking" and "speaking" about business ethics have or should have an ambition of inspiring and influencing "acting" ethically in business (cf. his distinction, developed for comparing North American and European Business ethics, across three system levels, in Enderle 1996a, e.g., p. 34). In another article, he outlines what he calls "problem- and action oriented" business ethics and his thoughts about the "priority of practice over theory" (Enderle 1996b, e.g., pp. 46–50).

For following up the subheading of this chapter, a modest but realistic ambition of reducing the theory–practice divide could be to inspire our target groups, such as business people, business organization members and (if they count) business faculty and students, to "talk" and "think" about their "acting", by entering, trying out and learning "moral conversations" on their own terms, in controlled situations such as Socratic dialogue in the design presented in this chapter. The label (and desirability) of such "moral conversations" has been suggested and elaborated by a third author worthwhile referring to in the context of this chapter: *Frederick B. Bird* (1996, see esp. pp. 191–250). Bird develops this best remedy against moral muteness, moral silence, moral deafness, and moral blindness in a few steps. "Good moral communications[13] are constructive. They help to clarify and do not obscure issues. They elicit and foster ongoing participation, helping people to overcome their shyness and reticence to speak and to attend to the concerns of others. They occasion and do not stifle interactions. They assume the form of good conversations" (Bird 1996, p. 205). Good conversations are characterized by seven features, they are "recognizable; speakers are attentive; conversations move forward reciprocally; communications are rational (i.e. intelligible, reasonable, thought-provoking) and honest; speakers keep the promises they make; the exchanges remain civil" (Bird 1996, p. 207). If this is so, good conversations can help with overcoming moral silence, deafness, and blindness, by productive features and communicative functions (p. 226; cf. Table 12.4 below). Eventually, Bird suggests a wide range of organizational–ethical climate development measures (see Bird's text table on p. 239 about five "general" and five "organizational ways of cultivating good conversations").

Table 12.4   Good conversations, features and functions

How do Good Conversations Help to Overcome Moral Silence, Deafness and Blindness?

Features of Good Conversations	Communicative Functions
Occur over time	Allow time for reconsidering and for negotiating
Cultivate the sense of partnership	Develop as part of the process
Educational	Allow for imagination, learning, mutually instructing
Foster trust	Encourage people to take more risks, to collaborate
Strengthen conscience	Help in the forming of conscience, in decentering and recentering
Occasion gracious initiatives	Occasion acts of forgiveness, humor, wit, face-saving, and "reckoning with-out sharing"

Source: Bird (1996).

In the context of this chapter, the question is if, to what extent and perhaps under which conditions SD could fit in as a catalyst for improving the ethical climate in business contexts, at least as a good way to start, since SD represents a well-tested design, after all. Not surprisingly perhaps, the SD community had a dialogue about the threats and opportunities of going practical, including its potential moral obligation to do so – during a dedicated conference in Loccum, Germany in 2000 (see Brune and Krohn 2005, esp. the lectures, pp. 15–60). The most convincing or at least inspiring arguments can be documented here in the format of selective quotations:

"'Ethics' requires us to extend conducting Socratic Dialogues from the customary contexts to business organizations and to adjust the method to these specific circumstances" (Boers 2005, p. 15). Even if there might be some potential risks of being "instrumentalised" and "corrupted", it is "both possible and advisable to conduct a Socratic Dialogue in business organizations. In practice, of course, all kinds of tensions appear" (ibid., p. 20). Different contexts of use require of course "adjustments" of the method, but since there is no "standard practice", "protecting the method" would be "inappropriate" (p. 21).

Another Dutch business philosopher, J. Kessels, claims that Socrates himself would have been pragmatic when it comes to reaching business target groups: "If Socrates wants to talk with them, get them to investigate themselves and inquire into virtue, the first thing he must do is speak their language. To link up with their concerns he will take over their terminology, avoid big words and ask questions that do not seem to have any ethical relevance, even though his final aim and focus is always the same: truth, goodness, virtue, or whatever you name it" (Kessels 2005, p. 41).

Two of the German contributors are more concerned with defining and protecting the identity boundaries of SD than testing and stretching them. For H. Gronke, SD is not only a "method but also an attitude – and a principle", and in the Nelson–Heckmann tradition, inspired by and bound to the post-Kantian "Critical Philosophy" tradition. It is *not* a "pragmatic means to help people and organizations to reach their several aims" (Gronke 2005, p. 25), but introduced "to clarify people's claims in matters of truth and justice in a radically critical manner, (as a) court of reason. ... In short: Socrates may *go on* the market, but he must *not become part of* the market (p. 26). For preventing irresponsible use or abuse of the SD approach, by for example consultants, Gronke suggests then to distinguish between a narrow sense or idealistic SD, carefully kept in the Critical Philosophy tradition, and admittedly pragmatic or golden mean "*Socratic-Oriented Dialogues*", so to speak responsibly marketed and conducted SDs, for example in business contexts, which are as close as possible to the narrow sense SD but which do not pretend to practice them as if context didn't matter. Both such legitimate dialogue forms need to be distinguished from what is clearly irresponsible and illegitimate: *Para-Socratic Dialogues*.

H. Gronke's key argument is in favor of boundaries and clarity (SD-trademark protection is mentioned explicitly, by the way). His academic colleague G. Raupach-Strey focuses on the core of the issue more abstractly, as a question of distinguishability between theory and practice. After examining the unity of theory and practice from an epistemological and an ethical perspective she concludes: "The presupposition of self-sufficiency of theory is not legitimate concerning Socratic Dialogues: searching for truth serves practical application, whereas focusing practice illustrates abstract notions and theoretical sentences, and both are ending in practical engagement" (Raupach-Strey 2005, p. 58). She then suggests to distinguish between dialogues "without purpose" and dialogues "under given conditions and serving certain purposes, especially as an instrument for making decisions" (which risk instrumentalization), and to use the relation between the intention of searching the truth and other intentions, as the key criterion. "Other" intentions must neither contradict nor compromise the intention of searching the truth, and any avoidance of critical reflection about the social and political conditions under which SD is offered is unacceptable. Or with another quotation (which can serve as a repetition and summary of the preceding paragraphs): "Socratic Dialogue can well be used in all aspects of life; in the tradition of critical philosophy it is even a duty to do so. But we have to be aware that the aim can be displaced or even falsified. Whenever and wherever we are practicing Socratic method, we have to listen to the warnings of Socrates. Philosophizing is not a matter of convenience. ... The more you are paid, the more you have to consider the interests at stake, rather than the reasons" (Raupach-Strey 2005, p. 60).

12.7 THREE FINAL REMARKS

As communicated in the subheading of this chapter, it is suggested to use or at least to try out Socratic dialogue design for offering present and future business professionals help with a catalyst for practical organizational development and learning (cf. Kessels 1996, or once more Boers 2005, Gronke 2005 and Kessels 2005), for learning consensus-development, in practice. If one wants to or needs to, one argument in favor of Socratic dialogue could be that it represents a possible operationalization of discourse or dialogue ethics (cf. e.g., Raupach-Strey in Birnbacher and Krohn 2002, pp. 106–139), as theory going practical. An opposite line of influence is another argument: taking practitioner participants' experience and reflections back to theory, as a potentially legitimate way of theory development, bottom-up, listening critically and carefully to "practice". Obviously, one could also consider a dialogue across the theory–practice divide, about such dialogue experienced as a way of reducing the theory–practice divide.

When it comes to future work (beyond learning Socratic dialogue by doing it rather than talking about it) one can note at least three topics for a continued discussion or dialogue:

How can one develop fruitful and productive *dialogue themes*, fitting well with life and business work life (or business school life) situations of the participants and in line with the initiator's *Erkenntnisinteressen* (knowledge-for-what interests)? Should one consider spending the time and effort to experiment with a dialogue stage 0, letting the participants themselves agree on the topic they find fruitful to have a dialogue about, on their own terms (and why, of course)?

If one hopes that Socratic dialogue can help with reducing the theory–practice divide, how far can one and how far should one go in compromising with the prospective business participants' tight schedules? Is there some acceptable *minimum time*, or in other words, is such minimum time better than no time at all, or is it compromising the very core thought that true consensus-building requires time and taking time off for that purpose is a key point of the whole project? (cf. Kessels et al. 2009, p. 57, Boers 2005 or Gronke 2005, who, as mentioned above, suggests to market such stretching of boundaries as Socratic-Oriented Dialogue, rather than SD in a narrow sense).

How necessary is the requirement of participant experience-sharing as a key definition criterion of Socratic dialogue, for example "wise responses to wrongdoing", or "what is moral wrongdoing"? Could (not or not-yet experienced) *future scenarios* become acceptable within the design, where the participants would be a decision maker or among the decision makers and share imagined options and contexts? Would this represent an interesting design for collective moral imagination development, a legitimate or illegitimate extension of the Nelson–Heckmann design (a Socratic-Oriented or Para-Socratic Dialogue, if one used Gronke's labels, 2005)?

As the reader might have learned by now: one could stage a Socratic dialogue for patiently reaching a well-justified consensus about these (and other) issues, for reducing the theory–practice divide.

NOTES

1. An earlier version of this chapter was presented in 2012 at the 7th TransAtlantic Business Ethics Conference (TABEC) in Bergen and at the 19th Annual International Conference Promoting Business Ethics, in Buffalo NY. It summarizes what I have learned from participating in a number of Socratic Dialogues, and out of reading much of the English and German literature written in the mentioned tradition. I also reuse fragments of two conference papers, presented together with colleague Kristian Alm, in Trento (2010) and in Antwerp (2011), respectively. A next paper (co-authored with Kristian), about Using Socratic Dialogue for teaching business ethics, is planned as an extension of this chapter.
2. See ibid for further elaboration. For a more thorough presentation of a typical Socratic dialogue process see also a paper by the above mentioned "inventor", German Leonard Nelson, see e.g., http://www.friesian.com/method.htm (accessed May 28, 2014) or van Rossem's presentation, http://www.dialogism.org/socratic_dialogue_KvRossem.pdf (accessed May 28, 2014).
3. Cf. also Birnbacher's arguments in favor of some flexibility (Birnbacher 2010, pp. 231–232). For longer lists of rules for procedures, participants , and facilitators see e.g., Krohn in Brune and Krohn 2005, pp. 9–10, or more generally Raupach-Strey in Brune and Krohn 2005, pp. 150–152. Cf. most clearly in a hands-on cook book format Kessels et al. 2009, pp. 36–45.
4. Cf. esp. Heckmann in Birnbacher and Krohn 2002 and even more detailed Heckmann 1981 (esp. pp. 14–15, 18, 35f, 79–86).

5. *Content or substantial dialogue*: question and example inquiry (if you don't understand, urged to stop content); *meta dialogue*: how we are investigating (behavioral areas to work out) and *strategic dialogue*: group decides where to go (different possibilities are offered, cf. Krohn 1998).

6. For a list with five criteria for assumed productive stories see Krohn in Brune and Krohn 2005, p. 10.

7. Cf. also Leonard Nelson's description: "By analyzing conceded judgments we go back to their presuppositions. We operate regressively from the consequences to the reason. In this regression we eliminate the accidental facts to which the particular judgment relates and by this separation bring into relief the originally obscure assumption that lies at the bottom of the judgment on the concrete instance. The regressive method of abstraction, which serves to disclose philosophical principles, produces no new knowledge either of facts or of laws. It merely utilizes reflection to transform into clear concepts what reposed in our reason as an original possession and made itself obscurely heard in every individual judgment" (Nelson 1949, p. 10). See also Heckmann 1981, pp. 59ff, or not least Kopfwerk Berlin in Brune and Krohn 2005, pp. 88ff, esp. pp. 96–110.

8. For additional examples of Socratic dialogues see e.g., Kessels 1998 (*Dismissal ethics*), Heckmann 1981, pp. 12–21 (*Über das Wollen*, intention) and pp. 46–52 (*Freedom*, with many meta-level reflections by the author), R. Saran in Brune and Krohn 2005, pp. 199–203 (When is unequal treatment acceptable?), Brinkmann and Lindemann 2014 (voicing of moral concerns), Knezic et al. 2010, pp. 1107–1110, for listings of topics see e.g., Krohn 1998, pp. 122–123 (translated in Saran and Neisser 2004, pp. 17–18), Krohn and Walter 1996, or e.g., http://www.philosophisch-politische-akademie.de/sgarchiv.html (accessed May 28, 2014).

9. These dialogues were facilitated by Norwegian colleague Pia Axell, about topics such as "integrity", "trust", or "moral intuition".

10. Various examples of Socratic dialogues can also be found e.g., in Krohn 1998, pp. 122–123 with further references or simply by a web-search.

11. See two EBEN conference papers where the present author and a colleague presented this design as a best practice reference for what has been recommended as a "moral conversation" alternative to moral muteness (cf. Bird 1996). This source (in particular Chapter 7) can be recommended as a popularized and easy to read alternative to Habermas' discourse ethics design, or with a few quotes as appetizers (Bird 1996, pp. 204–205): "Our concern is to limit, reduce and overcome moral silence, deafness, and blindness … by finding ways (that) … are interactive and take place over time, help individuals address and master their moral reluctance, inarticulateness, inattentiveness, and blurred visions. … Good moral communications are constructive. They help to clarify and do not obscure issues. They elicit and foster ongoing participation, helping people to overcome their shyness and reticence to speak and to attend to the concerns of others" Cf. also Bird's seven "marks of good conversations" (Bird 1996, p. 207, elaborated on the following pages), as well as his text tables about "communicative functions" (p. 226) and "ways of cultivating good conversations" (p. 239).

12. For avoiding even slight suspicions of instrumentalization of Socratic Dialogue, the word "catalyst" has replaced the word "tool" which was used in previous versions of this article. The risk of such instrumentalization of SD for other purposes, good ones or not so good ones, is discussed briefly below, and more thoroughly in Brune and Krohn 2005, pp. 15–60.

13. For Bird, moral communication is one of five social communication "types", typically "seeking voluntary cooperation by establishing, maintaining, and interpreting normative agreements" (Bird 1996, p. 196), or in other words, "not only do people attempt to establish, modify, and sustain agreed-upon understandings that set forth normative standards about how they are expected to act but they also seek to gain the consent of others to these arguments by providing intelligible arguments" (Bird 1996, p. 199).

REFERENCES AND ADDITIONAL READINGS

Bird, F.P. (1996), *The Muted Conscience*, Westport CT, USA: Quorum.

Birnbacher, D. (2010), 'Schule des Selbstdenkens – das sokratische Gespräch', in K. Meyer (ed.), *Texte zur Didaktik der Philosophie*, Stuttgart: Reclam, pp. 215–236.

Birnbacher, D. and D. Krohn (eds) (2002), *Das sokratische Gespräch*, Stuttgart: Reclam.

Boers, E. (2005), 'On Our Duty to Use the Socratic Dialogue in Business Organizations', in Brune and Krohn (2005), pp. 15–23.

Brinkmann, J. (2009), 'Using Ibsen in Business Ethics', *Journal of Business Ethics*, **84**, pp. 11–24.

Brinkmann, J. and B. Lindemann (2014), 'Voicing Moral Concerns: Yes, but how? The use of Socratic Dialogue Methodology', paper presented at the Annual EBEN conference, Berlin.

Brinkmann, J. and K. Peattie (2005), 'Exploring Business School Ethics', *Journal of Business Ethics Education*, **2**, pp. 151–170.

Brune, J.P. and D. Krohn (eds) (2005), *Socratic Dialogue and Ethics*, Münster: LIT.

Brune, J.P., H. Gronke and D. Krohn (eds) (2010), *The Challenge of Dialogue*, Münster: LIT.

Enderle, G. (1996a), 'A Comparison of Business Ethics in North America and Continental Europe', *Business Ethics: A European Review*, **5**, pp. 33–46.

Enderle, G. (1996b), 'Towards Business Ethics as an Academic Discipline', *Business Ethics Quarterly*, **6**, pp. 43–65.

Gronke, H. (2005), 'Socratic Dialogue or Para-Socratic Dialogue? Socratic-Oriented Dialogue as the Third Way of a Responsible Consulting and Counselling Practice', in Brune and Krohn (2005), pp. 24–35.

Heckmann, G. (1981), *Das Sokratische Gespräch – Erfahrungen in philosophischen Hochschulseminaren*, Hannover (for a translation of pp. 66–71 and 79–82 see Saran and Neisser, 2004, Chapter 12).

Herestad, H. (2002), 'Short Socratic Dialogue', in H. Herestad et al. (eds), *Philosophy and Society. Papers presented to the 6th International Conference on Philosophy in Practice*, Unipub, Oslo, pp. 91–102.

Kessels, J. (1996), 'The Socratic Dialogue as a Method of Organisational Learning', *Dialogue and Universalism*, **6** (5–6), pp. 53–67.

Kessels, J. (1998), 'The case of the shared values: An example of a Socratic Dialogue', in W. van der Burg and Th. van Willigenburg (eds), *Reflective Equilibrium. Essays in Honor of Robert Heeger*, Kluwer: Dordrecht, pp. 203–215.

Kessels, J. (2005), 'What Questions would Socrates ask? On Dialogue and Ethics in Organizations', in Brune and Krohn (2005), pp. 36–41.

Kessels, J., E. Boers and P. Mostert (2009), *Free Space. Field guide to conversations*, Amsterdam: Boom.

Knezic, D., Th. Wubbels, E. Elbers and M. Haijer (2010), 'The Socratic Dialogue and Teacher Education', *Teaching and Teacher Education*, **26**, pp. 1104–1111.

Krohn, D. (1998), 'Theorie und Praxis des Sokratischen Gesprächs', in K.H. Lohmann and Th. Schmidt (eds), *Akademische Philosophie zwschen Anspruch und Erwartung*, Frankfurt, pp. 119–132 (for a translation see Saran and Neisser, 2004, Chapter 3).

Krohn, D. and N. Walter (1996), 'Sokratische Gespräche der Philosophisch-Politischen Akademie seit 1966 – eine Dokumentation', in S. Knappe et al., (eds) *Vernunftbegriff und Menschenbild bei Leonard Nelson*, Frankfurt, Dipa, pp. 135–148.

Nelson, L. (1922), 'Die sokratische Methode', reprinted in Birnbacher and Krohn (2002). An English translation by Thomas K. Brown III, originally published in *Socratic Method and Critical Philosophy*, Yale University Press, 1949, partly reprinted in Saran and Neisser, 2004, Chapter 13. The text is also available online, see http://www.friesian.com/method.htm (accessed June 18, 2013).

Raupach-Strey, G. (2005), 'Searching for Truth versus Practical Application?', in Brune and Krohn (2005), pp. 53–60.

Rorty, R. (2006), 'Is Philosophy Relevant to Applied Ethics?', *Business Ethics Quarterly*, **16**, pp. 369–380.

Saran, R. and B. Neisser (eds) (2004), *Enquiring Minds. Socratic Dialogue in Education*, Stoke on Trent, UK: Trentham Books.

Schwartz, M.S. and A.B. Carroll (2008), 'Integrating and Unifying Competing and Complementary Frameworks. The Search for a Common Core in the Business and Society Field', *Business and Society*, **47**, pp. 148–186.

Shipley, P. and H. Mason (eds) (2004), *Ethics and Socratic Dialogue in Civil Society*, Münster: LIT.

Siebert, U. (2001), *Bildung vom Menschen aus*, Kassel: Weber & Zucht.

Van Hooft, S. (1999), 'What can Philosophy offer Enterprise?', *Business & Professional Ethics Journal*, **18**, pp. 113–124.

Van Rossem, K. (n.d.), 'What is a Socratic dialogue?', retrieved from http://www.dialogism.org/socratic_dialogue_KvRossem.pdf (accessed June 18, 2013).

13. The future of business ethics: a structured dialogue between the participants

Knut J. Ims and Lars Jacob Tynes Pedersen

13.1 INTRODUCTION

This book has addressed questions of relevance to contemporary business ethics. In various ways, the chapters herein are concerned with ethical issues that pertain to the relationship between business and the greater good – how the two may conflict, as well as how business can be transformed in order to align the goals of business and society. In this respect, this book is also oriented towards *the future of business* in general, and *the future of business ethics* in particular.

In this concluding chapter, we turn to the latter point. Business ethics as a field has matured and developed considerably. This is in part due to developments in the problem matter that business ethics is designed to address. As business practice becomes more globalized, as issues related to the climate become more pressing, as financial markets have a bigger – and to a significant degree detrimental – impact on business and society; business ethics develops in order to account for these developments and to be suited to address the challenges that arise from these developments. In addition, however, business ethics changes as a consequence of developing needs for competence in business. The professionalization of tools and approaches related to business ethics and corporate social responsibility – ISO-standards, reporting initiatives and frameworks, and so on – have introduced a set of competences that businesses expect business students to be familiar with. Such demand side developments also influence how business ethics develops. Finally, business ethics develops as new perspectives flourish, as new connections are made to other fields, and as the influence of new theoretical, intellectual and cultural traditions integrate into the knowledge base of the field.

The big question is, however, is the state of business ethics appropriate for the challenges that individuals, businesses and societies face? Can business ethics achieve the aim of bridging business and the greater good – the goal of creating and protecting economic, societal and environmental value(s) simultaneously? This leads us to ask the question of what the future of business ethics is, and what the future of business ethics should be, in order for it to serve its purpose of promoting ethical practices, behaviors and institutions in business.

This question was the point of departure of the structured dialogue that concluded the Seventh TransAtlantic Business Ethics Conference. All of the conference participants were asked to offer their vision of what the future of business ethics ought to be, and in particular what kinds of changes can create a business ethics suited to face the challenges of the future. The dialogue took place as a roundtable discussion, and gave the conference a thought-provoking and forward-looking ending that points forward towards future themes of interest for the scholarly community associated with the TABEC conferences, as well as for business ethics more broadly.

In this chapter, we aim to recreate the structured dialogue that took place at the conference. Each of the participants was asked to transcribe the ideas they presented at the conference; however, none of the texts reproduced here are exact transcripts of what participants said in the roundtable dialogue. Rather, this chapter represents the best efforts of the authors to give an account of the ideas they propagated in the dialogue.[1]

13.2 GEORGE G. BRENKERT ON THE FUTURE OF BUSINESS ETHICS AS A PRACTICAL EFFORT

George Brenkert addresses business ethics as a practical effort. He emphasizes the need for business ethics to develop in ways that make it possible to properly embed ethics in organizations, and discusses implications for how the field should develop as well as how teaching ought to be conducted.

> Business ethics is an ambiguous term encompassing a number of different activities. It can refer to the study of the ethics of business in either (to simplify) a normative and/or conceptual manner or to the social scientific study of the actual ethics of individuals, organizations and systems related to business. It can refer to the ethics by which businesses operate or should operate. And it may include the teaching of business ethics within businesses or at academic institutions such as colleges and universities.

Quite frequently business ethics has been distinguished from corporate social responsibility. On this view, business ethics refers to ethical issues between management and employees while corporate social responsibility refers to the (ethical) relations of business with society and the environment. I think that this distinction is not helpful because both areas concern various values and norms by which individuals and businesses either do or should relate to one another. I look forward to further criticism of this distinction and its increasing irrelevance in the future.

Over the past several decades, business ethics, in its broad sense, has expanded its reach in two different ways. First, a broader range of participants has entered the discussion of business ethics topics. Initially, business ethics was greatly influenced by philosophers who took up the banner. However, soon others from social science and practitioners from business entered the discussion, both changing and enriching the discussion. Second, the topics of business ethics have broadened. From issues of normative ethics, they have expanded to include empirical and legal topics. One of the interesting and valuable developments in the last couple of decades has been the study of ethics in economic decision-making both by economists and other social scientists. These studies will continue to add to our understanding of business ethics.

I am confident that we will see other changes in the future regarding the topics of business ethics. A great amount of time has been devoted over the past decades to employee/employer issues as well as stockholder/stakeholder issues. The different positions are fairly well known; and the lines dividing different camps are well marked. However, if business ethics is a practical effort, more time needs to be spent on how these ethical views might be embedded in actual organizations. For this too little time has been spent on how the ethics of organizations change, what the role of power is in effecting changes, and what the relation of business to other institutions in society is, for example to politics. In recent years there has been some tentative movement to address these questions. It is an area in need of further development because it is linked to a more general issue of the role of power in providing a context and a basis for ethical behavior. It is especially here, I think, that business ethics needs to move in a much more robust manner, both theoretically (i.e., philosophically) as well as empirically. Another area deserving of greater attention than it has received is the impact of digital technologies on the ethics of business and social relations promoted by business. Given the dynamic nature of this area it will be the locus of an ever changing set of ethical challenges.

Finally, there will be new developments in the teaching and inculcation of ethics both in academic contexts as well as in businesses. Within business, ethics officers have played an important role in moving beyond compliance responsibilities to those fostering ethical cultures in business. However, their responsibilities remain separated too strongly from the responsibilities of those who are linked with corporate social responsibility. Greater integration of these different functions and responsibilities in business is both desirable and likely. And both need to give greater attention to the ethical dimensions of the products produced, how produced, where produced, how marketed and how recycled.

Within the academic domain there have been important changes in the teaching of business ethics (and CSR). We have long since passed beyond the simple examination of philosophical theories of ethics and their application to business situations. Case studies, forms of casuistry, debates, ethics bowls, practical projects examining real-time ethical situations in business, video creation and the use of social media are expanding and deepening instruction in business ethics. I assume that there will continue to be an expansion of such innovative and engaging efforts to address business ethics with students. One of the most crucial directions that would benefit business ethics is the examination of mainline theories of finance, economics, strategy, and accounting as taught in business schools in an effort to uncover their ethical assumptions that many believe inhibit the role and place of business ethics within these academic institutions.

A business ethics that moves in these directions will be, I think, vastly interesting, rewarding, and potentially more effective than it has hitherto been.

13.3 PETER PRUZAN ON WHAT IS REQUIRED IF BUSINESS ETHICS IS TO HAVE A FUTURE

Peter Pruzan asks the fundamental question of how we can ensure that business ethics is to have a future at all. He addresses the need to move beyond purely rational perspectives, and sheds light on how spirituality may enrich business ethics as a field and as a practice.

I have little faith in my ability to see into the future. Therefore, instead of providing a scenario on the future of "Business Ethics", I will provide some reflections on developments that will be required *now* if the field is to *have* a future – if it is to continue to be regarded as a domain that is worthy of academic recognition and respect and that attracts inspired theoreticians and practitioners as well as the ears and eyes of the media and the rest of us.

My personal experience, my readings in the field and the continued stream of scandals one meets virtually every day in the international media have convinced me that the major challenge facing the field of "Business Ethics" (and of ethics in other fields such as the Bioethics, as well as the related fields of "Sustainability", "Environmental Accountability" and "Corporate Social Responsibility") is to help transform the mind-set of our leaders to a higher level of conscious awareness. And this is not just in business, but in all fields of organized activity.

By this I do not imply that it is not important for the future welfare of this globe and its inhabitants to improve research in and the teaching of "Business Ethics" as we know it today. It will continue to be important for organizations of all kinds and at all levels to develop shared and *healthy*[2] perspectives on values, to develop ethical codices and guidelines for employees and suppliers, to provide training on dealing with moral dilemmas – and other such practical tools and perspectives on ethical challenges in organized commercial activity.

However, and the following is my major concern here, unless we are able to complement the almost exclusively rational approaches to the field (e.g., analyzing complex decision situations employing consequentialist and deontological approaches) with approaches that emancipate and empower the individual's inner guidance, we will experience wide-spread and well-deserved skepticism with respect to the *raison d'être* of the field of "Business Ethics".

The shift in the consciousness referred to is such that "Business Ethics" will no longer primarily be regarded as providing limitations on the actions of corporations while they pursue their financial goals, so they are not challenged due to being *un*ethical. Instead, goals and limitations will be reversed – the overall goal will be contributing to the common good – to acting so as to contribute to the well-being of the organization's stakeholders – subject to the limitation that the organization is financially healthy and viable.

In order for such a reorientation as to goals and means to take place, what I have referred to earlier as a shift in consciousness, will require that decision makers supplement their traditional rational analyses with spiritual-based guidance from their "inner world" when faced with challenging decisions in the external world of business. And a condition for them to be able to do so will be that they actively focus on emancipating and empowering the inherent source of their ethicality. Providing the motivation and the means for so doing will be the main challenge to teachers of a revitalized "Business Ethics".

It is my strong conviction that unless such a shift takes place, we will continue to observe that concern for the common good remains subservient to ego-based aspirations for financial wealth and power. Blatant greed and a lack of sensitivity to the aspirations and needs of the constituencies affected by our organizations' actions will continue to undermine our trust in our business enterprises, their leaders and the institutional frameworks they function in – and therefore as well in "Business Ethics".

I realize that an appeal to complement rationality in the theory and practice of "Business Ethics" with spirituality can and will be seriously challenged in a world where economic rationality dominates the perspectives of both business academicians and practitioners. But unless the field of "Business Ethics", meaning the academic community and the active practitioners in various corporate, consulting, regulating and advisory bodies, actively focus on motivating and inspiring the individual decision maker to supplement their economically-based success criteria with perspectives on the "good life" for one self as well as the organization and its sundry stakeholders, "Business Ethics" will continue to deal more with *un*ethics than with ethics.

At a practical level, perhaps a primary operational challenge is for our theoreticians to inspire the practitioners to expand the standards and measures of performance they use to characterize business decisions, including inner promptings that are not subject to rational analysis. Inspiration can be obtained from such diverse and "unorthodox" sources as "happiness research",[3] research on the interrelationships between management, spirituality and religion[4] and research on spiritual-based leadership.[5] The footnotes provide just a few possible sources of inspiration.

But also other challenges to the field of "Business Ethics" will clearly arise from the above focus on a shift in consciousness and the emancipation and empowerment of one's inner guidance. These do not only include developing a widely accepted vocabulary and frame of reference (considered briefly above with respect to "success"), but also such matters as: Who will be qualified to teach and provide advice on such matters? Who can "teach the teachers" and "advise the advisors"? How to avoid confusing a call for spirituality in business with a return to religious dogma? How to develop decision-making environments and tools that facilitate the resolution and dissolution of conflicts in groups where the individual participants each refer to deeply felt convictions that are not in harmony with the convictions of the others, and where each participant strives to experience harmony between their thoughts, words and deeds?

The challenges are many as well as potentially hugely rewarding for theoreticians and practitioners of "Business Ethics" and for the well-being of our societies.

13.4 ELEANOR O'HIGGINS ON IDEALS AND REALITIES IN THE FUTURE OF BUSINESS ETHICS

Eleanor O'Higgins takes as point of departure the distinction between the ideals and realities of business ethics – what it is and what it ought to be. She discusses virtues that should be embraced in order for business practices to change fundamentally, and how this relates to the identities of business practitioners.

> The question about "the future of business ethics" can be approached from two perspectives. One is the "ideal", i.e., what *should* the future of business ethics be in practice? The other is the "reality", *what is it likely to be*? If the future state of business ethics resembles business ethics today, then it will certainly not be anywhere near the ideal.

When considering the ideal, it is common wisdom to expect business ethics to feature various characteristics – business practitioners, and especially leaders with a sense of values and principles that balance economic wealth creation with social and environmental sustainability. This can be achieved by mutual respect in human relationships, recognizing our interdependencies. It also requires actors or agents to appreciate the consequences of their actions on others and take personal responsibility for them.

In pondering questions about consequences and personal responsibility, business practitioners will necessarily consider their own identity, who they are, how they define themselves, the limits of what they would or would not do for the sake of economic success. Business ethics, at its best, should encompass the traditional cardinal virtues of prudence, justice, temperance/discipline, and fortitude. The theological virtue of charity would also not go amiss.

This may be seen in contrast to the situation at present, where mainstream business, rather than embracing virtues, may instead be seen to value many of the seven deadly sins, in particular greed and pride/arrogance, largely bolstered by envy. Not only are these not regarded as sins in contemporary business, they are perversely seen as facilitating social welfare, as embodied in economic man.

The definition of business ethics matters here. As long as business ethics is defined as outside the realm of general ethics, it is perceived as a special case, so that standards of moral right or wrong in our everyday lives – the virtues – are somehow suspended when it comes to business. This boils down to ways of justifying personal selfishness, an atomistic view of human beings where everyone is out for themselves, without considering the consequences for others and a sense of entitlement to materialistic goods without limit. This has enabled business actors to perpetrate harm to society, forcefully manifested in the global economic crisis.

This worldview of business is reinforced by some of those who inhabit the top echelons of business and their self-serving interest in maintaining the current culture. Moreover, research on corporations consistently shows a self-selection bias where many of those who choose and get ahead in business careers possess psychopathic traits like narcissism, egocentricity, cynicism and ruthlessness. Then, such traits are exacerbated when individuals reach the top as they abuse their power to ensure that no one else will wrest it from them.

So, if the future "reality" is to be brought closer to the "ideal" in business ethics, it means that we have to change our models of business, its purposes and its mores to a form that no longer rewards the practice of "sins". Such rewards attracted those who excelled most at unethical behavior. Instead, business has to be seen as a medium for practicing virtues. This is more easily said than done, but paradoxically, the financial crisis may present an opportunity for change, i.e., "You don't ever want a crisis to go to waste; it's an opportunity to do important things that you would otherwise avoid."[6]

13.5 KEVIN T. JACKSON ON HOW FUTURE BUSINESS ETHICS MAY TRANSMIT AUTHENTIC HUMAN VALUES

The point of departure of Kevin T. Jackson's views on the future of business ethics is that the content of business education conflicts with human nature. He argues that the very salvation of civilization is at stake when it comes to instilling moral and intellectual culture into business, and discusses how we may achieve the goal of transmitting authentic human values through business ethics education.

> The job of educating future business leaders is hampered by widespread intellectual weaknesses not just in business schools but in other institutions of learning too. The weaknesses are simultaneously causes and effects of sundry intellectual vices, methodologies, and ideologies that are hostile to, and incompatible with, a sound understanding of human nature and its relationship to business and economics.

> Business ethics needs to somehow absorb the worth and dignity of philosophy – not only for understanding the significance of business as a human endeavor, but also for successfully conducting business. I would exhort business people of all kinds and in all nations to think broader, bigger and deeper. By emphasizing the significance of philosophy for business and economics, our field of business ethics must be firmly rooted in questions of truth, goodness, and even beauty.

> The field of business ethics should foster understanding of the relationship between business and the wider moral and intellectual culture, not for the sake of solving mere intellectual puzzles but because in a very real way the salvation of civilization is at stake. It is of vital importance that business ethics be equipped to defend the ability of human reason to know the truth. A firm confidence in reason has been an integral part of the Western philosophical tradition, but it stands in need of reaffirmation today. At least part of the reason for this is connected with the global financial crisis. Economic crises are accompanied by disturbing perplexity about values, not only financial ones but moral, epistemological, and aesthetic ones as well. It is this aspect, I believe, that makes such crises particularly disquieting not just within financial institutions, but also across the wider culture.

> I believe that widespread misunderstanding of the relationship between economics (ultimately grounded in truth), ethics (ultimately grounded in goodness), and culture (ultimately grounded in beauty), particularly among those charged with teaching business, weakens the ability of both business schools and business organizations to cultivate and transmit authentic human values. The "ethics" that corporations and business schools try to transmit, when they badly misunderstand the relationship, is "business ethics" only in a superficial sense. All too often it is an agenda for political correctness

(motivated from either end of the political spectrum); or it sometimes amounts to "window dressing" to serve the narrow interests of the organization.

So, going forward, business ethics must continuously resist getting captured by corporate interests, political interests, and technocratic interests.

13.6 GEORGES ENDERLE ON DIFFERENT LEVELS AND CHALLENGES IN THE FUTURE OF BUSINESS ETHICS

Georges Enderle argues that the future of business needs to encompass multiple levels of analysis in order to address the complex challenges it faces. Furthermore, he argues that business ethics needs to combine descriptive–analytical and normative–ethical approaches for a sound treatment of those challenges.

> Since the 1980s business ethics has evolved to a fairly well-established field that covers academic activities such as teaching, training, and research as well as practical initiatives of business people and organizations, professional associations, governmental agencies and civil society organizations. Testament to this worldwide evolution in academia is the *Global Survey of Business Ethics in Teaching, Training, and Research* (Rossouw and Stückelberger 2012). Obviously, the terminology of key concepts varies a great deal according to different languages, cultures, and foci of interest. In English there are particularly three terms that characterize the field or parts of it: business ethics, economic ethics, and corporate responsibility/corporate social responsibility. While the terminology undoubtedly needs to be clarified (see Enderle 2010), I would like to emphasize some substantive features of "business ethics" (named in short) that are based on the Global Survey and my recent personal experience in the field.
>
> When dealing with business ethics, one should place it in the key context of "globalization" and strive for "sustainability" as a key goal (see the textbook *Business Ethics* by Crane and Matten 2010). Taking into account the different foci of interest around the world, business ethics should encompass (at least) three levels of analysis: the micro or individual level, the meso or organizational level, and the macro or systemic level. In order to address complex challenges such as climate change, trust in the financial system, poverty, and wealth creation, it is insufficient and often misleading to limit the analysis on one or two of those three levels. Individual ethics or organizational ethics (e.g., corporate responsibility) is no substitute for institutional ethics nationally and internationally. Remember that the neglect and ignorance of institutional ethics in the 1920s and 1930s in Continental Europe led to the disaster of the Second World War.

A second lesson from the evolution of business ethics in the global context can be described as "the need to walk on two legs." This means that business ethics would fail if it contented itself with only describing and analyzing the world (e.g., why it is "bad") or only postulating and arguing for how the world should be. Rather, business ethics should comprehend both the descriptive–analytical and the normative–ethical dimension of the challenges to be addressed.

A third lesson concerns the relationship between theory and practice. Academia can learn a great deal from good and bad business practices. The development of global standards such as the Global Reporting Initiative, the UN Global Compact and the UN Guiding Principles for Business and Human Rights is a good example while corporate scandals like Enron's and the global financial crisis have not only shocked the public but also shaked up many academics. At the same time, confronted with major challenges, business ethics as an academic endeavor bears a fair share of responsibility to provide guidance for addressing those challenges.

To be more specific, I suggest that three major challenges lay ahead of us, which have emerged with increasing clarity, urgency, and importance, concerning all levels of business, from the individual to the organizational and the systemic level: (1) a rich and comprehensive understanding of wealth creation as the purpose of business and economics; (2) the guarantee of securing all human rights to all people; and (3) the active involvement of the world's religions in meeting the challenges of creating wealth and securing human rights (see Enderle 2011).

13.7 JOHANNES BRINKMANN ON CRITICISM, COLLABORATION AND CONFRONTATION IN THE FUTURE OF BUSINESS ETHICS

Johannes Brinkmann emphasizes the multiple roles that business ethics needs to play in the broader field of business. He argues that business ethics should remain a criticism of business, yet develop as a collaborative partner of business, but that it should even – when it is necessary – confront business in order to improve business.

Where should business ethics go?

Our field should continue, elaborate and deepen our function as a well-founded *criticism* of business practice, business research and business education, together with (preferably in cooperation with, if necessary in confrontation with) our business school colleagues, but at the same time, we should:

Stay constructive, that is participate actively, together with business practitioners, in drafting and *staging positive examples of and for business
practice*, for example in an action research format.

The interesting challenge is of course to weigh and balance our equally
important ideals of academic integrity (critique) and practical significance
(positive examples) for making the business world a better place.

I am not sure where to start: with business practitioners, with our business
school colleagues, or with our business students, and among these groups
with the interested and receptive ones or with the ones with the lowest
demand and presumably the highest need for business ethical enlightenment.
But we should start somewhere and walk, not only talk.

13.8 JOSEP M. LOZANO ON PERSONAL DEVELOPMENT IN THE FUTURE OF BUSINESS ETHICS

Josep M. Lozano's starting point is that business ethics is crucially about
personal development, and that this feature of business ethics needs to be
emphasized and clarified. He argues that business ethics has the potential
to create spaces of freedom, wherein individuals can go beyond reproduction of existing cultures, and rather improve those cultures through
criticism and personal development.

Where are we going with Business Ethics?

Business Ethics (BE) should be at the hearts of business schools. We have
confused offering BE courses with being trained in BE. The subjects are
there, but not the BE (or not enough of it, at any rate). It is not just a question
of integration and mainstreaming, as we usually say. It is mostly about the
fact that the management discourse and its various disciplines have been built
self-sufficiently without considering their ethical and value dimensions and,
once built, there has been endless debate as to how to incorporate, add and
inoculate them. And, if these dimensions are not intrinsically present from the
beginning, they will never be fully present.

BE should focus much more on the processes of learning and personal
development. Business schools are full of programmes that talk about
development (leadership development, management development, and so on)
but what it is that is to be developed is not always obvious. BE is so
concerned with the contents that it often only manages – if it does in fact do
so – to change the politically correct discourse and increase the complexity of
the analysis. But it scarcely accompanies processes of transformation and/or
personal development. Not least because the latter does not refer to a subject
but to the educational project of the respective institutions; a topic which,

curiously, has rarely impacted upon BE as a discipline. In the current debate on the contribution of business schools, ethics and the need for ethics, or not, as the case may be, comes under discussion. But, we will find little material on BE contributions in connection with business schools' educational models. It seems that BE is considered so important in its own right that it doesn't even bother to reflect on the institution that shapes its context (and, by the way, its credibility).

BE should be a catalyst capable of facilitating business schools, going beyond the reproduction of the dominant culture in relation to vision and business management. Being uncritical reproducers of what is generally accepted serves to train, but not to educate. Generally speaking, a business education has been much more business than education. When I talk about going beyond reinforcing and reproducing what has already been established and also to question it, I am not referring to techniques, capabilities and procedures, but to attitudes and mentalities, which is why we are talking about BE in the first place.

BE should help build the personal integration of the education received. It is a common misconception to draw attention over and over again to the risk that what is learned in business schools is a collection of disciplines without anyone taking responsibility for how this accumulation of fragments is personally articulated. It is left to chance, to personal journeys and to the school of life's hard knocks. And professional ethics has more of a role to play in how each person performs this articulation than the subjects of BE. The quality of business schools in the future will involve more than simply stating that there is a risk of becoming a provider of fragments. And, in this respect, if it is important to address this issue, BE should come up with something appropriate to remedy the situation.

BE should help create spaces of freedom in business schools, even at the price of reducing its own space as BE. By spaces of freedom, I mean that educating the future management world requires voices to be heard in business schools other than those that come from the world of management. We will neither improve management capacity nor will we be able to respond to the future needs of organizations or emerging societies if we understand management education as a closed loop, in which management only speaks *of* management *for* management. To better understand what it means to engage in management, business schools should hear other voices from other spheres: culture, spirituality, and politics. BE should be capable of producing spaces of freedom, not of joining in and replicating what goes on in the silos of repetition.

13.9 OVE JAKOBSEN ON THE FUTURE OF BUSINESS ETHICS

Ove D. Jakobsen addresses the interdependence between the economic system and the eco-systems within which economic activities operate. He proposes that a new paradigm is needed, whereby business ethics moves from a materialistic to a spiritual world-view.

> Business ethics could not be separated from the question: "Is economics a moral science?" In my opinion, economics is nothing but values. The goal in the economy is to transform nature to commodities that increase the well-being of human beings without disturbing the interplay between different eco-systems. To do this, knowledge is of great importance. Economic activities are in other words a combination of natural and cultural values. Production, distribution, consumption and redistribution (reprocessing of waste) are all necessary functions in the economy. Today the negative unintended consequences of the exploitation of nature and the unfair distribution of wealth are extremely serious. To solve these problems a deeper change in economics, business administration and private lifestyles are all necessary. This change has fundamental implications for business ethics.

> The present convergence of crises, "in money, energy, education, health, water, soil, climate, politics, the environment, and more – is a birth crisis, expelling us from the old world into a new (Eisenstein 2011, p. xx). Never in our history have humans faced so many interconnected global crises of our own making. We are now facing an unprecedented challenge, which requires us radically to rethink our worldview and to reflect on ecological and societal consequences of how we organize the local, national and global economy. Creating a viable future is about justice – for humans, for the Earth, and future generations of all species.

> Because most scholars today accept that the crises are symptoms of a deeper ontological, epistemological and ethical character I argue that it is necessary to change from a materialistic to a spiritual worldview. The consequences for business ethics are fundamental. Schopenhauer's and Nietzsche's criticism of the modern society represents an interesting introduction to this topic. In addition, Kierkegaard's (2004, 2012) three modes of existence represent an interesting reference to explore the need for a change in business ethics, and the driving forces behind the change processes.

> In the context of the spiritual worldview the religious mode of existence is of special interest. The reflections on the religious mode of existence represent the interpretative context for development in business ethics. Because spirituality is closer connected to intuition than rationality, the focus will change towards implications of intuitive ethics. To be conscious that we are integrated parts of the living Gaia leads to a kind of eco-centric moral responsibility with implications for business ethics.

The spiritual worldview represents an interesting contribution to the discussion on how to rethink and develop practical solutions to the most urging challenges in business ethics. Kierkegaard described the progress through the three modes of existence as a gradual appropriation of the individual's existence. "To have an authentic existence one must not be a mere spectator or passenger in life, but seize control of one's own destiny" (Kenny 1998, p. 300). That is to say, that the process is "an adventure, a risk, a self-commitment to an objective uncertainty" (Copleston 1985, p. 344).

In my opinion the development of business ethics goes along with a deep change from rational self-interest to a kind of intuitive holistic concern. This change process has the potential to unfold solutions to the most urgent challenges, locally, regionally and globally. Where governments and traditional leaders look at problems from the outside, spirituality comes to understand them intimately, in a holistic perspective from within. The return they seek are not in profits, "but in advances in education, environmental protection, rural development, poverty alleviation, human rights, healthcare, care for the disabled, care for children at risk, and other fields" (Bornstein 2007, p. 12).

13.10 KNUT J. IMS AND LARS JACOB TYNES PEDERSEN ON CHARACTER BUILDING AND THE DEVELOPMENT OF MORAL IMAGINATION

In a joint reflection, Knut J. Ims and Lars Jacob Pedersen take a virtue ethical approach and focus on character building and the development of moral imagination to secure ethical behavior in business and organizational life.

With Hannah Arendt's conception of Adolf Eichmann as a super-efficient manager in mind, empathy and compassion should play an important role in the teaching of business ethics. Adolf Eichmann was one of Adolf Hitler's faithful servants and he was able to plan, organize and implement a huge project – framed as the project of "Endlösung" that ultimately resulted in sending six million Jews to concentration camps. The term "the banality of evil" was coined as a way of seeing Eichmann as a leader who did not have strong negative feelings for the Jews, but rather saw it as his honor to do a good job – to be an effective manager. Bandura, Caprara and Zsolnai (2002) write about moral disengagement strategies, practices that form a slippery slope to corporate transgressions. Such mechanisms enable "eminent members of the business community" who are not "dangerous, criminally oriented mavericks" to commit unethical acts without experiencing moral guilt.

How can education contribute to avoiding that managers carry out harmful acts towards other people or other sentient beings? In our view, character building is central, and a main emphasis should be to have a balanced approach between heart and mind. This means to apply at least two perspectives to the same phenomenon – a perspective characterized both by proximity and distance. It means that one should not start with aggregating humans or any other kind of being, one should start with seeing their face. We should think of everybody as a face, and that everybody has a name and address, and thereafter we may proceed towards more distanced, abstract perspectives. This would be in line with Martin Buber's (1958) two ways of living: *I-Thou* before *I-it*. It is also very fruitful to view business through the lens of Ian Mitroff's (1998) four dimensional perspective: the scientific–technical perspective, the social–interpersonal perspective, the systemic perspective and, not at least, the spiritual–existential perspective. The latter involves posing profound questions related to meaning and purpose in life, and questions about having a "ground (life) project that is worthy and noble."

A main purpose of business ethics should be the development of empathy. Many methodological tools may promote this end, including the use of role play and literature for character development. For more than a decade, we have experimented with such methods in the ethics classroom, and students have engaged in and appreciated this approach. By reading classical works such as Henrik Ibsen's *Peer Gynt* and *The Enemy of the People*, students may engage in ethical reflection aimed at opening their minds and hearts. Cases and literature may enable students to develop a moral language that they can master in the environment of business and the culture of particular organizations. This involves understanding that "business ethics embraces much more than simply cultivating the ability to 'Just say no' or 'Just say yes' to clear-cut alternatives. It includes the discovering, anticipating, encountering, and constructing of moral problems" – many of which are dilemmas that require wisdom in order for the actor to create workable solutions (cf. Ciulla 1991, p. 212). By exploring the moral shades of business life using economic know-how as well as wisdom, students will be better able to invent sustainable, multicolored solutions. In a larger sense, character building is an attempt to build a link between wisdom and empathy. This should be the main objective of business ethics in the future, in order to stimulate sensitivity, compassion and wisdom in future business practitioners.

13.11 LASZLO ZSOLNAI AND ANTONIO TENCATI ON REGAINING LEGITIMACY AND RELEVANCE IN THE FUTURE OF BUSINESS ETHICS

Concluding the dialogue, Laszlo Zsolnai and Antonio Tencati jointly voice the concern that business ethics has lost credibility and relevance, and they ask the question of what is required to regain its legitimacy. They argue that new paradigms and practices are necessary, and highlight four levels on which innovative approaches are necessary.

The recent economic and financial crisis shows that business ethics lost its credibility and relevance. It became evident that business ethics teaching did not change the general attitude of managers in mainstream business. Ethics and compliance programs were not able to prevent major banks and big corporations to enter into questionable practices and make dirty businesses all over the world.

One explanation of the betrayal of business ethics is that our discipline did not question the underlying models of mainstream business, namely profit maximization and agency theory. Also, business ethics did not have the courage to challenge the institutional structure of contemporary global capitalism. The consequence is that exploitation of our planet's finite sources is continued, the basic needs of society are disregarded and the interest of future generations is neglected. By its institutionalized greed culture and the "enrich yourself" mentality mainstream business became a retrograde force in the development of humanity in the 21st century.

Therefore, alternative managerial paradigms and business practices are badly needed. This calls for an in-depth reframing of the prevailing assumptions in economics and management based on a negativistic and reductionist view of human nature. If business ethics scholars want to foster careful, collaborative, and responsible attitudes in doing business, they have to foster innovative research at four levels:

- individual (individual level), beyond the unrealistic homo oeconomicus conception;
- firm (micro level), beyond profit maximization and agency theory;
- districts, clusters, industries, and sectors (meso level), beyond the five forces model;
- the economy as a whole (macro level), beyond the infinite growth idea.

These research efforts need to aim at building a new vision of management for really sustainable patterns of development beyond the current competitive, disruptive, and, thus, self-defeating approach. This should also have a huge impact on universities and business schools and their role in educating future practitioners.

In conclusion, to gain legitimacy and relevance business ethics should aim to develop a normative but usable theory of ethical management. This theory needs to address systemic and operational issues of managing business in a sustainable, future respecting and pro-social way. It implies that (i) business activities may not harm nature or allow others to come to harm, (ii) business activities must respect the freedom of future generations, and (iii) business activities must serve the well-being of society. Ecology, respect for future generations and serving the well-being of society call for a radical transformation of business. If business ethics cannot contribute to the much needed transformation of business it may disappear as a discipline which did not delivered its promised benefits.

13.12 SUMMARY

This chapter has presented views on the future of business ethics that were voiced in the structured dialogue at the closing session of the Seventh TransAtlantic Business Ethics Conference. The dialogue partners all expressed that ethics should be a vital part of the teaching and practice of management and that faced with serious crises in business and society in the new millennium, the need for critical and innovative thinking is even more pressing than earlier.

As some of the participants voiced, business ethics has lost credibility and relevance, and therefore we are in great need of new paradigms and practices. We believe that the central ideas, beliefs and insights expressed by this panel of business ethicists offer new windows into the rich complexity of moral reasoning that is necessary for business ethics to develop and regain its legitimacy and true meaning, and for it to be the important challenger of mainstream business thinking and practice that is necessary.

NOTES

1. The following conference attendees also participated in the dialogue, but their contributions are not reproduced here: Thomas Donaldson, Prakash Sethi, Wesley Cragg, Andrew Crane and Thomas Beschorner.
2. I note that organizations such as the mafia and Hells Angels may excel in developing shared values and norms, with clear guidelines for behavior and strictly enforced sanctions for behavior that deviates from the norms – yet most of us would feel that it would be a serious misnomer to characterize such organizations as "ethical"; the values and norms disregard the values and norms of the many constituencies that are affected by their actions.
3. See for example http://www1.eur.nl/fsw/happiness/, the website of the *World Database of Happiness: Continuous register of scientific research on subjective appreciation of life* and http://www.springer.com/social+sciences/well-being/journal/10902, the website of the *Journal of Happiness Studies* published by Springer.
4. See for example http://www.tandfonline.com/toc/rmsr20/current, the website of the *Journal of Management, Spirituality and Religion*, published by Taylor & Francis.
5. See for example http://www.globaldharma.org/sbl-research.htm, the website of the Spiritual-based Leadership Research Programme for a knowledge-base of interviews and materials. In 2013, this research program and knowledge base was transferred to the Tyson Center for Faith and Spirituality in the Workplace at the University of Arkansas: http://tfsw.uark.edu/.
6. Quote from Rahm Emanuel (Mayor of Chicago) in 2008.

REFERENCES

Bandura, A., G-V. Caprara and L. Zsolnai (2002), 'Corporate Transgressions', in *Ethics in the Economy. Handbook of Business Ethics* (ed. L. Zsolnai), Bern: Peter Lang, pp. 151–164.

Bornstein, D. (2007), *How to Change the World – Social Entrepreneurs and the Power of New Ideas*, Oxford, UK: Oxford University Press.

Buber, M. (1958), *I and Thou* (2nd revised edition) (R.G. Smith, Trans.), New York: Charles Scribner's Sons.

Ciulla, J.B. (1991), 'Business Ethics as Moral Imagination', in *Business Ethics. The State of the Art* (ed. R.E. Freeman), New York: Oxford University Press,

Copleston, F.C. (1985), *A History of Philosophy* (Book 3), London, UK: Doubleday.

Crane, A. and D. Matten (2010), *Business Ethics. Managing Corporate Citizenship and Sustainability in the Age of Globalization*, Third edition, Oxford, UK: Oxford University Press.

Eisenstein, C. (2011), *Sacred Economics – Money, Gift and Society in the Age of Transition*, Berkeley, CA, USA: Evolver Editions.

Enderle, G. (2010), 'Clarifying the Terms of Business Ethics and Corporate Social Responsibility', *Business Ethics Quarterly*, **20** (4), pp. 730–732.

Enderle, G. (2011), 'Three Major Challenges for Business and Economic Ethics in the Next Ten Years: Wealth Creation, Human Rights, and Active Involvement of the World's Religions', *Business and Professional Ethics Journal*, **30** (3–4), pp. 231–252.

Kenny, Anthony (1998), *A Brief History of Western Philosophy*, Oxford, UK: Blackwell Publishers.

Kierkegaard, S. (2004), *Either/Or – A Fragment of Life*, London: Penguin Books.

Kierkegaard, S. (2012), *Fear & Trembling*, New York, USA: Merchant Books.

Mitroff, I. (1998), *Smart Thinking for Crazy Times: The Art of Solving the Right Problems*. San Francisco: Berrett-Koehler Publishers, Inc.

Rossouw, D. and C. Stückelberger (eds) (2012), *Global Survey of Business Ethics in Teaching, Training, and Research*, Geneva: Globethics.

Index